Why Peace Breaks Out

Why Peace Breaks Out

Great Power Rapprochement in Historical Perspective

Stephen R. Rock

THE UNIVERSITY OF
NORTH CAROLINA PRESS

Chapel Hill | *London*

Library of Congress Cataloging-in-Publication Data

Rock, Stephen R.
Why peace breaks out.

Bibliography: p.
Includes index.
1. World politics—1900–1914.
2. Great powers. 3. Peace—History—
20th century. I. Title.
D445.R58 1989   909.82'1   88-33824
ISBN 0-8078-1857-7 (alk. paper)

Printed in the United States of America

93 92 91 90 89   5 4 3 2 1

To My Mother and Father

Contents

Tables

Preface

Thomas Hardy once wrote that "War makes rattling good history; but Peace is poor reading."[1] Apparently, most scholars agree. While hundreds, even thousands, of books have been written on the causes, conduct, and consequences of war, little attention has been devoted to identifying the factors that might incline states toward peace. This is particularly true if one conceives of peace as not merely the absence of war, but as a condition in which even the possibility of armed conflict has been virtually eliminated.

The situation is unfortunate. Although avoiding open hostilities— which studies of war may help us do—is certainly a laudable objective, a more ambitious goal can be imagined. Indeed, a condition of cold war (or hot peace?), in which one relies on deterrence, crisis prevention, and/or crisis management to prevent latent tension and animosity from erupting into battle is far from ideal, especially in the nuclear age. If we are ever to have security, in the truest sense of the word, then stable, amicable relations among the world's leading powers—and above all between the Soviet Union and the United States—will have to be achieved.

This study seeks, by examining historical cases of great power reconciliation, to gain some understanding of how and why such a development might come about. It does not claim that a fundamental transformation of the Soviet-American relationship is likely, or could be easily obtained. Nor does it purport to offer the final word on a subject that is far from simple. It does, however, suggest that there is reason for hope, and that scholars and policymakers alike may want to begin thinking about how the Soviet-American antagonism, which has dominated international politics for almost half a century, might someday end.

This book, like most, reflects the efforts of many persons besides its author. I am indebted to Richard Rosecrance, a source of ideas, inspiration, and oft-needed encouragement; George Quester, who praised the good aspects of my work and criticized constructively the not-so-good; and Myron Rush, whose close and patient reading of every chapter remains for me the very model of professional dedication. I am also grateful to the Institute for the Study of World Politics, the Cornell University Graduate School, and the Cornell University Peace Studies Program for financial assistance during the early stages of this study.

I had the excellent fortune to complete this book in large part while a Research Fellow of the Avoiding Nuclear War Project at Harvard University's Center for Science and International Affairs. During my tenure at CSIA, I benefited from the comments and suggestions of a number of people. I especially wish to thank Joseph Nye, Stephen Van Evera, Sean Lynn-Jones, and James Miller, who read much or all of the manuscript and offered valuable advice as to how it might be improved. Jennifer Laurendeau and Eckhard Lübkemeier provided expert assistance with translations.

My greatest debts are more personal than intellectual. Writing a book is a solitary and sometimes frustrating task. Like many authors, I suspect, I enjoy "having written" as much or more than the process of writing itself. Three persons merit my deepest appreciation for their support. My mother and father accomplished the difficult feat of inquiring often about my progress without ever once implying that it was too slow. It is impossible for me to convey adequately to them the full measure of my thanks for their unfailing interest and countless expressions of love and confidence. My wife, Jenny, provided me with a life of personal fulfillment and a sense of perspective, reminding me that some things are more important than books. Because of all they have done, and continue to do for me, I am profoundly grateful for the opportunity to share the publication of this book with the members of my family.

Poughkeepsie, New York

Why Peace Breaks Out

1

Introduction:
Why Peace Breaks Out

The Question

The problem of national security commands today, as in the past, considerable attention in the United States. More than forty years after the beginning of the cold war, Americans remain fearful of the Soviet Union and concerned about the consequences of a confrontation with that power, consequences which could include a catastrophic nuclear exchange. Three basic strategies have dominated the policy debate: arms control and disarmament, deterrence, and, most recently, defense. Each of these approaches is in essence military and/or technological. The last two involve the development and deployment of weapons and weapons systems designed to strengthen America's posture, while the first entails limiting or reducing armaments that would produce a weakening in the U.S. position. All assume the continuation, into the foreseeable future, of the present Soviet-American antagonism.

What has been almost ignored in the widespread fascination with military-technological fixes is the possibility of a *political* solution to the problem, the idea that American (and Soviet) security might best be guaranteed by the amelioration, or even the elimination, of hostility between the superpowers. Such a fundamental transformation of the Soviet-American relationship may seem highly improbable. But given the difficulty of maintaining a reliable deterrent, the problematic prospects for a truly effective defense, and the dismal record of arms control, it is surely worth exploring. And history counsels us to consider the matter with an open mind. For there have, in the past, been instances in which major world powers have overcome virulent and virtually hereditary hostility to achieve a stable and lasting reconciliation. By examining these cases and attempting to explain them, we can shed some light on the nature of the

Soviet-American problem and the chances, if any, for its pacific resolution.

This is a study of two such cases: England and France during the last years of the nineteenth century and the first years of the twentieth, the era culminating in the famed Entente Cordiale of 1904; and Britain and the United States from 1895 to about 1905, the period of what historian Bradford Perkins has called the "great rapprochement." To facilitate an understanding of the circumstances that led these erstwhile enemies to compose their differences and form firm and enduring friendships, these cases are contrasted with two others in which adversaries failed to come together and relations deteriorated rather than improved: England and Germany in the several decades prior to World War I, and Germany and the United States during the same prewar epoch.

In broader conceptual terms, this study seeks to explore the historical process by which nations may make a transition in their mutual relations from a state of war to a state of peace—that is, why peace breaks out. War, in this sense, does not refer solely to a situation marked by the presence of open hostilities but to a more general condition in which the potential for such hostilities clearly exists. Likewise, peace does not mean merely the absence of armed conflict but denotes a special and more stable condition in which the threat itself of such conflict is effectively lacking.[1] These notions have long been employed by political philosophers and follow the formulations of Thomas Hobbes, who wrote that "WAR consists not in battle only, or the act of fighting, but in a tract of time wherein the will to contend by battle is sufficiently known. . . . For as the nature of foul weather lies not in a shower or two of rain but in an inclination thereto of many days together, so the nature of war consists not in actual fighting but in the known disposition thereto during all the time there is no assurance to the contrary. All other time is PEACE."[2]

Hobbes, of course, believed that a state of peace could be attained only through the coercive power of Leviathan, or some form of civil government. In this respect, he differed from a second great philosopher, John Locke. For whereas Hobbes considered the state of nature to be necessarily a state of war, Locke conceived of a precontractual society of "men living together according to reason, without a common superior." Thus, he wrote, there is a "plain difference between the state of nature and the state of war which . . . are as far distant as a state of peace, good-will, mutual assistance, and preservation, and a state of enmity, malice, violence, and mutual destruction are from one another."[3]

Given the lengthy catalogue of human conflict, it can hardly be surprising that most scholars have adopted a Hobbesian rather than a Lockean view of international politics, holding that its essentially anarchic character places every nation in a perpetual state of war with every other.[4] A few, it is true, have recognized in passing that some nations do enter into relationships approaching a state of peace.[5] To date, however, only a single volume has been devoted to answering the question of how and why this may occur. In *Political Community and the North Atlantic Area*, Karl W. Deutsch and a group of associates at the Center for Research on World Political Institutions at Princeton University attempted to explain the formation of what they termed "security-communities."[6] By way of definition, the authors wrote:

> A SECURITY-COMMUNITY is a group of people which has become "integrated."
> By INTEGRATION we mean the attainment, within a territory, of a "sense of community" and of institutions and practices strong enough and widespread enough to assure, for a "long" time, dependable expectations of "peaceful change" among its population.
> By SENSE OF COMMUNITY we mean a belief on the part of individuals in a group that they have come to agreement on at least this one point: that common social problems must and can be resolved by processes of "peaceful change."
> By PEACEFUL CHANGE we mean the resolution of social problems, normally by institutionalized procedures, without resort to large-scale physical force.
> A security-community, therefore, is one in which there is real assurance that the members of that community will not fight each other physically, but will settle their disputes in some other way.[7]

Deutsch and his colleagues examined two different varieties of security-communities. One, which they called "amalgamated," was characterized by the "formal merger of two or more previously independent units into a single unit, with some type of common government." The other, which they labeled "pluralistic," was marked by the retention of separate governments and decision-making centers on the part of the units involved.[8] The scholars determined, not surprisingly, that this latter kind of security-community was more readily developed and more easily preserved; thus the factors and conditions conducive to the formation and maintenance of pluralistic security-communities were held to constitute a set of minimum requirements for security-communities in general. According to the authors, three elements could be deemed essential: (1) the compatibility of major values relevant to political decision making; (2) the capacity of participating political units or governments to respond to each other's needs, messages, and actions quickly, adequately, and without resort to violence; and (3) mutual predictability of behavior.[9] Another dozen could be considered helpful: a distinctive way of life, a strong core area, superior economic growth, the expectation of joint economic reward, a wide range of mutual transactions, broadening of elites, links of social communication, mobility of persons, reluctance to wage "fratricidal" war, an outside military threat, strong economic ties, and ethnic and linguistic assimilation.[10]

The Princeton project, in both originality and scope, stands as a landmark inquiry into the foundations of international peace. Additional investigation, however, is clearly warranted. In the first place, the explanation offered by Deutsch and his colleagues is not a particularly parsimonious one. All told, fifteen conditions are either necessary or helpful for the formation of security-communities. While a certain amount of complexity is unavoidable given the multicausal nature of historical phenomena, a more concise formulation is obviously desirable. Moreover, these scholars do not present more than the barest minimum of historical evidence to support their numerous generalizations. A second volume containing such material was originally planned but was, unfortunately, never published.[11] Finally, the researchers, motivated mainly by an interest in the prospects for European unification, center their attention almost exclusively upon amalgamated rather than pluralistic security-communities. Of the cases selected for intensive analysis—Germany, the Hapsburg Empire, Italy, Norway-Sweden, Switzerland, the United Kingdom, and the United States—all but one fall into the former category. Most of these involve the integration of peripheral areas around a core of strength (e.g., Germany around Prussia, Great Britain around England), frequently by force. This process is hardly the same as that by which major world powers of roughly equal capabilities voluntarily enter into peaceful relationships. For these and other reasons, the findings generated by Deutsch and his associates, although suggestive, cannot be considered conclusive with respect to the problem posed here.

Looking for Answers

The emergence of amicable relations among formerly hostile powers may be conceptualized as occurring in two distinct stages. In the first, the states—or, more accurately, those within them who make and influence national policy—come to a decision that armed conflict is not an acceptable mechanism for settling their differences and that some reconciliation must be achieved. In the second, this *determination* is acted upon, outstanding disputes are liquidated, and an *expectation* of nonviolence develops.[12] Practically speaking, these processes may go on more or less simultaneously and be mutually reinforcing. Indeed, some belief in the possibility (though not necessarily the expectation) of a pacific relationship would seem to be a prerequisite to any serious determination to pursue one.

Although completion of both these stages is necessary before a state of peace can be said to have been established, the second is a logical (though perhaps not entirely inevitable) outgrowth of the first. Thus, to the extent that one can distinguish between them, this study concentrates on explaining the former stage. In other words, it seeks to identify factors that cause states to decide that armed conflict is not an appropriate method for resolving their disagreements.

Balance of Power and Balance of Threat

Our quest for the factors that lead hostile powers to establish friendly relations is perhaps best begun by considering some of the more enduring notions regarding states' attitudes and behaviors toward one another.

Among contemporary scholars, a realist or power-politics perspective has been the most popular. Although the realist school is by no means monolithic, its members share the basic belief that relations between states are determined by considerations of power. All other influences, including those of economics and ideology, are subordinate or even derivative. Some adherents to the realist paradigm find especially revealing an analogy between international politics and microeconomics. States, they argue, are like firms in a competitive industry. They are homogeneous, undifferentiated actors pursuing identical goals—at a minimum, survival, at a maximum, hegemony. The international system thus resembles the domestic market. International politics is a constant-sum game in which an improvement in the position of one state implies a corresponding deterioration in the position of every other.

There are two main variants of realist theory. The classic version, embodied in the works of, among others, Martin Wight, Hans Morgenthau, Nicholas Spykman, and, most recently, Kenneth Waltz, revolves around the concept of the balance of power.[13] Its principal hypothesis is that a balance of power tends to promote stability within the international system, and it focuses upon the attempts of states to achieve a balance in order to prevent the supremacy of a single power or coalition of powers.[14]

A second branch of realist theory rejects the efficacy of a balance of power, and argues instead that international stability is the consequence of gross inequalities in the capabilities of states. From this viewpoint, reflected in the writings of A. F. K. Organski and Robert Gilpin, global or regional hegemony appears as the best of all possible worlds.[15] The presence of a dominant state able to coerce other nations into accepting the existing distribution of international spoils ensures nonviolent relations. Conflict emerges with the onset of a power transition, as nations growing in strength seek to obtain a larger share of the international pie while the hegemon struggles to maintain its ascendancy.[16]

Balance of power and power transition theory are similar in that each posits that states confronted with an external threat will engage in balancing behavior. For those involved in a balance-of-power situation, this means acting to prevent any state or coalition of states from upsetting the existing equilibrium by becoming too strong. For the hegemon in a power transition, it means acting to prevent a challenger from surpassing it and assuming its position of dominance. And for the challenger in a power transition, it means acting to prevent the hegemon from blocking, or even turning back the clock on, its own rise to ascendancy.

Balancing behavior has usually been held to manifest itself in two ways: increased mobilization of domestic resources and the formation of international alliances.[17] But states may also balance by entering into international arrangements—formal or informal—that do not involve the kind of positive military collaboration implied by an alliance. A state may have the essentially negative objective of removing another state from its list of potential enemies, of obtaining some assurance of neutrality or nonaggression.[18] Generally, balancing behavior can be said to occur whenever a state attempts to increase its own capabilities or seeks to better its relations with less threatening or nonthreatening states in order to improve its position vis-à-vis a more dangerous adversary.[19]

One difficulty with much—though not all—of realist theorizing is that, as Stephen Walt has noted, balancing is "usually framed solely in terms of power. Balancing is alignment with the weaker side," or, alternatively, opposition to the stronger. And, as Walt points out, "This view is seriously flawed . . . because it ignores the other factors that statesmen will consider when identifying potential threats and prospective allies." Indeed, "states may balance by allying with other strong states, if a weaker power is more dangerous for other reasons."[20]

Aspects of cases examined in this study suggest that the actions of states are more consistent with what Walt calls a "balance of threat" theory than with a balance-of-power theory narrowly defined.[21] After German unification in 1871, for example, Germany and England were by any objective standard the two most powerful members of the European state system. The former was, of course, rising, while the latter had begun a gradual decline. Each, according to realist wisdom, should have seen the other as its natural adversary, mobilized against it, and sought to draw allies to its side. In fact, for nearly a generation following the Franco-Prussian War, England and Germany remained on generally polite, though not entirely cordial, terms and engaged in a substantial measure of diplomatic cooperation. It was not until German power was directed toward the same ends as English power, initially in colonial endeavors and then in the building of a great fleet, that the two nations became bitter enemies.

A still more telling criticism of pure balance-of-power theory is implicit in the case of Great Britain and the United States. For the most rapid and decisive improvement in the relations of these countries took place during a period when the changing distribution of power pointed toward a clash, when America was emerging as a major international actor and the principal threat to Britain's global hegemony. Between 1890 and 1910, the United States passed Britain as the world's leading power on most indicators of economic strength, and by 1907 the American fleet ranked second only to the Royal Navy. Many British observers were in fact convinced that the United States was destined to take command of the seas because of her vast resources and immense industrial potential. By balance-of-power logic, a serious Anglo-American antagonism was inevitable, and an Anglo-German alliance directed against the United States or a German-American alliance against Great Britain might have been predicted.

Yet none of these eventualities occurred. Instead, Britain and the United States were reconciled, while Anglo-German and German-American relations deteriorated into bitter animosity and, ultimately, war.

The case of Britain and the United States suggests a second problem with realist theorizing also identified, though not stressed, by Walt: that "statesmen do not live by threat assessments alone."[22] At first glance, of course, the Anglo-American reconciliation might seem to be explicable entirely in terms of balance-of-threat theory. Britain, facing dangers from France, Russia, and Germany—and the United States, at odds with Germany and with Spain—reached an understanding that enhanced their ability to meet these more compelling threats. This argument possesses some validity. It is clear that common concern over Germany in particular helped to draw America and Britain together. It is not, however, evident that this was a necessary or even an especially influential motivation for accommodation on either side. Although they later became widespread, apprehensions of insecurity were in 1895–96 fairly minimal. Anxiety regarding the intentions of third powers thus contributed only marginally to the initial popular demand for better relations in the wake of the Venezuelan Boundary Crisis and to early enthusiasm for a rapprochement on the part of government officials. Moreover, the friendship between Britain and the United States endured after 1918, when the German menace had been eliminated.[23] A strong case can therefore be made that the Anglo-American reconciliation was largely a product of a mutual belief that war between the two countries had to be avoided for other reasons.

In sum, the cases examined in this study call into question a narrow realist interpretation of international political behavior on two counts. First, when states balance they do not necessarily do so on the basis of aggregate power. The question "What are they likely to do with their power?" may be as or more important than "How much power do they have?"[24] Second, states concluding a reconciliation after a period of mutual hostility may not be engaged in balancing maneuvers. The desire for an understanding may be rooted in their bilateral relationship and owe little to the existence of external threats.

All this suggests that nonpower variables, influencing the calculus of threat and/or providing a rationale for rapprochement independent of threat, can have a considerable impact on the relations of states. Of a number of potentially important factors, two have been mentioned most prominently in theorizing about international politics: the economic connections among states, both commercial and financial; and their societal characteristics—their ideologies, their modes of economic, social, and political organization, and their cultures.

Economic Relationships

As far as economic explanations of international political behavior are concerned, two general and opposing emphases can be identified. The first, perhaps best represented by Lenin's theory of imperialism, is on economic relationships as a source of interstate conflict.[25] This Marxist perspective, much like the realist, sees states as firms in a competitive industry, each striving to increase profits at the expense of others.[26] International politics, reduced to economics, is a constant-sum game in which competition for markets, both for goods and for capital, breeds hostility and war.[27]

In contrast to this negative view, another group of theorists has looked upon economic relationships as having a positive influence in international affairs. Grounded in the free trade doctrines of Adam Smith and David Ricardo, and associated with the nineteenth-century arguments of Richard Cobden, the "liberal" paradigm has seen states as engaging in mutually advantageous economic exchange, ultimately becoming so dependent upon one another for their prosperity that warfare among them is virtually ruled out. More recently, elements of this perspective have surfaced in the "interdependence" and "transnationalist" approaches of such authors as Robert Keohane and Joseph Nye, who have suggested that the proliferation of commercial and financial interconnections among states may promote peace by rendering too high the costs of employing force.[28] In this conception, world politics is not a constant-sum, but an increasing-sum, game. States are not alike, but perform specialized functions in an international division of labor. By operating in accordance with the laws of comparative advantage, they act in their own individual interests but to the benefit of all.

Ideological Solidarity

The idea that "birds of a feather flock together" has been a persistent one in theorizing about international politics.[29] In 1796, Edmund Burke, opposing British peace overtures to the Jacobin government of revolutionary France, argued, "Men are not tied to one another by papers and seals. They are led to associate by resemblances, by conformities, by sympathies. It is with nations as with individuals. Nothing is so strong a tie of amity between nation and nation as correspondence in laws, customs, manners, and habits of life."[30] Burke added that such correspondence, though "incapable, like everything else, of preserving perfect trust and tranquillity among men, has a strong tendency to facilitate accommodation, and to produce a generous oblivion of the rancor of their quarrels."[31] More recently, Hans Morgenthau, known for his emphasis on the role of power in the relations among states, has acknowledged that "ideological solidarity" may form the basis of some alliances.[32] And the notion that states similar in terms of their societal attributes—not only political ideology and its manifestation in institutions of government, but also language, tradition, and culture broadly defined—are most likely to get along underlies much of Deutsch's analysis and is evident in his stress on shared values and a distinctive way of life.[33]

Theorists suggest that states sharing certain societal characteristics are more apt to have friendly relations for two main reasons. Initially, such similarity may lead them to develop a sense of common identity and the feeling that a conflict between them would be fratricidal and must therefore be avoided.[34] Second, it may cause the states to discount the importance of other issues that divide them, especially geopolitical ones. This could be a crucial factor in the assessment of threats. As Walt notes, "States with similar traits may fear each other less, because they will find it harder to imagine an inherently 'good' state deciding to attack them."[35] By contrast, dissimilarity of societal characteristics would be expected to have opposite effects, promoting mutual distaste and probably suspicion as well.

Recent research has lent new credence to the old idea that a shared political ideology binds states together, while a differing philosophical orientation splits them apart. Michael Doyle, in his essay on "Kant, Liberal Legacies, and Foreign Affairs," offers evidence that liberal states, for reasons similar to those advanced above, are extremely reluctant to fight one another. At the same time, he argues persuasively that attitudes and values held in common by liberal states tend to exacerbate disputes between these states and nonliberal ones. Most critical is "the perception by liberal states that nonliberal states are in a permanent state of aggression against their own people."[36] States that do not respect the rights of their own citizens cannot be expected to respect the rights of other states; they are inherently dangerous. The implications of this belief for threat assessment by liberal states should be quite evident.

Motivating and Facilitating Factors

Balance-of-power/threat, economic, and ideological/cultural theories point to a variety of factors that could be involved in the establishment of pacific relations between once hostile states. It may be useful to think of these factors as falling into two basic categories. "Motivating factors" are those that provide states with positive inducements to pursue amicable relations. "Facilitating factors" are those that enable states to act upon these incentives. They are usually defined negatively, as the absence of some obstacle to friendship.

The theories discussed above suggest these as the most important motivating factors in great power rapprochement: (1) the need to balance against an adversary or adversaries constituting a more serious threat; (2) the desire to preserve vital economic connections; and (3) the wish to avoid a fratricidal or civil war. They suggest these as the most important facilitating factors: (1) a sufficiently low level of geopolitical competition to allow for compromise and the resolution of major issues; (2) the absence of economic rivalry; and (3) ideological compatibility or, alternatively, the absence of ideological disaffection.

It must be emphasized that both types of factors are important and that the absence of facilitating factors may prevent a reconciliation even if strong incentives to an understanding exist. This may be particularly true in the case of balance-of-threat motivations. Scholars have long recognized that states prefer to balance by domestic mobilization rather than the formation of international coalitions because of the sacrifices required to sustain an alliance or alignment relationship. The absence of facilitating factors can only magnify this predilection, making it more likely that balancing behavior will be internal and will not, therefore, be reflected in a rapprochement. Thus, as we shall see, Germany in the years before 1914 made no serious effort to come to terms with the United States, her geopolitical competitor, economic rival, and ideological antagonist, despite the fact that American goodwill would have strengthened her against Britain, her principal enemy.[37] Similarly, in a case not examined in this study, the liberal-democratic Western Powers of the interwar period failed to seek an understanding with the communist Soviet Union despite the fact that they and the USSR were increasingly menaced by Germany and Japan.[38] As late as March 1939, Neville Chamberlain, responding to calls for an Anglo-French-Russian alliance, refused to consider collaboration with Russia because, he said, "I distrust her motives, which seem to me to have little connection with our ideas of liberty."[39]

Some Hypotheses and a Framework for Analysis

The preceding discussion has identified a number of possible explanations for the emergence of peace between formerly antagonistic powers. Evidence presented in the following four chapters lends support to several propositions synthesized to a considerable extent from this discussion and subsuming many of the motivating and facilitating factors mentioned above. Whether these hypotheses are generalizable to other cases in other periods of international history, including our own, cannot be determined without additional investigation. But, as I will argue with respect to Soviet-American relations, they are surely suggestive.

> HYPOTHESIS I: A state of peace is most likely to emerge among states that are heterogeneous in the exercise of national power.

The concept of heterogeneity/homogeneity in the exercise of power can best be defined as the degree to which the geopolitical ambitions of states overlap. It is a function of both the range of overlapping aims and of the attachment to these aims on the part of the states. Two states whose objectives conflict in very few matters and whose commitment to them is marginal will be highly heterogeneous, while those whose objectives conflict in many areas and whose commitment is strong will be highly homogeneous. Of the two dimensions, intensity of commitment is probably the more important since even a single issue can seriously divide states that regard it as vital. The range of overlapping aims may itself be seen as the product of two separate factors: the direction of each state's interests and the scope of these interests. Two states whose ambitions run in different directions or are narrow in scope will suffer relatively little overlap, while those whose ambitions run in the same direction and are extensive in scope will encounter substantial conflict.

The logic of this hypothesis should be fairly obvious, incorporating as it does much of the reasoning behind balance-of-power and balance-of-threat theory. States whose geopolitical ambitions do not overlap at all (a rare situation among major powers, of course)[40] will lack an important—perhaps the most important—obstacle to good relations. For states whose aims do conflict, the less the overlap, the more likely that the resultant animosity can be overridden by economic and ideological incentives. Finally, all other things being equal, a given state would be expected to see its greatest menace as coming from the other state whose strategic and territorial objectives clash most directly with its own. Operating in accordance with balance-of-threat theory, the state should seek to counter this danger by aligning itself with other states whose designs are less incompatible with the protection of its vital interests.

> HYPOTHESIS 2: A state of peace is most likely to emerge among states that are heterogeneous in their economic activities.

The notion of heterogeneity/homogeneity in economic activities refers to the inputs and outputs of states' economic systems, especially as these relate to international trade and finance. States that produce and/or export different commodities may be considered heterogeneous, while those that produce and/or export similar commodities are homogeneous. Likewise, when one state is primarily a lender of capital and another a borrower, we may say they are heterogeneous; when both lend or both borrow, they are homogeneous.

Liberal, Marxist, and mercantilist theories discussed above hint at the logic of this hypothesis. States whose economies are heterogeneous are likely to be interdependent, furnishing one another with goods and services each does not itself produce.[41] Such mutual reliance, when costly to disrupt, may provide a significant incentive to achieve and maintain cordial relations.[42] States whose economies are homogeneous, on the other hand, will be likely to compete with one another in their home and/or foreign markets. This is bound to cause resentment, particularly if the states are guided by a mercantilist world view in which success at commercial and financial endeavors appears critical to national political and military power. Although trade wars are not often prone to become shooting wars, economic competition that reinforces a geopolitical rivalry may be severely divisive and may solidify or magnify perceptions of threat.

Commercial transactions do, of course, take place between states even when their economies are essentially homogeneous because of the law of comparative advantage. And competitive trade does result in some degree of interdependence. Exporters in one country depend on the other to furnish markets for their products, importers who buy and then sell these products derive their livelihood from them, and, most importantly, consumers benefit from lower prices and/or greater availability of merchandise. International trade theory posits, in fact, that even competitive trade increases the level of welfare in the countries involved.[43]

For several reasons, however, interdependence flowing from competitive trade is much less likely to produce positive political results than interdependence flowing from complementary trade. In the first place, interdependence based on price differentials rather than on heterogeneity of production is almost by definition of a lower order.[44] Trading with another country to obtain goods at a reduced cost is not the same as trading to obtain goods one does not or cannot produce at all.[45] Disruption of commerce in the latter situation, particularly if the items in question are foodstuffs or vital raw materials, is a considerably more serious problem. Second, although even competitive trade makes a country better off as a whole, it involves a redistribution of income from producers to consumers. Gains on the consumption side are spread across the entire society, while losses on the production side—in terms of reduced profits, lower wages, and unemployment—are borne only by those in the import-competing sector. The per capita loss among the losers is thus much higher and more keenly felt than the individual gain among the gainers, and the former are therefore much more likely to act politically in an attempt to influence national policy. Finally, and most crucially, while competition in the home market leaves a country better off, competition in third markets, where no consumption advantages compensate for losses to producers, manifestly does not. In sum, the positive effects of the interdependence inherent in competitive trade are apt to be more than outweighed by the negative impact of the competition itself.

The salience of economic heterogeneity/homogeneity in the political relations of states almost certainly depends heavily on the level of transactions among them. States that are heterogeneous—that have complementary economies—but do not exchange goods and capital with one another will not be interdependent. Similarly, states that are homogeneous but do not exchange goods and capital with one another or with third countries will not be competitive. In general, the greater the volume of trade and financial flows, the stronger the effects of their composition or structure.

It should be noted that economic interdependence may not foster harmony and goodwill in every situation. Respected scholars have contended that interdependence may be more a source of conflict than of amity.[46] If interdependence is to exercise a beneficent influence on the relations of states, two conditions would seem essential. First, the dependence must be genuinely mutual, or at least sufficiently symmetrical that neither party is willing or able to manipulate it for political or economic purposes. And second, escape from a position of dependence via military action (conquest of third countries or an attack on the state upon which one relies) must be either an infeasible or an unacceptably costly policy. Neither of these conditions was present in Japanese-American diplomacy of the late 1930s and early 1940s, a case often cited as evidence of the deleterious effects of interdependence.[47] Nor, as we shall see, did they exist in Anglo-German relations during the period before the First World War.

The impact of interdependence, as it is being treated here, is a function of ostensibly rational calculations of economic interest grounded in commercial and financial exchange rather than the sociological effects of transnational interpersonal contacts that accompany such exchange. Some authors have postulated that high levels of economic transactions (and athletic, artistic, and scientific exchanges) between peoples can lead to greater understanding and thereby contribute to improved relations.[48] This argument is plausible, but it seems more likely that increased contacts between nations of similar outlooks, beliefs, and values would be beneficial, while increased contacts between nations that differ markedly on these dimensions might actually be harmful. In some instances, "familiarity breeds contempt" may be the operative rule. Should this be so, any sociological effects of interdependence would be dependent on the similarity of the societies involved, which is the subject of the following hypothesis.[49]

> HYPOTHESIS 3: A state of peace is most likely to emerge among states that are homogeneous in their societal attributes.

Heterogeneity/homogeneity of societal attributes refers to the degree to which states are similar on a number of dimensions, including language, ideology, form of government, and culture broadly defined. States that are alike in these respects are homogeneous; those that are unlike are heterogeneous.

The logic of this hypothesis has been discussed previously and needs only brief repetition here.[50] Generally, states homogeneous in their societal attributes might be expected to have pacific relations for two principal reasons. First, homogeneity may lead them to develop a sense of common identity and the feeling that a conflict between them would be fratricidal and must therefore be avoided. Second, homogeneity may cause the states to discount the importance of other issues that divide them, especially geopolitical ones. By contrast, heterogeneity of societal characteristics would be expected to have opposite effects, promoting mutual distaste, distrust, and an exaggerated perception of threat.

Of all the societal attributes possessed by states, political ideology—and its institutional and procedural manifestations—may be the most salient. Here it is necessary to modify the hypothesis out of the recognition that not every ideology, commonly held, appears to facilitate friendly relations. Rather, it seems crucial to distinguish between what Walt calls "unifying ideologies" and what he terms "divisive ideologies."[51] The former, which include liberalism and monarchism, imply a basic respect for national sovereignty and suggest no authority by one state over the affairs of others. Relatively minor differences within the general philosophical tradition cause little or no concern. The latter, however, of which communism and Christianity are prime examples, call upon adherents to form a centralized movement under a single leadership responsible for defining and disseminating a single, absolute truth. This type of ideology is almost guaranteed to produce discord at some point. Fairly modest doctrinal disputes or variations in practice will assume epic proportions as advocates of rival interpretations try to establish their legitimacy and thus their right to existence and/or control. In sum, homogeneity of political ideology may be conducive to peace only when the ideology that is shared is a unifying one.

Taken together, these three hypotheses constitute a framework for analyzing the political relations among states. They do not, in the strictest sense, represent a theory. Construction of a theory would require one to specify the relative importance of each of the dimensions—exercise of power, economic activities, and societal attributes. It would further require one to specify the level of heterogeneity/homogeneity necessary for peace along each dimension, should there exist some minimum threshold, and on all three dimensions combined. This would, in turn, require one to develop a formula for measuring these levels with satisfactory precision and an index capable of combining them. While such an undertaking might be feasible, it would clearly demand the examination of a much larger number of cases than are considered here.

The Need for a Catalyst

Although the motivating and facilitating factors implicit in the above hypotheses deserve the bulk of our attention, they do not exhaust the list of potential causes of great power rapprochement. There also exists a third type of factor that some theorists have seen as important: a catalytic factor. Even if strong incentives to an understanding are present and serious obstacles appear to be lacking, some sort of catalyst may be necessary to set the process of reconciliation in motion. The most likely candidate for this role is an acute crisis between two states. Indeed, Ned Lebow, in his study of international crises, concluded that such events may "prove essential to rapprochement in some instances."[52]

The need for a catalyst in bringing about a rapprochement flows mainly from the fact that there is a kind of inertia inherent in states' perceptions of one another and of their interests. Images, once solidified, are difficult to change and may persist long after the conditions in which they were formed have been altered.[53] Crises, by taking states to the brink of war and forcing them to contemplate its implications, can shatter old patterns of thought. As Lebow explains, "Short of war, crises are the most salient and visible points of conflict between states. . . . Crises can accordingly put interstate conflicts into sharper focus by providing insights into the state of mind and objectives of the protagonists. Acute crises also produce a kind of collective trauma in that they confront leaders on both sides with serious threats to their personal and national interests and are likely to leave them somewhat shaken even after the successful mastery of such challenges. Both characteristics of crisis can act as catalysts prompting reassessment of the basic premises of a nation's foreign policy."[54] In all, Lebow offers five possible reasons for a crisis to act as a catalyst to better relations: (1) defeat in the crisis forces policymakers to reevaluate basic policy assumptions; (2) defeat diminishes the influence of hard-liners in the government who were responsible for the policy that led to the crisis; (3) outstanding issues are resolved; (4) a fear of war is inculcated; and (5) mutual empathy and trust are promoted if the crisis settlement is negotiated with a problem-solving rather than a competitive orientation.[55] As I shall argue later, the Venezuelan Boundary Crisis of the winter of 1895–96 exhibited many of these characteristics and served as catalyst for the Anglo-American reconciliation, while the Fashoda Crisis of 1898 also had many of the same results and performed a similar function in the case of Britain and France.

The evidence presented in this work thus lends support to a fourth hypothesis:

> HYPOTHESIS 4: Even if the exercise of power, economic activities, and societal attributes favor pacific relations, some catalytic event may be required to set the process of reconciliation in motion. The most probable candidate for this role is an acute crisis between the two states.

Methodology

The basic strategy of inquiry employed in this study is that of the comparative method. Also known, with minor variations, as controlled comparison; structured, focused comparison; and comparative historical analysis; the comparative method allows for the systematic examination of social and political phenomena that cannot be analyzed by generally superior experimental or statistical means. Its aim, like that of the other modes of scientific investigation, is to establish causal connections between certain factors and conditions and a given phenomenon one wishes to explain.[56]

In pursuing a comparative research strategy, scholars may follow either (or both) of two paths. On the one hand, they may choose what is usually called the "positive method" or the "method of agreement." This procedure requires scholars to consider together several cases of the particular phenomenon they wish to explain. Out of a number of potential causal influences, they identify as causally relevant only those factors and conditions common to each case, eliminating those that are not. Control of extraneous variables, in the scientific sense, is obtained by selecting cases that differ as greatly as possible along the range of hypothesized explanatory factors. On the other hand, scholars may opt for what is usually labeled the "negative method" or the "method of difference." This procedure is, in essence, the opposite of the first. It requires investigators to contrast cases that exhibit the phenomenon in question with other cases that do not. Only those factors and conditions that vary across the two sets of cases are held to be causal, while those present in both instances are ruled to be unrelated to their outcomes. Control within this method is achieved by selecting sets of cases that are as similar as possible along the range of potential explanatory elements.

This study relies primarily upon the negative method or the method of difference. It considers two historical instances in which a state of peace emerged between nations: England and France during the first years of the twentieth century, the era of the Entente Cordiale; and Britain and the United States from 1896 to roughly 1905, the period of the so-called great rapprochement. It contrasts with these "positive" cases two others in which a state of peace might have developed but did not: England and Germany, and Germany and the United States, in the generation or so prior to the First World War. These "negative" cases provide, with respect to the logic of the method of difference, suitable counterexamples to the positive cases because they are of the same historical context and involve two of the same countries. The logic of the method of agreement, comparison across the positive cases themselves, is also present in this study. However, its utility independent of the method of difference is somewhat weak since the two cases are too similar on too many dimensions to allow for a substantial degree of control. Thus, the method of agreement must, in this instance, serve mainly to reinforce and to elaborate upon conclusions derived mainly from the method of difference.

There are, it should be noted, several limitations commonly attributed to the comparative method. One of these concerns the logic of elimination according to which the strategy operates and the level of scientific control that it allows. In many situations, it proves impossible to satisfy completely the requirements of this logic. A researcher either cannot identify cases different in enough respects to employ the method of agreement, or is unable to find cases sufficiently alike to pursue the method of difference. Further, even if one of these designs can be successfully implemented, the problem of "many variables, few cases" means that perfect control can never be obtained. There will always remain some danger that the scholar will identify as having causal significance a relationship that is in reality nothing more than a spurious association.[57]

A second, and related, shortcoming of the comparative method is its inability to deal effectively with multiple causes. The logic of elimination provides no mechanism for discovering the interactive effects among various determinants, or even for assessing their relative importance. This problem becomes still more acute if one is concerned not with the presence or absence of certain variables, but with degrees of presence or absence. Indeed, in some instances the logic of elimination could actually lead a researcher to reject as non-causal a factor of considerable significance.[58]

A third difficulty sometimes held to plague the comparative method has to do with the independence of cases. It is an accepted principle that in multivariate analysis of any type the cases must be fully independent. But this requirement can rarely, if ever, be met with respect to international political phenomena. A certain amount of historical learning is inevitable, and cases selected from the same time period or involving the same countries may have a more direct impact upon one another. This, in fact, is true of several of the cases analyzed in this study. For example, the emergence of peaceful relations between England and France was clearly facilitated by the deterioration of relations between England and Germany. Likewise, the development of Anglo-French amity appears to have constituted an obstacle in the path of Anglo-German friendship.

Fortunately, none of these problems is as intractable as some authors have supposed. They can be greatly mitigated, if not entirely surmounted, by the use of traditional, historical, "within-case" explanation in conjunction with the comparative logic of elimination.[59] By examining each case in detail, and by tracing the causal sequence involved, it is possible to test, and to modify if necessary, the presumed causal linkages established through the comparative method. In this manner, the researcher can not only identify the various factors motivating and influencing individual decision makers and public opinion, but can also discover their interactive effects and assess their relative significance. Use of such historical "process tracing" makes it unlikely that a spurious association will be mistaken for a valid causal relationship. Similarly, process tracing lessens, if not removes, the need for completely independent cases. When this technique is employed, the influences of the cases on one another can be taken into account as part of the causal configuration of each case, to be woven into the more general analysis. It is, in fact, one of the great virtues of the comparative method that the scholar utilizing this strategy can derive explanations that are both generalizable across cases and sensitive to the particular idiosyncracies of individual case histories.

Selection of Cases

The four cases that comprise this study were, of course, selected for specific reasons. England-France and Britain-United States were chosen because they constitute outstanding examples of the transition by nations from a state of war to a state of peace. They represent the only instances in modern history in which this transformation was achieved by major powers without a decisive and immediately antecedent war and occupation.[60] And they are cases in which the change has proved enduring. For more than three-quarters of a century, the threat of mutual warfare has been, for all practical purposes, absent from the relations of these countries. Indeed, the Anglo-French and Anglo-American security-communities might almost be described as permanent, insofar as that term can be applied to any aspect of international politics.

In other respects, too, the Anglo-American and Anglo-French rapprochements of the late nineteenth and early twentieth centuries were especially attractive cases. First, in each instance, the development of peaceful relations marked a radical departure from traditional patterns of conflict and hostility that had persisted for hundreds of years. France and England had been hereditary enemies dating back to the Norman invasion, while Britain and the United States had quarreled since the days of American independence. Moreover, this transformation was sudden and dramatic, a change revolutionary rather than evolutionary in nature. Although some general improvement had occurred in the tenor of both Anglo-French and Anglo-American diplomacy since 1815, when these nations had last been at war, the decisive movement toward reconciliation was, in each case, contained within a brief and fairly circumscribed span of time. A mere six years after the famous Fashoda Crisis of 1898, England and France concluded the Entente Cordiale, symbolic of their newfound friendship. Similarly, within a decade following their bitter dispute of 1895–96 over the Venezuelan boundary, Britain and the United States had resolved not only that thorny question but a host of other potentially explosive issues, and Anglo-American amity had been placed on firm ground.

The fact that the emergence of amicable relations in these two cases was so rapid and at such variance with previously existing attitudes and actions greatly facilitated the task of research. It meant that the development of peace involved deliberate and conscious foreign policy decisions and was the object of considerable attention on the part of political leaders, interest groups, and the presses of these and other countries. This, in turn, meant that the opinions and activities of persons relevant to the process could be determined and the factors and conditions explaining it identified. A thorough and adequate investigation of instances in which peace emerged incrementally and imperceptibly over an extended period of time would have been far more difficult to achieve.

Of the two contrasting cases, England-Germany and Germany-United States, less needs to be said. These cases were selected because they were opposed to the Anglo-French and Anglo-American cases in outcome, yet sufficiently similar in other respects to permit effective use of the method of difference. In particular, they were drawn from the same pre-World War I epoch, included two of the same countries, and, more generally, involved relationships between great, or at least major, powers in the international arena.

Did Peace Break Out?

In this work I claim that relations approximating a state of peace—as defined above—developed between Britain and the United States and between England and France around the turn of the century. Ascertaining when or whether a state of peace has emerged is not, of course, an exact science. Expectations of nonviolence, ultimately the defining characteristic, can be measured along at least three dimensions: popular attitudes, elite opinion, and military planning. These expectations will rarely, if ever, be held universally; persons with contrary predictions can almost always be identified. Moreover, the three indicators themselves will be prone to yield inconsistent evidence. In particular, military plans (or rather, the absence thereof) suggestive of a state of peace may lag well behind popular and elite perceptions because of bureaucratic inertia and the desire of the armed services to be prepared for any conceivable contingency, no matter how remote the chances of its actually arising.[61]

This study depends primarily upon evidence of elite, and to the degree possible, popular expectations in its characterizations of the relations between states. In doing so, it follows what might be termed the "preponderance of evidence rule," based on the notion that while dissenting voices will always be heard, at some point expectations of nonviolence are so pervasive that a state of peace may be said to exist. The presence or absence of military preparations for conflict, although taken into account, is for reasons just mentioned assigned lesser weight. In addition, the study relies on the assessments of other scholars who have previously examined the cases. Finally, it may be argued (though I hesitate to do so) that in the final analysis it is not necessary to establish conclusively that a state of peace emerged. It is, I think, beyond contention that Anglo-American and Anglo-French relations improved dramatically and decisively during the late years of the last century and the early years of the present one. What is important is to gain some understanding of the factors responsible for these profound transformations.

2

Great Britain and
the United States,
1895–1905

Narrative: The Rapprochement

For most of us, it is difficult to imagine a time when Great Britain and the United States were not on friendly terms. The idea of a special relationship between these nations, encouraged by their alliance in two world wars and by their economic and military collaboration since 1945, has become deeply ingrained. We recognize, of course, that Anglo-American relations have not always been amicable. The mother country and her former colonies fought twice, in 1776 and again in 1812. But from our present-day perspective these episodes appear as historical accidents, unfortunate aberrations in an otherwise unblemished tradition of natural harmony.

In fact, the relations between Great Britain and the United States remained gravely strained long after the two countries last met in battle.[1] The American Revolution and the War of 1812 left a bitter legacy on both sides of the Atlantic, and a series of subsequent incidents periodically threatened to explode into further conflict. In the 1830s and 1840s, hostilities nearly broke out over boundary disputes in Maine and Oregon. The 1860s and 1870s saw the *Alabama* claims controversy and acrimony regarding Britain's role in the American Civil War. Toward the end of the century, differences arose over northeastern fisheries and the hunting of fur seals in the Bering Sea, so that throughout the 1880s and 1890s "talk of war was not uncommon."[2] This brief list of disagreements is by no means exhaustive. But it amply illustrates the tension, suspicion, and outright antagonism that plagued Anglo-American diplomacy for more than a hundred years. Given this background, "the wonder is," as one historian has put it, "that despite the two wars, threats of a third war, and decades of animosity, America and Britain achieved a lasting rapprochement around 1900."[3]

The decisive movement toward the reconciliation of Great Britain and the United States began late in 1895. It followed, and was in part prompted by, the sharpest crisis in Anglo-American relations since the Civil War era. At issue was the boundary between Venezuela and the neighboring colony of British Guiana. Although efforts had been made since the 1840s to resolve this dispute, each had failed. The Venezuelans had, in fact, inflated their claims over the years, while the British, who had offered concessions on several occasions, hardened their position after the discovery of gold in the contested areas during the 1870s. As the century drew to a close, Venezuela, citing the Monroe Doctrine, appealed to the United States for help.[4]

The American government, sympathetic to Venezuelan concerns, repeatedly expressed to London its wish for a negotiated settlement, but took no real action until the summer of 1895. On 20 July, the secretary of state, Richard Olney, sent a message through the American ambassador to the British government asking that the matter be submitted to arbitration. The dispatch invoked the Monroe Doctrine in asserting the right of the United States to intervene in the dispute and requested that London reply before President Grover Cleveland's annual speech to Congress in December.[5]

The British prime minister, Lord Salisbury, waited four long months before responding to Olney's message. His reply, delivered by the British ambassador in Washington, Julian Pauncefote, was a blunt rejection of the Monroe Doctrine as international law and a firm refusal to arbitrate.[6] The delay in the response from London, which arrived too late for Cleveland's speech, its condescending tone, and its denial of American standing in the issue outraged the president. In a special message to Congress on 17 December, Cleveland said that

> the dispute has reached such a stage as to make it now incumbent upon the United States to take measures to determine with sufficient certainty for its justification what is the true divisional line between the Republic of Venezuela and British Guiana. . . .
>
> In order that such an examination should be prosecuted in a thorough and satisfactory manner, I suggest that the Congress make an adequate appropriation for the expenses of a commission, to be appointed by the Executive, who shall make the necessary investigation and report upon the matter with the least possible delay. When such report is made and accepted it will, in my opinion, be the duty of the United States to resist, by every means in its power, as a willful aggression upon its rights and interests, the appropriation by Great Britain of any lands or the exercise of governmental jurisdiction over any territory which, after investi-

gation, we have determined of right belongs to Venezuela.

In making these recommendations I am fully alive to the responsibility incurred, and keenly realize all the consequences that may
follow.[7]

Cleveland's message burst like a bombshell upon Anglo-American
relations. The *New York Sun* ran the headline, "War If Necessary,"
and jingoes throughout the United States rallied to support the president.[8] In London, where the depth of American feeling on the issue
was not generally understood, the explosion came as a considerable
shock.[9] However, the British were not initially anxious to back down
and "on both sides of the Atlantic there was talk of war."[10]

In retrospect, the Venezuelan Boundary Crisis appears somewhat
contrived. Cleveland's speech, on closer examination, left substantial room for maneuver, providing as it did that the United States
should take no action until the commission had completed its investigation and its report had been accepted. Nevertheless, at the time,
the danger of war seemed all too real. And it was, ironically, this
danger that pushed Great Britain and the United States along the
path to peace.

Within a week after the president's message, the tide of bellicosity
fell in the face of rising revulsion at the prospect of conflict. In England and in the United States there was an "extraordinary outburst
of demand . . . for some kind of permanent arbitration system that
would banish for ever all possibility of Anglo-American war." Letters
and resolutions from individuals, civic groups, and religious organizations streamed into London and Washington.[11] The enormous outpouring of pacifist sentiment in the United States so disgusted Theodore Roosevelt that he wrote to his friend Henry Cabot Lodge that
"the clamor of the peace faction has convinced me that this country
needs a war."[12] In the wake of this reaction, an agreement to arbitrate
the boundary question was soon reached and a final settlement
achieved.

The popular enthusiasm for an Anglo-American reconciliation
that was demonstrated during the Venezuelan episode provided
powerful momentum toward further efforts at accommodation.
American and British officials now felt themselves free to pursue
closer relations, and perhaps in some measure compelled to do so by
their aroused electorates. On 11 January 1897, the two governments
concluded the Olney-Pauncefote Arbitration Treaty. This pact bound
England and the United States to submit to arbitration all future
disputes; a simple majority would be sufficient to decide minor

issues, while decisions regarding territorial and other matters of vital interest would be reached via a more complex process that would in effect enable either nation to veto a settlement it found unacceptable.[13]

The Olney-Pauncefote Treaty was hailed almost universally on both sides of the Atlantic. In England, the *Economist* argued that "unless either nation becomes wilfully blind to the rights of the other, and, in fact, attacks its essential rights and interests, there is no reason why the treaty should not put an end to the fear of war between the two branches of the Anglo-Saxon kin."[14] In America, the *St. Louis Republic* declared that "this arbitration treaty definitely provides, within its scope and term of life, for the abolition of war."[15] A *New York World* survey of 400 newspapers throughout the United States found 361 in favor of the agreement and a mere 39 opposed.[16] It was an unexpected turn of events, therefore, when the American Senate first radically amended the treaty and then refused to ratify it. Fortunately, the British did not see in this action any resurgence of the old Anglophobia. The *Economist* admitted that "it is not the people of the United States who have wrecked the treaty. Instead they have been no less earnest than our own people in the cause of arbitration. Not only all the best and most thoughtful influences in the States, but public opinion as a whole has shown itself most strongly in favour of ratifying the treaty. The opposition in the Senate has thus no sort of popular feeling behind it."[17] And most Englishmen, while disappointed, would have agreed with an American newspaper, the *Rochester Herald*, which claimed, "After all, it is the spirit of the treaty rather than its technical form that counts. Treaty or no treaty, it is unlikely that England and the United States will go to war during this generation, at least."[18]

The remarkable change that was now coming over Anglo-American diplomacy was demonstrated upon, and reinforced by, the outbreak of hostilities between the United States and Spain in April 1898. In contrast to the continental countries of Europe, British public opinion was almost wholly on the side of the American cause. The United States embassy in London was so besieged by Englishmen seeking to enlist in the American forces that the ambassador had to announce, through the *Times*, that "American Diplomatic and Consular officials in this country have no authority to entertain such applications."[19] The British government, while ostensibly neutral, maintained a distinctly pro-American attitude throughout the conflict, and effectively blocked a European proposal to intercede on behalf of the Spanish.[20] This sympathy and even support could not pass unnoticed in the United States, and Americans loudly voiced their appreciation. The British ambassador, Lord Pauncefote, noted that they had been suddenly seized by "the most exuberant affection for England and 'Britishers' in general."[21] His second secretary in Washington, Reginald Tower, agreed, reporting that "unanimous, or almost unanimous friendliness to England is now manifested by the Press throughout the length and breadth of the country, and . . . bid[s] fair to pass the bound of moderation in as great degree as the dislike and distrust of yesterday."[22]

Indeed, Anglo-American relations had by this time improved so dramatically that many persons believed the two countries had concluded a secret alliance.[23] They had not, but statements of political leaders in both England and the United States provided ample fuel for such speculation. In the British Parliament, H. H. Asquith boasted that "the closer union of Great Britain and America, not only in sympathy and thought, but political co-operation, is no longer merely the ideal of those who see visions and dream dreams."[24] Joseph Chamberlain, Britain's colonial secretary, and a rabid proponent of Anglo-American amity, spoke openly of alliance on several occasions.[25] Perhaps most astonishing, however, was a speech delivered by Richard Olney, in which the once Anglophobic former secretary of state argued that the United States should abandon her traditional policy of isolation, based on Washington's farewell address, and begin cooperating with England, her "best friend."[26]

By the end of 1898, then, a very considerable transformation had been effected in the relations of Great Britain and the United States. But their rapprochement was still new and somewhat tenuous, and there remained outstanding issues that threatened to slow, or even to reverse, the process of Anglo-American peace. The most dangerous of these questions was that of the isthmian canal. Under the terms of the Clayton-Bulwer Treaty of 1850, any passage through Central America was to be constructed and controlled by Great Britain and the United States together. Since that time, however, strong feeling had developed in the United States that the project should be an entirely American endeavor. In 1900, a bill to study possible routes across the isthmus was introduced in Congress, and the unilateral abrogation of the Clayton-Bulwer pact became more than a vague threat. Had the British government adopted a hard line, conflict over the canal issue could not have been ruled out. But London was not prepared to sacrifice so quickly her newfound friendship with the

United States, and she thus negotiated, and then acceded to, Washington's demands. After an initial accord was rejected by the typically intransigent Senate, a second agreement was soon reached, giving the United States the sole right to build and maintain an isthmian canal. By the Hay-Pauncefote Treaty, proclaimed in February 1902, Great Britain effectively granted the United States maritime supremacy in the Western Hemisphere and removed from the agenda of Anglo-American relations a source of serious strain.[27]

The importance of the conciliatory nature of British policy, and the willingness of London to make concessions to the United States during this period, cannot be overstated. It was demonstrated again the following year in the successful resolution of another potentially volatile issue, that of the Alaskan boundary. The border between Alaska and the Canadian Yukon had been legally established by Anglo-Russian treaty in 1825, when the former territory was part of the tsarist empire. The geographic features on which the line was based were, however, exceedingly ill defined, and considerable ambiguity existed. The problem was brought to a head by the discovery of gold in the Klondike region in 1896. A modus vivendi was achieved in 1899, but it rapidly became evident that a permanent solution would be required.

Throughout the negotiations that ensued, Britain made it clear to Dominion leaders that she would not jeopardize her good relations with America. The Hay-Herbert Treaty, signed on 24 January 1903, provided for a binational commission of six impartial jurists, three from each side, to adjudicate the matter. When President Theodore Roosevelt violated the agreement by appointing to the tribunal men who were far from impartial, London acquiesced and bullied Ottawa into acceptance. The final judgment, which was substantially in accordance with the American position, was widely approved in England for having allowed her to settle the dispute at such a minor expense.[28]

The conclusion of the Alaskan boundary episode may be said to mark the point at which the Anglo-American rapprochement became secure. Other controversies were to arise in the coming years, most notably over Anglo-German efforts at debt collection in Venezuela and Panama Canal tolls. But these were not so dangerous and were resolved without great difficulty. After 1903, an Anglo-American war was virtually unthinkable. The relations of Great Britain and the United States had become those of peace.

The Exercise of Power

The late nineteenth and early twentieth centuries saw the potential for a vigorous power rivalry between Great Britain and the United States. From her role as a minor actor on the world stage, America rose to a position of international influence and became capable of mounting a formidable challenge to British ascendancy. Portents of this development had been apparent for some time. Since the 1820s, England's former colonies had possessed a population larger than that of the mother country, and the gap had grown wider with each passing year. The gross national product of the United States had by steadily increasing margins outstripped that of Britain since the 1850s. And around 1900 America began to approach and then to surpass Britain in other important indicators of national strength.

In 1899, the United States replaced Britain as the world's primary consumer of pig iron. Within six years she had become its principal manufacturer as well. American output of crude steel exceeded British output by 1890. Consumption and production of coal were larger in the United States by 1891 and 1899, respectively. And this transformation was equally impressive when translated into per capita terms. By 1900, per capita output of crude steel was higher in the United States than in Britain. By 1904, per capita production and consumption of pig iron were greater. By 1908, the average American citizen consumed more coal than his English counterpart. And about 1910, America's per capita gross national product overtook that of Britain. When one stops to consider that in that year the population of the United States stood at 92 million persons to Britain's 36 million, it is evident that in many respects the United States had already supplanted Britain as the world's leading power.[29]

Nor was America's growth confined to the economic sphere. During this period, the United States began to rapidly expand her military capabilities, particularly on the seas. As late as 1890, the American navy did not contain a single battleship. But sparked by the Samoan episode of 1889 and the writings of Alfred Mahan, the United States embarked on a massive program of naval construction. By 1905, America owned a total of twenty-four battleships built or in construction, a figure higher than that of Germany. By 1907, the American navy had surpassed the German navy in overall tonnage, and *Jane's Fighting Ships*, the authoritative publication on naval affairs, ranked the American fleet number two in the world.[30]

Prior to 1914, most American naval and political leaders professed themselves satisfied with a navy "second to that of Great Britain." A persistent and vocal minority, however, demanded a fleet "second to none."[31] In a 1902 article for the *North American Review*, naval constructor, and later congressman, Richmond P. Hobson of Alabama, a leader of this faction, argued that "the United States should have the largest navy in the world; indeed, the proportions would not be strained if the Navy of the United States equalled the combined navies of the earth." He then went on to propose a plan by which the American navy would become stronger than the British navy by 1920.[32]

The British were not unaware of America's naval ambitions or ignorant of her ultimate potential. Many foresaw a day, in the not-too-distant future, when the United States would become the world's leading maritime power.[33] In 1901, Selborne, first lord of the Admiralty, stated his belief that "if the Americans choose to pay for what they can easily afford, they can gradually build up a navy, fully as large and then larger than ours." He added, "I am not sure they will not do it."[34] A report by the British naval attaché in Washington several years later provided additional confirmation of this already prevailing view.[35]

From a narrow realist perspective, Great Britain and America were almost destined to be enemies. Long the leading international power, Britain found herself being eclipsed by the United States on significant indicators of economic capacity and industrial might.[36] Her ability to remain mistress of the seas, on which she had staked her survival for centuries, would be seriously jeopardized by further expansion of the American fleet. At the same time, however, she retained a substantial advantage over the United States in terms of her existing naval strength. Although other nations, most notably Germany, had also entered into a period of rapid growth, none possessed either the power of Great Britain or the enormous potential of the United States. Under such circumstances, one might have expected Britain to see America as the gravest menace to her international position and the United States to view Britain as the main impediment to her future advancement. Indeed, the late nineteenth and early twentieth centuries did witness a number of geopolitical disputes between the two countries. The most important of these have been discussed above. Confrontations over the Venezuelan boundary, the isthmian canal, and the Alaskan-Canadian border were all symptomatic of attempts by the United States to advance its strategic and territorial interests and attempts by Great Britain to resist.

What is surprising, at least from the realist standpoint, is that the Anglo-American power rivalry did not end in an apparently inevitable hegemonic war, but was resolved through peaceful accommodation. Most of the sacrifices involved in this achievement were made by Great Britain. Between 1895 and 1905, Britain gradually retreated from the Western Hemisphere and removed herself as an effective obstacle to the exercise of American authority in that region of the world. The Hay-Pauncefote Treaty, which granted Washington the sole right to construct and control the isthmian canal, symbolized Britain's acceptance of naval inferiority in American waters and her new commitment to a geographic division of labor with the United States. Henceforth, she would concentrate on the protection of her empire in other areas of the globe, leaving the Americans unchallenged in their own backyard. The subsequent elimination of the North Atlantic naval station at Halifax and the reduction of the Caribbean station to a cruiser squadron based in England were further manifestations of this commitment. In 1903, Prime Minister Arthur Balfour publicly enunciated Britain's policy of withdrawal from American affairs when he proclaimed his government's support for the Monroe Doctrine, saying, "The Monroe doctrine has no enemies in this country that I know of. We welcome any increase of the influence of the United States of America upon the great Western Hemisphere."[37] A comparison of this statement with Salisbury's unyielding response to Olney's message of but eight years before shows just how far and how quickly the British position had changed.

Britain's decision to abandon the Western Hemisphere to the United States was, in part, determined by the need to somehow improve the security of the British Empire. For most of the nineteenth century, Britain had maintained a posture of "splendid isolation," distancing herself from continental affairs and relying upon the Royal Navy to protect her far-flung possessions. By the late 1890s, however, Britain's isolation appeared to be much less splendid as the danger to her imperial position became more and more acute.

The pressures on British imperial defense flowed from a number of sources.[38] In Afghanistan and Persia, as well as in Turkey, London was confronted with a Russian appetite for territory that seemed more voracious with each passing year. The specter of a tsarist invasion of India, which had haunted British policymakers for decades, loomed larger as the Orenburg-Tashkent Railway neared completion. In North Africa and South Asia, British interests clashed with those of France. And the Franco-Russian Alliance of 1894 had united these two foes and ended Britain's domination of the Mediterranean Sea. To these difficulties were added complications of still more recent origin. The United States, especially after 1898, emerged as a major force on the international scene. At the same time, Germany embarked upon an ambitious program of naval expansion that threatened to deny Britain her traditional maritime supremacy. Finally, as the ancient Chinese Empire began to disintegrate, and the various powers jockeyed for position, there arose the likelihood of involvement in a conflict in the Far East. The situation facing Britain was, to put it mildly, an uncomfortable one. As Joseph Chamberlain commented somewhat morosely in 1898, "We have in hand difficulties of the most serious character with France, Russia and Germany. We are engaged in an important expedition in the Soudan; and it is uncertain as yet whether the war on the North-west frontier of India has been finally concluded. We may emerge from all these troubles without a war, but I cannot conceal from myself that the prospect is more gloomy than it has ever been in my recollection."[39]

Britain's desire, naturally, was to resist all of these pressures.[40] Her efforts to do so, however, quickly encountered formidable economic constraints. Paul Kennedy has noted, "The simplistic remedy of increasing the defence budget until Britain's navy and army were capable of satisfying all the demands which were placed upon them was financially impossible."[41] Excluding those amounts appropriated for prosecution of the war in South Africa, British military and naval estimates rose by 38 percent from 1895–96 to 1901–2. Total government expenditures grew from £105 million to £147 million over the same period. The chancellor of the exchequer, Hicks Beach, concluded that the extra tax levied to meet the costs associated with the South African War would have to be maintained in peacetime, and he argued that if spending continued to climb a radical change in English fiscal policy would be required.[42]

Not all British statesmen feared a fiscal revolution. Indeed, if funds sufficient for imperial defense could have been obtained through higher direct taxation or by the introduction of some form of protection, Balfour and Chamberlain, among others, would have been prepared to take such action. But even this was doubtful. For despite the bloated defense budgets, Britain's security position continued to deteriorate. By 1901, in the opinion of War Secretary St. John Brodrick, the British army was short 50,000 troops.[43] Worse, as Selborne, at the Admiralty, informed his colleagues in January of that year, Britain's once commanding naval lead over France and Russia had practically vanished. Since 1895–96, while British shipyards had built twelve battleships, those of France and Russia had turned out nineteen. The Royal Navy now had forty-five battleships at its disposal; the combined fleets of the Dual Alliance, forty-three. According to the Admiralty's projections, a state of parity might be reached as early as 1906.[44] The "two-power standard," by which Britain had long guided her naval policy, was thus gravely threatened. And the new construction programs of other rising powers had already significantly diluted its value. By 1901 Germany had built a total of fourteen battleships; the United States, seven; and Japan, five—with plans for many more.[45]

The difficulty of Britain's security position was most forcefully revealed, to those not previously aware of it, by the war in South Africa, which began in 1899. To cover the expenses incurred by the British expedition, London was forced to raise taxes. The nearly 400,-000 British troops dispatched to the scene required more than two years of bloody fighting to subdue a group of only 80,000 Boers. Although their biggest fear, intervention by a continental coalition, never materialized, British officials felt their freedom of diplomatic and military action severely circumscribed.[46] In particular, Britain was forced to tread lightly in her relations with France and Russia. According to the War Office, the South African conflict had rendered Britain incapable of mustering the forces needed to fight these two powers.[47] Curzon, the British viceroy in India, was warned by both Lord Goschen, head of the Admiralty, and Brodrick, the war secretary, to avoid confrontations in Persia and the Persian Gulf during this period.[48] Arthur Balfour, first lord of the Treasury and later prime minister, complained that as a result of the conflict Britain had, for the moment, become a "third-rate Power."[49] And Lord Lansdowne, Brodrick's predecessor at the War Office, and then foreign secretary, contended that unless Britain were able to procure the assistance of another power, "our South African entanglements make it impossible for us to commit ourselves to a policy which might involve us in war."[50]

By the last years of the nineteenth century, then, and certainly by the early years of the twentieth, it had become apparent to British statesmen, and more gradually to public opinion, that Britain's imperial reach was badly overextended. "The truth is," lamented Sir

Henry Campbell-Bannerman shortly before taking office as prime minister, "we cannot provide for a fighting Empire, and nothing will give us the power."[51] It was clear that Britain's strength was no longer sufficient to enable her to meet all her defense commitments and face all her potential enemies. The government in London began, therefore, to seek to extricate Britain from her predicament. One means of doing so was to reach an accommodation with some of her possible adversaries, including the United States.

Given the deeply rooted tradition of isolation in America, not to mention her long history of Anglophobia, few British officials expected Washington to play a positive role in support of British interests. Francis Bertie, under-secretary in the Foreign Office, argued in 1901 that Britain could safely depend upon the United States to counter German ambitions in the American seas, but his notion that she might become an active partner in imperial defense did not gain wide acceptance until much later.[52] Most British statesmen had less ambitious designs. Mainly, they hoped to remove the United States from the list of potential foes so that badly overtaxed resources could be utilized elsewhere.[53] This was first manifested in the British approach to the Venezuelan boundary dispute, when the ill-fated Jameson Raid, the subsequent Kruger Telegram, and the hostility of the continental powers prompted the cabinet to reverse Salisbury's original position and to agree to a negotiated settlement.[54] It reached its logical conclusion in the fleet reorganization program of 1904–6, which closed the North Atlantic naval station at Halifax and reduced the Caribbean station to a cruiser squadron based in England, effectively ending Britain's permanent naval presence in the Western Hemisphere so that her maritime power could be concentrated in European waters.[55]

The elimination of the United States as a likely adversary was particularly important to Britain in view of the almost insurmountable obstacles that she would have faced in any Anglo-American war. British statesmen had long recognized that in the event of a conflict with the United States an invasion of Canada could not be prevented. Indeed, they had not bothered to maintain a land presence on Canadian soil for nearly three decades. However, the British government had hoped to offset such an invasion by a decisive naval victory, bombarding American cities and blockading the coast. Now, with the advent of American sea power, this hope appeared lost. To defeat the Americans, Britain would be forced to devote a large portion of her fleet to the effort. And this she could not do. As early as 1895, when the United States threatened war over the Venezuelan issue, Britain found herself unable, because of the international situation, to increase her forces in the Western Hemisphere, and her position only worsened with each passing year.[56] The virtual impossibility of successfully prosecuting a war against the United States, and the grave risks associated with any attempt to do so, were spelled out in an Admiralty memorandum:

> Centuries of triumphant conflict with her European rivals have left Great Britain the double legacy of world-wide Empire and of a jealousy (of which we had a sad glimpse during the South African war) which would render it hazardous indeed to denude our home waters of the battle squadrons, which stand between our own land and foreign invasion.
>
> America, it seems, can employ every ship she possesses in the Western Atlantic, but the conditions under which England could employ her whole naval force in such a distant locality are hardly conceivable. . . .
>
> . . . It appears, then, that however unwelcome, the conclusion is inevitable that, in the event of an occurrence so much to be deprecated as the rupture of friendly relations with the United States, the position of Canada is one of extreme danger, and, so far as the navy is concerned, any effective assistance would be exceedingly difficult. . . .
>
> Generally, the more carefully this problem is considered, the more tremendous do the difficulties which would confront Great Britain in a war with the United States appear. It may be hoped that the policy of the British Government will ever be to use all possible means to avoid such a war.[57]

To an extent, then, Britain's cultivation of American friendship was part of a broader policy of imperial consolidation, a cautious retreat dictated by the exigencies of her strategic position.[58] Hostilities with the United States, unpalatable under the best of circumstances, could not be contemplated in a world where other, more serious, dangers loomed. British statesmen had good reason for thinking that America was not the principal threat to their security. The United States, unlike the continental powers of Europe, was geographically distant from the British Isles and from much of the British Empire. Moreover, in contrast to Britain's other rivals, the United States harbored no real designs on British possessions or spheres of influence. Even American opinion favoring the annexation of Canada had by this time almost completely disappeared. Given the relatively minor nature of America's territorial ambitions—a narrow strip of land along the Canadian border and a Central American canal—plus the disproportionately large expenditure of resources that would have been required in order to sustain her position, accommodation with the United States appeared to offer great strategic benefits at fairly little cost.

In this sense, it was a relatively high level of heterogeneity in the exercise of British and American power—as compared to the exercise of British and German, British and Russian, and British and French, power—that contributed to the rapprochement. It was no coincidence that Britain reconciled first with the United States, whose ambitions clashed least with her vital interests, then with France, whose aims posed a more significant threat, and not at all with Germany, whose objectives were most fundamentally incompatible with her own.

While Britain actively sought an accommodation with the United States in order to bolster her strategic position, Americans were also beginning to feel a similar—though less compelling—need for an understanding. The concern with security that pervaded British political discourse at the turn of the century was not, it must be admitted, so prevalent in the United States. Objectively speaking, Americans at this time had little to worry about. Separated from their potential enemies by a vast expanse of ocean, they were further protected by the heated rivalries among the European powers that forced those countries to keep their fleets in home waters. Nevertheless, it would not be accurate to state, as one scholar has done, that there was in the United States "no keen intimation of danger, no well-defined fear of a specific menace."[59] For, despite the relative safety of the American position, considerable apprehension, particularly of German ambitions, existed among the general public and extended to high levels within the government as well.

The diplomatic relations between the United States and Germany had been deteriorating since about 1890 as various disputes over trade and tariff policies poisoned the air. The first suggestion that Germany might actually pose a threat to America's vital interests did not come, however, until 1896, when Charles de Kay, the American consul-general in Berlin, warned that "should the Emperor's desire to have a great fleet become the wish of a sufficiently powerful section of the population, the United States must be prepared for an 'aggressive' colonial policy in Germany and this aggression points towards South America."[60] American distrust of German objectives in the Western Hemisphere quickly intensified. This distrust had at its

foundation the rapid expansion of German maritime power, and it
was fueled by a series of specific incidents, including a confrontation
over Samoa in 1898–99, the maneuvers of German Vice-Admiral von
Diederichs in Manila Bay during the Spanish-American War, and the
heavy-handed German efforts at debt collecting in Venezuela in
1902–3. By 1900, the influential senator from Massachusetts, Henry
Cabot Lodge, was convinced that Germany sought to destroy the
Monroe Doctrine and to establish a colonial empire in Brazil.[61]
Harper's Weekly agreed that Germany intended to "blow the Monroe
Doctrine sky-high,"[62] and the British ambassador in Washington,
Michael Herbert, reported back to London that "suspicion of the
German Emperor's designs in the Caribbean is shared by the Admin-
istration, the press, and the public alike."[63] For President Theodore
Roosevelt, "the specter of German aggression" was a "veritable
nightmare."[64]

The precise degree to which fear of Germany and, to a lesser
extent, other European powers such as Spain contributed to American desires for a reconciliation with Great Britain is difficult to determine. It is doubtful whether a majority of the population perceived
that cordial relations with England could prove helpful in thwarting
continental ambitions. But the value of British friendship to American defense interests was not unknown to those in positions of
authority and influence. Roosevelt himself appreciated the fact that
British neutrality, if nothing more, was vital to American hopes of
resisting German advances. In 1901, at a time when public clamor for
the unilateral construction of an isthmian canal was building, the
soon-to-be chief executive warned that "we should be exceedingly
cautious about embroiling ourselves with England, from whom we
have not the least little particle of danger to fear in any way or shape;
while the only power which may be a menace to us in anything like
the immediate future is Germany."[65]

Meanwhile, others in the United States saw Britain as an active,
though informal, partner in the protection of the hemisphere. As
early as 1898, in the wake of the Spanish-American War, Brooks
Adams argued that only the benevolent exercise of British sea power
could provide an effective guarantee of American security. Writing in
the *Forum*, Adams stated that "England is essential to the United
States, in the face of enemies who fear and hate us, and who, but for
her, would already have fleets upon our shores."[66] Similar sentiments
were expressed by another American observer, who informed his
English readers in a *Westminster Review* article of 1900:

There is not a thinking man in America to-day, who does not recog-
nise that the further the policy of expansion is pushed the less
disposition will the Continental Powers of Europe have to respect
the Monroe Doctrine as applied to South America, after Asia, the
most promising scene in the world for European Colonial aggrandisement. It is by no means improbable that Germany, strengthened
by the proposed increase in her naval force, and still burning to
extend the field of her Colonial influence, will seize the first pretext
to plant her foot upon the Southern pampas and defy the United
States to expel her from the soil.

   This is one of the probabilities of the future, while another, still
stronger, is a complication with some other, or even the same foreign
Power, growing out of the new territory the United States already
holds outside of her continental boundaries. Which European nation
is likely to support her in the enforcement of the Monroe Doctrine?
England, and England alone. Which European country is apt to be
her ally in case of complications on other grounds? Again, England,
and England alone.[67]

The belief that Anglo-American friendship was beneficial, if not
indispensable, to American security interests was most strongly held
by the United States Navy. In January 1905, following an extensive
tour of naval installations in the western United States, the British
naval attaché, Captain D. R. Dechair, reported to London his discovery of the conviction among American officers that a firm understanding should be established with Great Britain. This would not be
"an alliance exactly, but an understanding approaching cooperation,
which would, in the event of a hostile coalition of European Powers
against the United States, ensure her the support of the British
Navy."[68] The official position of the American navy was explicitly
laid out in a report by the General Board the following year:

   Germany is desirous of extending her colonial possessions.
   Especially is it thought that she is desirous of obtaining a foothold in
   the Western Hemisphere, and many things indicate that she has her
   eyes on localities in the West Indies, on the shores of the Caribbean,
   and in parts of South America. It is believed in many quarters that
   she is planning to test the Monroe Doctrine by the annexation or by
   the establishment of a protectorate over a portion of South America,
   even going to the extent of war with the United States when her fleet
   is ready.

   It is asserted on good authority that Great Britain does not wish to
   acquire any additional colonial possessions. Should it be true that
   Germany wishes to extend her colonial possessions to the Western
   Hemisphere, our interests are here bound up with those of England,

and we can reasonably expect passive, if not active, assistance from Great Britain should it become necessary for the United States to prevent German acquisition of territory in this hemisphere.

The welfare of the United States and its immunity from entanglements with the other Powers is greatly strengthened by strong ties of friendship and by unanimity of action with Great Britain.[69]

It is unclear whether mistrust of German ambitions would have exceeded suspicion of British intentions sufficiently to cause the United States to make geopolitical concessions to Britain had Britain been unwilling to withdraw from the Western Hemisphere. The pressures on British defense were so substantial that London surrendered her commitments without ever truly testing the depth of American resolve. Certainly the United States appeared more obstinate and more reluctant to compromise her objectives in the pursuit of an accommodation. But it is arguable that had push come to shove, Americans might well have taken a more conciliatory stance. At any rate, as German power began to be projected more and more into areas overlapping with American power, the exercise of British power became less and less a worry, and the United States came to see the possibility and the strategic value of Britain's friendship.

The role of power and power politics in the relations of Great Britain and the United States during the late nineteenth and early twentieth centuries indicates the need for a modification of conventional realist wisdom. From the realist standpoint, these two countries were natural, almost certain enemies, for they stood at the apex of the international power structure. America, rising, approached or surpassed Britain as the world's mightiest nation in terms of industrial base and underlying capabilities. Britain, declining, still possessed her traditional mastery of the seas, but by 1907 the American fleet had gained the second ranking, and knowledgeable British officials believed that American supremacy was only a matter of time. Under these circumstances, Britain ought to have seen in the United States the chief menace to her international position, while America ought to have viewed Britain as the principal obstacle to her future advancement. Yet this was not what happened. Instead of meeting in battle, Britain and the United States were reconciled, drawn together in part by a common desire to counter other potential adversaries, which, by the yardstick of aggregate power, should have been judged to constitute lesser threats.

This was so in some measure because Americans and Englishmen alike were not concerned solely with the distribution of power among nations but also with its exercise, actual and intended. In point of fact, the tangible geopolitical disputes between Britain and the United States were fairly minor. Differences over the Venezuelan and Alaskan boundaries appear in retrospect almost trivial, while the issue of the isthmian canal was of greater, but hardly earth-shattering, significance. Neither country harbored ambitions that seemed to threaten the other's most vital interests. Britain sought no territorial aggrandizement in the Western Hemisphere. The United States no longer coveted Canada, nor did she wish for colonies in Asia or Africa. Geographically separated from the British Isles by a broad expanse of ocean, her growth posed no real danger to Britain's home security. By contrast, French and Russian aims menaced British possessions in several areas, while Germany threatened to seize from Britain naval supremacy in the waters nearest British shores. Similarly, German desires to obtain coaling stations in the Caribbean, to claim parts of the Spanish Empire there and in the Pacific, and to establish colonies in Latin America were well documented, even if the government in Berlin pursued these objectives with less vigor than Americans feared and Germans hoped.[70]

The case of Britain and the United States suggests, then, that it is not aggregate power relationships that determine friendships and hostilities among states as much as the ends toward which this power is employed. In this respect, Britain and America, despite their considerable similarity as insular, maritime powers, were more heterogeneous with regard to one another than with regard to other possible opponents. And this relative heterogeneity—primarily geographic—in the exercise of power contributed to their rapprochement.

The Anglo-American reconciliation cannot, however, be explained entirely, or even mainly, as a function of differences in the levels of geopolitical competition between these and other states. In the first place, perceptions of the relative salience of various international rivalries and the degree to which vital interests overlapped were based less on an objective evaluation of aims and ambitions than a subjective assessment, strongly influenced by the ideological and cultural affinity between the United States and Britain on the one hand, and the ideological/cultural disaffection and economic competition between these and other powers (especially Germany) on the other. Furthermore, even ostensibly rational strategic calculations did not lie behind much of either the public agitation or the official enthusiasm for an accommodation. It is instructive that the initial movement toward improved relations began in late 1895 and early 1896, before most persons in the United States or in Britain (some members of the British cabinet excepted) had much sense of insecurity. Finally, the Anglo-American friendship forged during this era continued, albeit not without some strain, after 1918, when no external dangers loomed on the horizon.

This suggests that, in fact, the Anglo-American rapprochement was more the product of incentives internal to the relationship of the two countries than a response to any external imperatives. Indeed, as we shall see, the understanding appears to have been prompted mainly by desires on the part of both Englishmen and Americans to preserve vital economic connections and to avoid a fratricidal war with Anglo-Saxon kin. In this sense, the degree of heterogeneity that did exist in the exercise of British and American power may have made a second contribution—as a facilitating factor—to the Anglo-American reconciliation, independent of threat assessments and balancing motivations. Because the specific points of conflict between the two countries were fairly minor and did not really involve national security or other perceived vital interests, they could be negotiated and compromised if other factors militated in favor of their pacific resolution.

Economic Activities

The economies of Great Britain and the United States were already intimately linked when the American Revolution drew to a close. America had, of course, long been a part of the British Empire and an integral component of the British mercantile system. But the economic relationship between the mother country and her former colonies broadened and deepened after American independence. Toward the end of the nineteenth century it emerged as a potent force for Anglo-American peace.

During the decade from 1896 to 1905, trade between Great Britain and the United States averaged about $681 million annually. Merchandise worth $524 million flowed from America to England every year, while $157 million passed from Britain to the United States. Anglo-American commerce in this period accounted for more than

40 percent of all U.S. exports and about 18 percent of all American imports. For Great Britain, these figures were 7.5 percent of total exports and 24 percent of total imports. The pattern of trans-Atlantic trade had changed considerably from the mid-1800s, when the volumes of goods and services traveling in each direction were roughly equal, and even more from the 1820s, when the United States consistently imported more from Great Britain than she exported to her. The value of annual shipments from Britain to the United States had, in fact, been declining since the 1840s. But the flow from America to England had continued to increase, in absolute terms, throughout the century. Although their relationship was no longer as exclusive as it once had been, the United States and Great Britain remained each other's most important commercial partners.[71]

The great volume of Anglo-American commerce was in part a reflection of the essentially heterogeneous and complementary nature of the two economies and was indicative of the fact that Britain and the United States relied heavily on one another for needed goods and services. This interdependence revolved mainly around trade in agricultural products and raw materials. Approximately 80 percent of all goods exported by the United States to England fell into this category. Of these commodities, two possessed special significance: cotton and wheat. From 1896 to 1905, more than three-quarters of all raw cotton used in British textile mills came from the United States. Roughly 40 percent of American cotton exports went to England, and about one-quarter of the total domestic production. During the period from 1897 to 1901, Great Britain obtained more than 60 percent of her imports of wheat and wheat flour from the United States, a figure representing nearly half of total British consumption. Almost 50 percent of all American exports of wheat and wheat flour were purchased by England, and about 15 percent of the entire amount produced in the United States.[72]

The importance of this commercial connection was recognized in both countries. In the midst of the crisis over the Venezuelan boundary in 1895, wheat interests in the United States telegraphed Washington to express their fears that exports to England would be endangered and their desire for a swift and peaceful accommodation.[73] Shortly thereafter, a writer in the *Forum* argued that

> the interruption of our commerce with Great Britain, would at once deprive a great number . . . of their customary occupation and means of subsistence. That privation would immediately act upon the entire products of agriculture, reducing prices to less than cost and

depriving nearly every branch of agriculture of any profit. But the evil would not end at that point. The prosperity of the railways and of the manufacturers, whose chief market is among the farmers and those engaged in the conversion of farm products, would be instantly impaired. Although the prices of a few articles might be extravagantly raised by the obstruction to imports, the great mass of our industries would be paralyzed and brought to a state of extreme depression.[74]

And George Harvey, at various times the editor of *Harper's Weekly* and the *North American Review*, wrote that "a quarrel with Great Britain would be disastrous. If her ports were closed to us, we should lose our principal customer, not only for our surplus cotton, but for our surplus breadstuffs. To the farmers of our prairie States and to the planters of our Southern States, such an obstruction to the export of their staples would mean catastrophe."[75]

For Britain, which depended on the products exported by the United States, stable Anglo-American trade was still more vital. The British economy was highly vulnerable to a disruption of commerce with America, a fact recognized by many Englishmen. In an article entitled "American Control of England's Food Supply," J. D. Whelpley claimed that if the United States were to cut off exports of foodstuffs to Britain it would be but a few weeks before the English people were threatened by famine. Moreover, he wrote, a stoppage of cotton shipments would close down the textile mills, throwing thousands out of work. Ultimately, in his words, "War itself against the United States, the English base of supplies, could only result in speedy capitulation or inevitable ruin."[76] This opinion was shared by Norman Angell of the *Daily Mail*, who also wrote of the futility of any British attempt to engage in a conflict with the United States: "We could, it is true, destroy her navy, bombard her ports, blockade her coasts and by doing so create a position far more onerous for us than for her. She would be embarrassed; we should starve—Lancashire from lack of cotton, and other parts of our population from the high prices of food."[77]

The cost of food was, in fact, a constant worry to British officials and was seen by them to constrain British policy toward the United States. During Parliamentary debate on tariff reform, the government steadfastly refused to consider the imposition of import duties on American agricultural products, an action which would have led to increased prices for English consumers.[78] Of course, the complete cessation of imports from the United States in time of war would have presented a far graver problem. Concern over just such a prospect existed in London and was heightened by the chronically poor relations between England and Russia, the other major purveyor of British foodstuffs. So long as conflict with St. Petersburg seemed possible, even likely, Britain could ill afford to contemplate becoming embroiled with the United States.[79] This difficulty was alluded to, though rather obliquely, by the House of Commons when, in 1897, it unanimously passed a resolution stating that "in the opinion of this House, the dependence of the United Kingdom on foreign imports for the necessities of life, and the consequences that might arise therefrom in the event of war, demands the serious attention of Her Majesty's Government."[80] The peril of Britain's position was further compounded by the vulnerability to American naval and military power of still other sources of food. A War Office memorandum noted pessimistically that should hostilities with the United States occur, not only would exports of grain from that country be suspended, but the flow of Canadian and Latin American grain might also be cut off. The War Office concluded that "such a condition of affairs might result in our being compelled to sue for peace on humiliating terms."[81]

In addition to their close commercial ties, the economies of Great Britain and the United States were also bound together in matters of finance. British investment in America, important in the days before independence, grew steadily throughout the nineteenth century. In 1899, it was estimated that British investors held about $2.5 billion in American stocks and bonds, roughly 75 percent of all American securities in foreign hands. By 1908, this figure had risen to $3.5 billion, and by 1914 to $4.25 billion.[82] The overwhelming preponderance of British money on the American market was noted by the German ambassador in Washington, Holleben, who lamented in 1900 that "Wall Street has almost become an English enclave."[83]

The dependence of the American securities market on British funds was dramatically demonstrated by the events of December 1895. Following President Cleveland's bellicose address to Congress on the Venezuelan issue, British financiers sought to divest themselves of their American holdings, thus precipitating a crash. Five firms failed, total losses of $170 million were recorded, and loan rates jumped to 80 percent.[84] The effect on railway stocks, in which Britons had invested heavily, was especially severe. By the end of that business week, prices had fallen as much as $16.75 per share.[85]

Historians have since pointed out that the stock market crash of 20 December 1895 was not merely a response to Cleveland's message but also the consequence of a long-term weakness in the American dollar.[86] However, this was not so apparent at the time. In both England and the United States, the financial crisis was attributed to the sudden threat of Anglo-American war.[87] And, in the United States at least, it seems to have contributed to the popular reaction against Cleveland's policy and to the clamor for peace. Certainly Lord Pauncefote thought so. On 24 December, the British ambassador cabled London that "the extraordinary state of excitement into which the Congress of the United States and the whole country were thrown by the warlike message of the President . . . has given way . . . to consternation at the financial panic which it caused."[88] Even Cleveland's own resolve may have been shaken. According to John Hay, admittedly no great admirer of the president, he was "terrified" by the crash.[89]

It is important to note that the Anglo-American rapprochement occurred at a point when the complementarity of the British and American economies was actually declining. Capital accumulation in America had reached such a level that foreign sources were no longer so essential; indeed, the United States began to move toward a position as lender rather than borrower in international financial markets. American funds found their way even into Great Britain. A modest flow around 1900 provoked fears of an "American invasion," and when U.S. financier J. Pierpont Morgan gained control of a substantial share of British shipping, public outcry was sufficient to compel the government to intervene to prevent the prestigious Cunard Line from falling into American hands.[90] In the area of trade, a parallel transformation was under way. The United States, rapidly industrializing, began to produce increasing quantities of manufactured articles that competed directly with comparable British goods. American exports of iron and steel rose almost sixfold between 1895 and 1905, while exports of machinery nearly quadrupled during the same period.[91] Englishmen chafed at high American import duties, and the United States figured prominently in British discussions of tariff reform and imperial preference.[92] Ernest E. Williams, who created a sensation in 1896 with a series of articles, "Made in Germany," had by 1901 decided that the United States was "an even more powerful rival."[93] J. A. Hobson, too, believed that Britain had less to fear from Germany than from America.[94] In fact, one student of the era has claimed that "if there had been an Anglo-American war, there would have been enough historical material to prove economic rivalry as a cause of the conflict."[95]

Despite this trend—which was greatly accelerated during the First World War—the damaging impact of the growing economic competition on the relations of Great Britain and the United States did not offset the salutary effects of their still close commercial and financial ties. In large part, this was because the structure of British and American trade remained broadly complementary. American exports continued to consist mainly of agricultural items England did not produce. Rivalry, while present, was not that severe. An 1897 study initiated by the British colonial secretary and designed to measure the displacement in colonial markets of British goods by foreign merchandise found only twelve instances of such displacement by American products, ranking the United States behind both Belgium, mentioned fourteen times, and Germany, cited forty-five times.[96]

The close commercial and financial connections that existed between Great Britain and the United States during the last years of the nineteenth century and the early years of the twentieth provided a significant incentive for the maintenance of amicable relations. America supplied Britain with raw materials and agricultural commodities that the latter was unable to produce herself, receiving in return a valuable market for export items. Similarly, Britain furnished the United States with large amounts of needed capital, obtaining at the same time a profitable outlet for her own surplus funds. Although these linkages became looser after about 1900 and were to some degree balanced by an increasing competitiveness, the British and American economies retained a substantial measure of complementarity.

In addition to the fact that elements of competition were outweighed by those of complementarity, it was also significant that the interdependence relationship between the two countries remained fairly symmetrical. While the United States began to depend on British markets for sales of some manufactured goods as well as agricultural products (and was therefore perhaps somewhat more dependent than before), Britain continued to rely heavily on the United States for foodstuffs and industrial raw materials. For this reason, although Englishmen occasionally resented America's progress and worried about her eventual supremacy, they could not afford to retaliate by closing British markets to the bulk of American goods, a situation recognized across the Atlantic. Joseph Chamberlain's proposals for tariff reform and imperial preference aroused little apprehension in the United States, and Americans generally did not perceive Britain to stand in the path of their economic expansion.[97] As we shall see in the next chapter, the German need for Britain's markets was not matched by British dependence on German merchandise, a situation that had quite different consequences.

Societal Attributes

It is the role of societal attributes in the Anglo-American rapprochement that most strikingly distinguishes this case from the others examined in this study. The phenomenon of Anglo-Saxonism, with its powerful yet often subtle influence on the attitudes of statesmen, politicians, and the public alike, is unique to the relations of Great Britain and the United States. In essence, Anglo-Saxonism was English-speaking nationalism, a belief that Englishmen and Americans, though they inhabited different lands, were a single people. It was based on the perception of a number of similarities between the two societies, including those of language, literature, religion, culture, and political and governmental ideology and institutions. At a minimum, Anglo-Saxonists held that conflict between the United States and Britain was unthinkable because it would be fratricidal, a civil war. At the maximum, they argued that the Anglo-Saxon race was superior to all others and that England and America shared a mission to spread enlightenment and civilization around the globe.[98]

The theory of Anglo-Saxonism was, of course, grounded in objective reality. Great Britain and the United States did possess certain common characteristics, among them the English language and its literature, a Protestant-Christian religious orientation, a commitment to liberalism, representative government, and the rule of law, and other vaguer cultural characteristics. But this had always been true, and it had not prevented the American War of Independence, nor had it preserved the peace in 1812. Indeed, the shared language had actually proved to be a bone of bitter contention throughout much of the nineteenth century. Many Britons were distressed at the proliferation of "Americanisms," which they saw as corrupting the mother tongue, and British criticism of American literature was frequently haughty and condescending.[99] The *Annual Review* in 1808 railed against the "torrent of barbarous phraseology with which

American writers threaten to destroy the purity of the English language,"[100] while the *Edinburgh Review*, evaluating John Quincy Adams's *Letters on Silesia*, commented that "the style of Mr. Adams is in general very tolerable English; which, for American composition, is no moderate praise."[101] Americans, for their part, deeply resented this contemptuous tone, and tended to dismiss British usage as "puerile" and "idiotic." Some even attempted to dissociate the United States from the English language, at least in name. William Marcy, U.S. secretary of state from 1853 to 1857, stipulated that only the "American language" be used in diplomatic reports. And when Indiana University was founded in 1838, the state legislature decreed that the school should instruct its students "in the American, learned and foreign languages."[102]

That Anglo-Saxonism emerged as a major force in the relations of Great Britain and the United States toward the end of the nineteenth century was the result of several factors. In terms of basic social and political philosophy, the two countries did seem more alike than had previously been the case. The reform bills of 1867 and 1884, which extended the franchise in England, had largely dissolved "the traditional American stereotype of that country as archaic, hopelessly feudal, and aristocratic."[103] Similarly, Britain's granting of self-governing dominion status to Canada had helped to erase longstanding American notions of British monarchical tyranny.[104] In addition, social ties between the two nations were becoming increasingly intimate, especially among the upper classes. By 1903, more than seventy Americans had married English noblemen, and the number nearly doubled during the following decade. Among the English elite, Randolph Churchill, George Curzon, Michael Herbert, William Harcourt, and Joseph Chamberlain all had American wives. Most of these women were themselves the daughters of prominent business or political leaders in the United States. Such unions surely contributed something to the feeling that Americans and Englishmen were one people.[105]

More important than these trends, however, was the fact that the intellectual climate of the time was right for the ripening of Anglo-Saxonism. The works of Charles Darwin, Arthur de Gobineau, and Edward Freeman, among others, were being widely read and discussed. The idea of natural selection and the survival of the fittest was enthusiastically applied to human relations in the form of Social Darwinism, and the rival imperialisms of Great Britain, Russia, France, America, and Japan lent considerable credence to the belief that a struggle for world supremacy among the Anglo-Saxon, Slavic, Latin, and Oriental races was indeed under way. It was, in short, an era highly favorable to the development of race nationalism, and not only in England and the United States, but in many other countries as well.[106]

The first significant wave of Anglo-Saxonist sentiment swept over Britain and the United States during the Venezuelan Boundary Crisis of 1895–96. In the words of historian Stuart Anderson:

> The brief war scare following President Cleveland's belligerent message of 17 December 1895, and the long negotiations which followed to end the Venezuela squabble and arrange for the arbitration of future Anglo-American disputes, elicited countless expressions of kinship and good feeling from the public of both countries. Much of the public reaction against the prospect of an Anglo-American war and in favor of an arbitration treaty was rooted in the widely held belief that Englishmen and Americans were fellow Anglo-Saxons, and that a war between them would be fratricidal. The emergence of a strong sense of racial brotherhood during 1895–96 meant that an important new factor had been injected into British-American relations. Englishmen and Americans, adversaries and rivals for a century and a quarter, would never look at each other in the same way again.[107]

For the next decade or so, Anglo-Saxonism remained a vital force in Anglo-American diplomacy. Innumerable references to the fundamental unity of the English-speaking peoples appeared in the presses of both countries. In 1896, a British paper, the *Spectator,* quoted from a textbook, newly published for use in English schools, to express its affection for "a nation which no right-feeling Englishman will ever call foreign. That nation is the United States of America. It is peopled by men of our blood and faith, enjoys in a great measure the same laws as we do, reads the same Bible, and acknowledges like us the rule of King Shakespeare. . . . Let us remember, then, that the United States is not and never can be in reality a foreign country, nor an American a foreigner. They and we are one flesh."[108]

Across the Atlantic, American journals and authors adopted similar positions. In a *North American Review* article of 1898, entitled "The English-Speaking Brotherhood," Charles Waldstein argued that Britain and the United States shared "a common nationality; a common language; common forms of government; common culture, including customs and institutions; a common history; a common religion, in so far as religion stands for the same basis of morality;

and, finally, common interests." As a result, he wrote, the two countries "ought to develop some close form of lasting amity."[109]

The prevalence of Anglo-Saxonist feeling among the general populations of Great Britain and the United States was clearly conducive
to the development of harmonious relations. But it was equally if not
more significant that the doctrine of English-speaking unity possessed influential adherents in positions of governmental and decision-making authority. Among British statesmen, Joseph Chamberlain, colonial secretary until 1903, and Arthur Balfour, prime minister
from 1902 to 1905, were the foremost Anglo-Saxonists. As early as 1887,
Chamberlain had stated that he refused "to speak or to think of the
United States as a foreign nation. They are," he said, "our flesh and
blood."[110] In 1896, he wrote to the American secretary of state, Richard
Olney, of his belief that England and America shared a "sympathy
which . . . must and ought to exist between peoples with common
origins, common literature, common laws and common standards of
right and wrong."[111] And in his famous Birmingham speech of 13 May
1898, the colonial secretary stated that it was a fundamental duty of
British policy "to establish and maintain bonds of amity with our
kinsmen across the Atlantic. They are a powerful and a generous
nation. They speak our language, they are bred of our race. Their
laws, their literature, their standpoint on every question are the same
as ours; their feeling, their interest, in the cause of humanity and the
peaceful development of the world, are identical with ours."[112] Balfour, in a letter to Henry White, wrote that "the fact that [America's]
laws, its language, its literature, and its religion, to say nothing of its
constitution are essentially the same as those of English-speaking
peoples elsewhere, ought surely to produce a fundamental harmony—a permanent sympathy."[113]

Chamberlain and Balfour, while the leading Anglo-Saxonists in
British political circles, were by no means the only ones. Cecil Spring
Rice of the Foreign Office, a close friend of Theodore Roosevelt, held
strong Anglo-Saxonist beliefs.[114] So did future prime minister Herbert
Henry Asquith and the many other members of Parliament who
belonged to the Anglo-American League, an organization which
emphasized that Britain and the United States were "closely allied by
blood, inherit the same literature and laws, hold the same principles
of self-government, [and] recognize the same ideas of freedom and
humanity" in its call for "the most cordial and constant cooperation
on the part of the two nations."[115]

Across the Atlantic, the array of governmental leaders who professed Anglo-Saxonism was no less impressive. John Hay, ambassador to England and then secretary of state under McKinley and Roosevelt, was easily the most prominent of the American Anglophiles. In an unpublished sonnet, probably composed during the 1890s, Hay, a poet of some reputation, eloquently revealed the depth of his feeling:

> Hail to thee, England! Happy is the day
>   When from wide wandering I hither fare,
>   Touch thy wave-warded shore and breathe thine air,
>   And see, as now, thy hedges white with May.
> Rich memories throng in every flower-gemmed way;
>   Old names ring out as with a trumpet's blare;
>   While on, with quickened pulse we journey where
>   London's vast thunder roars like seas at play.
> To thee, the cradle of our race we come—
> Not breaking fealty to a dearer home—
>   To warm our hearts by ancient altar-fires;
> Thy children's children, from whatever skies,
> Greet the high welcome of thy deathless eyes,
>   Thou fair and mighty mother of our sires![116]

Publicly, though in words somewhat less florid, Hay expressed identical sentiments. In a speech to the American Society in London in 1897, he noted that Americans were "the fortunate heirs of English liberty and English law."[117] And in his well-known "Partnership in Beneficence" speech, delivered in London the following year at the Lord Mayor's Easter Banquet, he commented that the people of the United States were "knitted . . . to the people of Great Britain by a thousand ties of origin, of language, and of kindred pursuits."[118]

Hay's Anglo-Saxonism was matched by that of other prominent Americans. Alfred T. Mahan, whose *Influence of Sea Power on History* was probably the most widely discussed book of the period, was the driving force behind American naval development and the primary exponent of American naval policy. As a military man, Mahan might have been expected to confine his considerations to matters of power, but he did not. In 1892, he wrote to his English friend, George Sydenham Clarke, that he was "impressed with the feeling that to work together for our mutual good . . . would be the highest statesmanship—for in political traditions as well as by blood we are kin, the rest alien."[119] In 1896, he claimed that his "own belief [had] long since passed . . . from faith in, and ambition for my country alone, to the same for the Anglo-Saxon race."[120] And that same year, Mahan penned these words: "In my honor, reverence, and affection, Great

Britain stands only second to my own country. As the head of the English-speaking race outside our borders, I feel for her what Mr. Balfour has not ineptly called race patriotism."[121]

Richard Olney, the secretary of state whose "twenty-inch gun" blast, as Grover Cleveland called it, precipitated the crisis over the Venezuelan boundary, was also caught up in the Anglo-Saxonist tide. A letter to Joseph Chamberlain in September 1896 carried Olney's conviction that "if there is anything the Americans are proud of, it is their right to describe themselves as of the English race—if there is anything they are attached to, it is to ideas and principles which are distinctly English in their origin and development." As a result, he continued, "nothing would more gratify the mass of the American people than to stand . . . shoulder to shoulder with England."[122] Less than a year later, when the U.S. Senate refused to ratify the arbitration treaty he had negotiated, the recently retired Olney sent a dispatch to an American diplomat in London, Henry White, with instructions to show it to the British government. In this correspondence, Olney sought to assure Englishmen that the Senate's action was not supported by the public in the United States and that "the American people are proud of their lineage; set the highest value upon the laws, the institutions, the literature, and the language they have inherited; glory in all the achievements of the Anglo-Saxon race . . . and feel themselves to be not merely in name but in fact, part of one great English-speaking family whose proud destiny it is to lead and control the world."[123]

Additional expressions of Anglo-Saxonist feeling came from even more unexpected sources. Sen. Henry Cabot Lodge, who for years had taken pleasure in "twisting the Lion's tail," suddenly developed an acute case of Anglophilia. Responding to Britain's support for the United States upon the outbreak of the Spanish-American War, he gleefully declared that "race, blood, language, identity of beliefs and aspirations, all assert themselves."[124] Lodge, however, was from an old Massachusetts family of English background, so his sentiments could not be considered completely surprising. Theodore Roosevelt, on the other hand, was of Dutch descent, yet he sympathized with Britain in the Boer War, holding that it was in "the interest of civilization that the English-speaking race should be dominant in South Africa."[125] Moreover, when invited by Augustus Lowell to deliver a series of lectures at the Lowell Institute, Roosevelt accepted, saying that he would like to discuss the history of the western movement in the United States, "which established the dominance of the English blood, tongue and law from the seacoast of the Atlantic to the Pacific." In his view, "the expansion of the English-speaking peoples [was] infinitely the greatest feature in the world's history."[126]

The homogeneity of British and American language, culture, and ideology, reflected in Anglo-Saxon nationalism, contributed to the Anglo-American rapprochement in two major respects. First, it played a significant role in the threat assessments of the two countries, leading Britain in particular to discount the danger posed by the United States. Although well aware of America's rapid growth and of her awesome military and industrial potential, most Englishmen simply could not see the United States as a menace to Britain or to her vital interests. The contrast with British (and American) perceptions of Germany in this regard is striking. As Philip Kerr, later Lord Lothian, explained, "During the years of her supremacy has she [England] lifted a finger against the United States, which have now a population twice her own and resources immeasurably greater? No, for the ideals of the United States, like her own, are essentially unaggressive and threaten their neighbours no harm. But Germanism, in its want of liberalism, its pride, its aggressive nationalism, is dangerous, and so she feels instinctively that if it is allowed to become all powerful it will destroy her freedom, and with it the foundation of liberty on which the Empire rests."[127]

Indeed, the force of Anglo-Saxon nationalism was such that potentially conflictual aspects of the Anglo-American relationship were not merely discounted but were actually given quite favorable interpretations. This, again, was particularly true in Britain. Englishmen who saw in German commercial competition sinister plans to ruthlessly destroy the British Empire and reduce Britain to an impoverished island frequently attributed American economic success to diligence and ingenuity—English traits—to be congratulated and emulated rather than feared. The *Saturday Review,* the most anti-American of the British papers, complained, "In the department to which the Americans have chosen to consecrate themselves, they are ousting everyone else. That is the plain truth and the Continent is beginning to see it. So does everybody here see it, but because the Americans are what the Briton calls 'Anglo-Saxons,' he thinks he must not whisper of their hurting him and so lets loose all his volubility in scolding on the Germans, who in comparison are hardly damaging him at all."[128]

This same tendency was even more marked with respect to the issue of imperialism. While British officials, and the public, too, strongly opposed French, German, and Russian colonial efforts,

American attempts at expansion were, for the most part, greeted with warm approval. For Britons, American imperialism meant that the United States was following in the glorious British tradition. It was a further confirmation that the American people were truly Anglo-Saxons and welcome evidence that they were now prepared to take up the burden of their race.[129] An article by Edward Dicey in the *Nineteenth Century* reflected British attitudes at the time. Following the Spanish-American War and the seizure of Cuba and the Philippines by the United States, Dicey wrote, "The mere abandonment by America of her attitude of isolation in all foreign affairs cannot fail to bring together more closely two kindred nations, whose ideas, ambitions, and institutions are almost as identical as their language. Thus in the Imperialist movement, which has led the United States to embark on a career of annexation, I see the promise of gain rather than loss to our own country. Even if this were not so, I should still find cause for congratulation in the fact that the American Republic has now reverted to the hereditary policy of the Anglo-Saxon race."[130]

The second way in which the ideological/cultural affinity between the United States and Britain contributed to their reconciliation was perhaps less subtle but no less important. Anglo-Saxonism was, in essence, a statement of a common identity among Britons and Americans. Those who embraced it believed strongly that an Anglo-American war would be fratricidal and had therefore to be avoided at almost any cost. Arthur Balfour, British prime minister from 1902 to 1905, spoke for millions on both sides of the Atlantic when he said, "The idea of war with the United States carries with it some of the unnatural horror of a civil war. . . . The time will come, the time must come, when someone, some statesman of authority . . . will lay down the doctrine that between English-speaking peoples war is impossible."[131]

Public proclamations of Anglo-Saxon unity began to wane about 1905. This was due in part to the fact that Anglo-American solidarity had become taken for granted and was no longer novel, and in part to the fact that such statements were not politically expedient at a time when Britain was striving to reach agreements with non-Anglo-Saxon powers—Japan in 1902, France in 1904, and Russia in 1907. But the assumption that the United States and Britain, by virtue of certain common characteristics, shared a unique and special relationship did not die out. In the period after 1918, it emerged once again as a critical force in Anglo-American diplomacy.[132]

The homogeneity of the societal attributes of Great Britain and the United States, reflected in Anglo-Saxon nationalism, was instrumental in the reconciliation of these powers. It lay behind the initial outpouring of pacifist sentiment during the Venezuelan boundary controversy and was a central element in popular and official desires for the settlement of that and other issues that subsequently arose. Its influence was manifested in two basic ways. First, it colored the perceptions of both Englishmen and Americans, causing them to underestimate the importance of the conflict of geopolitical and economic interests between the two countries and to discount the significance of the concessions necessary to achieve an understanding. Second, it led many persons to conclude that the benefits of avoiding a fratricidal war with "racial" kin outweighed the costs of the sacrifices required for this to be accomplished. As will become apparent in later chapters, these effects were devastatingly absent—or reversed— in the Anglo-German and German-American cases. In each of these instances, heterogeneity of societal attributes encouraged the exaggeration of geopolitical and economic competition, while the incentive of averting a fratricidal war was almost completely lacking.

Crisis as Catalyst

The economic and ideological/cultural factors that favored a reconciliation between Britain and the United States in 1895–96 did not come into existence overnight. There had, naturally, been important developments since the days of American independence. The commercial and financial links between the two countries had become broader and deeper, particularly after Britain's repeal of the Corn Laws in 1846 forced her to rely on American grain. Increasing democratization of the British political system through a series of reform bills, and the granting of self-government to Canada, had allowed for a greater sense of ideological solidarity. But the question can still be asked: why did these factors succeed in bringing about a rapprochement in 1895–96 but not at some previous point in time?

One answer is, of course, that geopolitical conditions were a crucial factor and that neither Britain nor the United States required an accommodation for strategic reasons prior to 1895–96. In other words, economic and societal relationships gained influence only when the two countries, confronted with their insecurity, included them in threat assessments and in calculations of the costs and benefits of alternative alignments. This argument is a logical one and may possess some validity. But it cannot be the whole story, for in late 1895 and early 1896, as we have seen, Americans and Britons evinced limited concern over the international situation.

A more satisfactory explanation, and one that is supported by evidence presented elsewhere in this chapter, is that some sort of catalyst was needed to precipitate the rapprochement. Americans and Britons, to a considerable extent, still viewed one another through lenses ground during the American Revolution and the War of 1812. Subsequent disagreements had, for the most part, served to perpetuate and reinforce these negative images. The Venezuelan Boundary Crisis of 1895–96 was the worst crisis in Anglo-American relations since the Civil War era. It brought Britain and the United States sufficiently close to war that persons on each side were forced to seriously consider the implications of such a conflict. Attention was focused on both the economic and the ideological/cultural incentives for an understanding. In the end, the need to preserve vital commercial and financial connections, as well as to avoid a fratricidal war with racial kin, was deemed to outweigh the geopolitical issues at hand, and the reconciliation proceeded.

The Venezuelan episode has been identified as the catalyst for the Anglo-American rapprochement by a number of historians. Ernest May, for example, states that "in effect, Cleveland and Olney startled England and the United States into one another's arms."[133] Stuart Anderson writes that "Grover Cleveland's veritable ultimatum to the British government in December 1895 had the eventual consequence of moving the two countries toward improved relations. . . . Under the stress of the Venezuela boundary dispute, Anglo-Saxon race sentiment emerged as a new and potent influence on British-American relations."[134] And, according to Charles Campbell, the incident produced a "massive revulsion from the prospect of a fratricidal war, and the spontaneous demand that such a dreadful moment must never recur. The public reaction revealed the presence of reciprocal good will in the United States and Great Britain that was much more pervasive and deeply rooted than had been suspected. Evidently basic underlying influences, such powerful influences as the booming Anglo-American commerce and the common heritage, had already had a considerable effect by the mid-1890s."[135]

Epilogue: Anglo-American Relations after 1918

The course of Anglo-American diplomacy in the years after 1918 further confirms the significance of nonpower factors—and especially of societal attributes—in the relationship between the two countries. Following the defeat of Germany, Britain and the United States were indisputably the two strongest actors on the international stage. Like Germany before her, America appeared poised to challenge Britain as master of the world economy and, more importantly, as mistress of the seas. An incipient naval race developed that bore a disturbing resemblance to the Anglo-German competition of the prewar era. Some observers at the time suggested, in fact, that relations between Britain and the United States had assumed the character of those between England and Germany during that earlier period.[136]

Yet, in contrast to the Anglo-German case—and surprisingly, from a purely power-political standpoint—armed conflict between Britain and America failed to break out.[137] Indeed, the Hearst newspapers in the United States excepted, it was not seriously considered outside of naval circles in either country. This is not to say, of course, that relations were not strained. They were, and responsible statesmen on both sides of the Atlantic expressed grave concern. But unlike England and Germany, Britain and the United States were able to resolve the most dangerous and divisive of their differences, those relating to naval construction and the size of their fleets. At the Washington Conference of 1921–22, the two nations agreed upon parity in battleships and aircraft carriers, while at the London Conference of 1930 they agreed to equality in cruisers, destroyers, and submarines as well. The negotiations leading to the accords were difficult, and the settlements involved sacrifices by both parties. For Great Britain, they meant the abandonment of maritime supremacy that had been hers for centuries and that she had long held to be essential to her security and the defense of her empire. For the United States, they meant the renunciation of naval predominance, which, given her vastly superior economic position, could have been hers for the taking.[138]

A variety of elements contributed to this willingness to compromise. The sorry experience of England and Germany in the years before 1914 was still fresh in the minds of many persons. It seemed as if unrestrained naval competition had been a major cause of the conflict just ended, and both Americans and Britons were tired of fighting and reluctant to risk another war. In addition, neither British nor American leaders wished to expend the huge sums of money required to carry on such a rivalry. This was particularly true of the British Labour Party under the guidance of Ramsay MacDonald, who became prime minister in 1924 and again in 1929, but Conservatives were also concerned with the financial implications, and one Tory M.P. stated flatly that he regarded "British taxes as being more dangerous than United States ships."[139] An American congressman likewise warned against excessive taxation, saying, "If we enter upon a policy of naval competition with Great Britain we can not offer to the people of this country any hope of a lessening of the burden for generations to come."[140] Among British statesmen, the desire for economy was coupled with the hardheaded recognition that if America chose to do so, she could outbuild Britain regardless of British expenditures. Lieutenant-Commander J. M. Kenworthy told the House of Commons in 1920 that "if we are going to enter into naval rivalry against the United States . . . one of two things is going to happen. . . . we are going to be outbuilt or bankrupt."[141] His sentiments were echoed by Noel Baker a decade later when he informed the House that in the absence of an agreement "there will be unlimited competition and the United States will outbuild us at every point."[142]

War-weariness and fiscal constraints notwithstanding, the crucial factor in the Anglo-American accommodation appears to have been a continued appreciation of the ideological and cultural bonds between the two nations. The idea of Anglo-Saxon solidarity was not dead; consciously and subconsciously it affected the attitudes of both Englishmen and Americans. Those who advocated restraint repeatedly accused proponents of unlimited naval expansion of preparing specifically and exclusively for an Anglo-American war, an event which they themselves viewed as being either impossible, owing to the common origins and ideals of the two peoples, or a fratricidal conflict too horrible to contemplate.[143] In their opinion, equality of fleets might be desirable from the perspective of pride and prestige, but superiority was not necessary since warfare between the two countries was unthinkable. The *New York Times* wrote that the United States was "bound to the mother country by too many ties of kin and common interest and understanding. . . . In American thought, our own navy and Great Britain's are regarded, not as rivals or possible opponents, but as parts of one sea power."[144] The same paper later editorialized, "The United States need not be nervous about British

sea power. . . . to talk about British aggression today would be gro-
tesque."¹⁴⁵ An aging Theodore Roosevelt agreed, writing that the British navy was "probably the most potent instrumentality for peace in
the world," adding, "I do not believe we should try to build a navy in
rivalry to it."¹⁴⁶ Similarly, the *Seattle Post-Intelligencer* spoke of "our
identity of language, our common culture, and the parallel trend of
our political thought." Said the paper, "We can gaze with equanimity
on England's great Navy, knowing that the democratic people of the
British Empire will never use that Navy wrongly."¹⁴⁷ And the *Providence Journal* likewise argued:

> While America is a land of diverse nationalistic strains, it is still
> English-speaking, still bound by peculiar ties of sentiment, history
> and tradition to the British people. Its political and social institu-
> tions are based chiefly on Anglo-Saxon models. Its ideals are the
> ideals of the British democracy, now more in evidence than ever
> before both at home and in the far-reaching empire which Mr. Lloyd
> George significantly calls the British Commonwealth. Throughout
> the earth there has grown up under the British flag a Union of States
> with whose prosperity and development we are in natural sympathy,
> for they speak our tongue, live under laws analogous to ours, and
> have often shown by word and deed their fundamental friendship for
> us.
>   It is a commonplace to say that toward these English-speaking
> nations America's future attitude should be that of confidence and
> good-will.¹⁴⁸

This attitude found further expression in the halls of government,
where Congress became increasingly reluctant to appropriate the
funds required to seek maritime predominance. Clarence Lea of California held that "no one will assert that we should build the biggest
of all navies with the expectation that some day we will contend with
the British Empire for the physical supremacy of the sea." It was, he
said, "unthinkable that we should ever contemplate a war with that
nation to whom we are bound by ties of kinship and race and from
which we inherited our law, our language, our ideals, and our Chris-
tian faith."¹⁴⁹ His colleague from Iowa, William Green, concurred,
asking, "Mr. Chairman, why should we quarrel with England? . . .
between the two great English-speaking nations there are sacred ties
that ought never to be broken. It is not merely that we are both of the
same speech and largely of the same blood, although that is much.
Beyond and above that is the fact that our sentiments, our hopes, our
aspirations are the same. Alike in our veins courses the spirit of

freedom. Alike our minds are filled with a determination to make all men equal before the law. . . . We have no occasion to be suspicious or jealous of the other, but each should rejoice as the other develops in strength and power."[150]

Across the Atlantic, such feelings were reciprocated. Even that most ardent of naval enthusiasts, Winston Churchill himself, insisted that "war between the two great English speaking peoples is completely excluded from our minds," a position taken by other Conservative leaders as well.[151] The *Times* called the building of a navy against the United States "unnecessary, hateful," and "a treachery to the future welfare of mankind."[152] Former prime minister Asquith told the House of Commons that he had not "the faintest apprehension of the intention or effect of what America is doing in the way of building up a Navy, or that it is directed or ever will be directed against this country." Rather, Asquith stated, a more favorable moment for universal disarmament had never existed, as "the two supreme naval Powers of the world . . . are these two great English-speaking peoples, between whom fratricidal strife is, we hope and believe still, an absolute impossibility."[153] Likewise, Commander C. W. Bellairs told the House that "a fratricidal strike between this country and America is absolutely impossible." Said Bellairs, "I rejoice in the strength of America. I rejoice in any accession to that strength, because it is so much more towards the defence of the ideals of Anglo-Saxon civilisation for which we all contend."[154]

Without this sense of ideological and cultural solidarity, which both eased suspicions and provided heightened incentives to accommodation, Anglo-American diplomacy of the interwar period might well have foundered on the shoals of naval rivalry. It is doubtful, for example, whether Americans would have been willing to forgo, however temporarily, maritime supremacy in order to reach an understanding with Germany, a nation for which they felt little affinity. It is perhaps still more difficult to conceive of circumstances under which Britons would have abdicated, without a fight, their traditional mastery of the seas in favor of any country but the United States.[155] The importance of the unique nature of the Anglo-American relationship in this respect was made explicit by certain British leaders at the time. In 1921, Arthur Lee, then first lord of the Admiralty, noted that America's claim to naval equality was one "which this country has never accepted in the past and never would accept, save in connexion with a great English-speaking nation that sprang from our loins and must ever hold a special place in our regard and confidence."[156] Eight years later, Foreign Secretary Austen Chamberlain remarked that "parity between the United States naval forces and our own [was] an admission which we have never made to any other nation, which we should have made to no other nation."[157] Probably the most eloquent statement in this vein was made by Archibald Hurd, a well-known naval expert and coeditor of Brassey's *Annual*. In an article fairly dripping with melodrama, entitled "The British Fleet 'Dips Its Ensign,'" Hurd wrote of "the United States of America, . . . joint inheritors of our gradually evolved system of democratic government," linked to the mother country by "tradition, a common language, a common literature, and a common love of freedom." Britain, he said, "could only have dipped the flag which we have kept flying so many centuries to one nation. . . . the trident of Neptune passes into the joint guardianship of the English-speaking peoples of the world."[158]

The maintenance, by Britain and the United States, of pacific relations during the 1920s and 1930s illustrates the ability of nonpower factors to mitigate or even to override the effects of manifestly unfavorable geopolitical circumstances and suggests a final, and very interesting, question. What would have happened had Britain, rather than the Soviet Union, emerged after 1945 as the world's second leading power? At the very least, it seems reasonable to assume that ideological, cultural, and perhaps economic ties would have continued to smooth the path of Anglo-American diplomacy. Certainly it is difficult to imagine a cold war between Britain and the United States approaching in either magnitude or intensity that which actually occurred between America and the Soviet Union.[159]

Summary

During the last years of the nineteenth century and the first years of the twentieth, the relations between Great Britain and the United States underwent a profound transformation. At odds since the American War of Independence, these adversaries put aside their differences and formed a friendship that has continued to the present day. In this chapter, I have sought to account for this dramatic, and, in terms of world history, decisive, turn of events.

Table 1. Great Britain and the United States, 1895

Exercise of Power	Medium/Low Heterogeneity: similar in insularity and reliance on naval strength, but possessing different geographic areas of primary interest and varying ambitions.
Economic Activities	Medium/High Heterogeneity: increasing similarity and growing competition, but possessing important complementarities in trade and finance; strong interdependence.
Societal Attributes	High Homogeneity: Anglo-Saxon nationalism grounded in similarities of race, language, and political and social philosophy and institutions.

The basis of the Anglo-American reconciliation is summarized in table 1, which outlines the two countries' relationship at the beginning of the period. In the wake of the Venezuelan Boundary Crisis, this combination of factors proved sufficient to bring about a rapprochement.

It is perhaps worth repeating that conditions necessary to produce a reconciliation between Great Britain and the United States appear to have existed in an absolute sense, within the context of the Anglo-American dyad and without reference to each state's relations with other powers. However, balancing motivations were not entirely absent, and became increasingly important as time went on. Indeed, as later chapters will make clearer, the combination of geopolitical, economic, and ideological/cultural factors present in the Anglo-American relationship was still more favorable to peace from a relative, multilateral, perspective. When a dangerous international environment led both countries—and especially Britain—to feel the need for friends, prospects for an Anglo-American rapprochement were further enhanced.

3

Great Britain and Germany,
1898–1914

Introduction

The record of Anglo-German diplomacy in the years before 1914 stands in stark contrast to the portrait of Anglo-American relations sketched in the preceding chapter. While Britain and the United States left enmity behind to form a new and lasting friendship, Britain and Germany abandoned a tradition of relatively cordial cooperation in favor of bitter antagonism and, ultimately, war. The story of Anglo-German relations in this period is the tale of a peace that once seemed possible, even probable, but which, in the end, never emerged.[1]

It would be misleading, of course, to imply that Anglo-German affairs were ever completely free from difficulty. Even in the best of times, no warm sympathy or depth of mutual affection existed between Germany and Great Britain. British statesmen, and the public, too, always harbored some reservations about Prussian militarism, and Bismarck deeply distrusted England for her liberal proclivities, a suspicion he managed to ingrain in many of the German people. Moreover, occasional squabbles like the one arising from Germany's acquisition of colonies in 1884–85 periodically introduced a measure of tension into the relationship. Still, for nearly three decades following the founding of the German Empire in 1871, official Anglo-German diplomacy was generally satisfactory, and London and Berlin tended to lean toward one another on international questions. It was not uncommon for British Conservatives to speak of Germany as a natural ally, and German leaders reciprocated this feeling, especially during Caprivi's tenure as chancellor. Although no formal association of this type was ever concluded, the two countries did, in fact, register some impressive achievements in diplomatic cooperation. The most significant was the colonial settlement of June 1890, whereby Britain ceded to Germany the island of

Heligoland in exchange for territorial concessions in East Africa and Zanzibar.[2]

Despite this pattern of tacit alignment, intermittent collaboration, and effective compromise, however, Great Britain and Germany ultimately proved incapable of developing a stable and enduring friendship. The crucial years were from 1898 to 1914. At the popular level, this period was characterized by the growth of a virulent mutual antipathy so powerful that it constituted a formidable obstacle to any openly acknowledged diplomatic association. At the official level, it was marked by agreement on a series of fairly minor issues, including the partition of Samoa, the territorial integrity of China, the future disposition of Portugal's African colonies, and the collection of Venezuelan debts, but these, ironically, bred misunderstanding after misunderstanding, and only made good relations still more difficult. Most importantly, the governments of Germany and Great Britain found themselves utterly unable to bring to a successful conclusion negotiations on either of two major questions—a defensive alliance and the naval armaments race—the resolution of which might have helped to stem the tide of hostility and make possible a return to a more peaceful and harmonious relationship.

The sequence of events involved in this sad story is too well known to require detailed description here. Certainly no aspect of modern history has received so much attention as the diplomatic background of the First World War, a subject on which Anglo-German affairs has typically occupied center stage. What seems appropriate, then, is to move directly into an analysis of the factors and conditions that caused Great Britain and Germany to fail at the attainment and perpetuation of peace during this critical era.

The Exercise of Power

From a narrow realist perspective, the period immediately after 1871 should not have been a pleasant one in Anglo-German diplomacy. Britain, preeminent within the European state system since Waterloo and Trafalgar, faced a new potential challenge to her ascendancy. After the defeat of France and the unification of the German Empire, Germany was unarguably the greatest power on the continent. In alliance with Austria-Hungary and Italy, she became the dominant member of the strongest international coalition of the day. And her influence was clearly on the rise. Yet, despite this, Anglo-

German relations did not deteriorate rapidly in the years following the Franco-Prussian War. On the contrary, as noted above, Britain and Germany tended to work in concert on international questions, and leaders in one country referred to the other as a natural ally. It was not until several decades later, when German activity in colonial, naval, and continental affairs began to endanger important British interests, that the two countries became bitter enemies.

What this suggests is that in the case of Britain and Germany, as with Britain and the United States, aggregate power mattered less than the exercise of that power. Indeed, Sir Edward Grey, British foreign secretary during part of the period, said as much when he noted that

> the Triple Alliance in 1886 and the following years, when Lord Salisbury and Lord Rosebery were Prime Ministers, was indisputably the strongest political combination, the most powerful thing in Europe. Nevertheless, the policy of friendship with it was followed by the British Government even before the Franco-Russian Alliance had come into existence as a counterpoise; and this policy was continued for many years, while the Triple Alliance continued, in spite of the Franco-Russian Alliance, to be the dominant factor in European diplomacy. During this period, therefore, Great Britain did not attempt to create any counterpoise to the strongest group; on the contrary, the British Government sided with that group. . . .
>
> . . . The conclusion I would draw is that Great Britain has not in theory been adverse to the predominance of a strong group in Europe when it seemed to make for stability and peace. To support such a combination has generally been her first choice; it is only when the dominant Power becomes aggressive and she feels her own interests to be threatened that she, by an instinct of self-defence, if not by deliberate policy, gravitates to anything that can fairly be described as a Balance of Power.[3]

The increasing lack of heterogeneity in the exercise of British and German power during the last years of the nineteenth century and the early years of the twentieth was manifested in a contest for imperial possessions and then, more fundamentally, in a struggle for command of the seas. The first Anglo-German colonial dispute erupted in 1884–85, when Germany, under the leadership of Bismarck, made her initial bid for extra-European territories, laying claim to South-West Africa, East Africa, Togoland, New Guinea, and the Camaroons.[4] Not every British statesman was displeased by this development. Gladstone probably voiced his true sentiments when he told the House of Commons, "If Germany becomes a Colonizing Power, all I can say is 'God speed her.' She becomes our ally and partner in the execution of a great purpose of Providence for the benefit of mankind."[5] But his view was not shared by a majority of the cabinet, nor by Britain's self-governing colonies, which saw their security menaced and their prospects for future expansion limited, and which pressured London to oppose German acquisitions. The British government embarked upon a policy of firm resistance, then quickly reversed itself and acceded to Germany's demands in the face of Bismarck's threats to cause difficulties in Egypt. The episode resulted in bruised feelings on both sides: the Germans upset at Britain's obstructionism, the British annoyed by Berlin's aggressiveness and bullying tactics.[6]

For the next three decades, colonial issues continued to divide Germany and Great Britain. In 1894, the British government concluded a treaty with King Leopold of Belgium whereby England obtained a corridor through the Congo, thus completing the "Cape to Cairo" route for which British imperialists longed. However, the agreement had the added effect, intended or not, of encircling German East Africa with British-held territory, and Berlin mounted such a vociferous campaign against it that the pact had to be renounced.[7] Differences over South Africa, which did so much to poison Anglo-German relations, were also largely imperial in nature. Colonialist elements in Germany wished to see their country acquire the Transvaal. Many others, including the government, saw no immediate need for outright possession, but desired at least an independent Boer state, viewing it as a "barrier to British supremacy in South Africa and a means of reserving the future until Germany's interests were more clearly defined."[8] The British, for their part, were determined that South Africa should remain solidly within their sphere. German meddling in South African affairs could not be countenanced, and the British ambassador warned the German foreign minister in 1895 that further German interference would mean war.[9] The acrimonious exchanges and mutual recriminations over the Jameson Raid, the subsequent Kruger Telegram, and the Boer War were all, in some measure, manifestations of imperial competition.[10]

Even those instances in which Britain and Germany managed to resolve their colonial differences through negotiation and diplomatic accord tended to injure rather than aid the cause of friendship. The settlement of 1890, by which England ceded to Germany the island of Heligoland in return for Zanzibar and other African lands, was widely interpreted by Germans as an ignoble retreat and loss at British hands.[11] The partition of Samoa in 1899 satisfied neither country. Britain, primarily because of her problems in South Africa, had to give in to German demands, but did so grudgingly and only after a long period of obstinance.[12] And the agreement of 1898 respecting the future division of the Portuguese colonies proved a festering sore in Anglo-German affairs until 1914. While the pact provided for Germany to receive the lion's share of these territories, it was to come into effect only if it were "not found possible to maintain the integrity" of Portugal's African possessions, an occurrence which, to German chagrin, London worked diligently to prevent.[13]

Strictly speaking, this imperial rivalry did not constitute an insurmountable obstacle in the path of Anglo-German peace. Colonial competition between England and France was more severe, yet those nations were able to overcome their differences and enter into a lasting friendship.[14] Nevertheless, the territorial jousting between Great Britain and Germany did have a serious and damaging impact upon their relationship. British statesmen, and the public as well, came to see Germany as a restless, ambitious, and aggressive power, willing to stop at nothing in her drive to dominate. At the same time, Germans came to view Britain as an unreasoning and implacable foe, bent on denying their country her rightful place in the sun. The frustration felt in Germany was voiced by Karl Peters, explorer and propagandist, in a 1911 article in *Der Tag*. Peters complained that "if Germany carefully keeps away from British spheres of interest, Britain will be pleased to live in peace with her. But, what are British spheres of interest on this planet these days? Or rather, what is not a British sphere of interest? . . . I am first waiting until when and where London will find a German attempt at expansion 'justifiable.' "[15] As early as 1897, in fact, the German foreign minister, Marschall, had warned Curzon that Britain's colonial policies, especially in Africa, had caused considerable resentment among the public.[16] And frequent outbursts in the German press gave credence to his words. The *Schlesiche Zeitung* put things this way: "From Zanzibar to Samoa! An unbroken line of disappointments! The German people is gradually coming to recognize that England is Germany's worst enemy."[17]

These attitudes and perceptions naturally carried over into other aspects of Anglo-German affairs. Imperial setbacks in the face of British intransigence led many Germans to support a large navy as a means of forcing Britain to yield. Already by 1894, Hatzfeldt, the ambassador to London, was pleading for a policy of pressure because he was "*firmly* convinced that otherwise we will accomplish *nothing* with the niggardly people here, either in [the colonial] or in *other* questions."[18] The *Grenzboten* complained in 1896 that "a colonial policy in all oceans is naturally not possible without ships," asking rhetorically, "And have we ships?"[19] And the *Kolonialzeitung*, alarmed by Britain's alleged scheming to gain control of the Portuguese colonies, decried the fact that Germany had no navy with which to thwart her plans.[20] To British observers, on the other hand, Germany's aggressiveness in colonial efforts provided further rationale, if any were needed, for the maintenance of maritime supremacy, the crucial link in imperial defense.

The major geopolitical issue that emerged between Great Britain and Germany during the prewar period was, of course, a rivalry in naval armaments. This was a problem of considerably more recent origin.[21] In 1897, the British navy still owned the overwhelming maritime superiority it had enjoyed since the battle of Trafalgar. All told, Britain had sixty-two battleships built or under construction; her closest competitors, France and Russia, had but thirty-six and eighteen, respectively. The German fleet consisted of a mere twelve battleships, the same number possessed by Italy, plus eight coastal defense ships, ten large cruisers, and twenty-three small cruisers.[22] In 1898, however, a revolutionary naval bill was passed by the German Reichstag. Under the terms of this legislation, and a second bill passed in 1900, the German navy was to expand to unprecedented proportions. By 1916, if all went according to plan, Germany would have afloat a total of fifty-five battleships, fourteen large cruisers, thirty-four small cruisers, and ninety-six destroyers. Manning these vessels would be 60,000 officers and sailors, more than double the number in active service in 1897.[23]

The new German naval program reflected the so-called risk theory of Admiral Alfred von Tirpitz, recently appointed head of the Imperial Naval Ministry. Tirpitz hoped to construct a fleet so strong that "even for the adversary with the greatest sea power a war against it would involve such dangers as to imperil her position in the world."[24] As he explained to the German emperor, once this goal had been achieved, "England will have lost all inclination to attack us [and] will concede to Your Majesty such a measure of maritime influence which will make it possible for Your Majesty to conduct a great overseas policy."[25]

This plan, of course, posed a direct challenge to Britain's traditional naval supremacy and to the benefits in commerce, imperial expansion, and security that this preponderance bestowed upon her.[26] It could not be ignored. As early as 1900, the Naval Intelligence Department had concluded that Germany—not France—was Britain's most likely future foe.[27] By 1902, the British Admiralty believed that it possessed proof that the German fleet was being constructed for battle with the Royal Navy. Restricted cruising ranges, cramped crew quarters, and other characteristics indicated that German battleships were being designed to operate only in the North Sea.[28] In October, Selborne informed the cabinet that, in his opinion, "the great new German Navy is being carefully built up from the point of view of a war with us."[29]

It was to take only a bit more time for the British population as a whole to become conscious of the threat inherent in the rise of German naval power. By the beginning of 1903, a substantial segment of the English press had become convinced "that German hatred of Britain was irreversible and that the German fleet was aimed at wresting maritime superiority from the Royal Navy." Among the publications sounding the alarm were the *Times*, the *Morning Post*, the *Spectator*, the *Fortnightly Review*, the *Observer*, and the *Daily Mail*. The *National Review*, which featured a series of articles by H. W. Wilson, was probably the most outspoken of the British papers.[30] These journals rapidly alerted their readers to this new and pressing danger. Before long, in the words of Arthur Marder, "Public opinion, the government, and the Admiralty were as one in viewing the German fleet as a potential menace far greater than the fleets of the Dual Alliance."[31]

While the British feared that Germany intended to gain control of the seas, Germans, for their part, lived in terror of the prospect that London might launch a preventive attack before their navy had reached a sufficient size. It was understood that should England discern Germany's aims such a strike would be entirely logical, and Tirpitz and Bülow recognized from the outset that the German fleet would have to pass through a "danger zone" before becoming a useful political instrument. That the notion was occasionally canvassed in the British press did nothing to allay their apprehensions in this regard. In late 1904, both *Vanity Fair* and the *Army and Navy Gazette* called for a preventive war, and Admiral John Fisher, first sea lord, himself put the suggestion to Lansdowne the following spring.[32] Although the cabinet never contemplated taking such action, the possibility weighed heavily on German minds, and there developed a full-blown "Copenhagen Complex" among both the general population and high-ranking government officials.[33]

In a very real sense, these mutual fears and suspicions reflected an accurate perception of a fundamental truth. German and British naval aims during the pre-1914 era were patently irreconcilable. Germany could not possess a fleet capable of carrying out an ambitious world policy without automatically compromising Britain's naval supremacy. Nor, on the other hand, could Britain maintain her preponderance of maritime power without denying Germany this capacity. Over the long run, unless one side or the other renounced or modified its objectives, some sort of conflict was virtually inevitable. And throughout the negotiations on naval armaments that took place between the two countries, neither demonstrated a willingness to retreat.

This does not, of course, mean that Great Britain and Germany were destined to go to war in August of 1914. Indeed, Tirpitz, believing that the German navy was still unprepared, bitterly opposed Berlin's decision to risk a battle with England at that time.[34] What it does mean is that a significant threat of conflict was continually present in Anglo-German relations. And so long as this threat remained, a condition of peace could not prevail.

In the final analysis, the most damaging aspect of the Anglo-German naval rivalry was probably the reflection it cast upon the European balance of power. The notion that Germany might be capable of upsetting this balance and establishing a continental hegemony did not occur to most Englishmen until about 1905. It was, of course, evident to them that Germany had been gaining power steadily, especially in relation to France. By 1900, the German population stood at 56 million to France's 38 million. Her output of coal, 150 million tons, was far in excess of France's 33 million. And she led France in the production of crude steel, 6.5 million tons to 1.5.[35] Moreover, although her military expenditures were not substantially higher than those of France, her army was considered much the better in terms of training, discipline, and matériel.[36] But none of this concerned the British so long as France was looked upon as the principal enemy, and even after the conclusion of the Entente Cordiale in 1904 British statesmen were slow to take alarm, believing that France's alliance with Russia compensated for her inferiority vis-à-vis Germany.

In 1905, however, events conspired to divest Englishmen of this last comforting assumption. The most important of these was Russia's collapse and defeat in her war with Japan.[37] Nearly every contemporary observer had predicted a Russian victory; now the formidable reputation of Russian military might had been reduced to rubble. Russia, it was clear, would not serve as a counterweight to German ambitions. Her opposition would not deter Germany from the pursuit of territorial conquests. This was the fear of such British leaders as Foreign Secretary Edward Grey, who told Cecil Spring Rice in early 1906 that he was "impatient to see Russia re-established as a factor in European politics."[38]

That Britain was unwilling to tolerate a German continental hegemony was intimately connected to her apprehensions regarding Germany's growing power at sea. Had Germany remained essentially a land power, Englishmen might have viewed the prospect of her ascendancy with greater indifference; under the circumstances, however, they could not.[39] Statesmen and public alike worried that if Germany were to consolidate her hold on Europe and eliminate every potential adversary there, she would then be free to devote all her energies to maritime expansion and the subjugation of Britain and her empire. As Leo Amery put it, "Then the German position from the point of view of [naval] competition with England will be enormously strengthened, so much so that it will be entirely beyond our capacity to meet. If we wish to prevent the consummation of those conditions and to preserve our supremacy on the sea, it is on the land that we must meet her."[40] Grey perceived the situation similarly. In 1912, he told the Committee of Imperial Defence that "if a European conflict, not of our making, arose, in which it was quite clear that the struggle was one for supremacy in Europe, in fact, that you got back to a situation something like that in the old Napoleonic days, then ... our concern in seeing that there did not arise a supremacy in Europe which entailed a combination that would deprive us of the command of the sea would be such that we might have to take part in that European war. That is why the naval position underlies our European policy."[41]

Britain's refusal to accept German hegemony on the continent had two implications for Anglo-German relations in the period before 1914. First, and more obviously, it meant that any act by Germany that was interpreted in England as a move toward European domination, whether or not it was so intended, could be expected to encounter British resistance. Already by 1905, the Admiralty and the War Office were united in their belief that "a second overthrow of France ... would end in the aggrandisement of Germany to an extent which would be prejudicial to the whole of Europe, and it might therefore be necessary for Great Britain in her own interests to lend France her active support should war of this nature break out."[42] As the above statements of Amery and Grey suggest, this view became increasingly prevalent as time went on, and by the summer of 1914 it was sufficiently strong to provide a significant, and perhaps the single, most compelling rationale for Britain's decision to enter the European conflict. Second, and more subtly, British anxiety about German continental domination meant that London was to become less and less willing to undertake steps to improve relations with Germany out of the fear that such measures would alienate France, and also Russia, forcing those countries into a dependence on Berlin. Hegemony through diplomacy as well as by conquest had to be prevented. As Bertie informed Mallet, "The danger for us to avoid will be to make the French lose confidence in our support and so drive them into some arrangement with Germany harmful to us while not being so harmful to the French."[43] Grey agreed, writing that "we cannot enter into a political understanding with Germany, which would separate us from Russia and France, and leave us isolated while the rest of Europe would be obliged to look to Germany."[44] His worry, therefore, was "not that relations with Germany were bad, but that they might become too good."[45] Indeed, Grey was so intent on keeping the faith of France and Russia that on one occasion he blocked a ceremonial visit to Germany by a band of the Coldstream Guards, threatening to resign over this apparently trivial issue.[46]

Although Germany and Britain became increasingly bitter geopolitical rivals during the late nineteenth and early twentieth centuries, it must be remembered that the two countries did engage in conversations aimed at the conclusion of a defensive alliance in 1898 and again in 1901.[47] Conducted in rather tentative fashion and without much sense of urgency, the talks never neared success, but they were sufficiently serious that at one point the two sides actually exchanged draft treaties.[48] These negotiations, and their ultimate failure, shed some additional light on the exercise of power and its role in Anglo-German relations of the prewar period.

The alliance talks between England and Germany at the turn of the century were motivated mainly by a common concern with the Franco-Russian Alliance. Germany was interested in procuring British aid to guarantee her borders in Europe, while Britain sought German assistance in colonial affairs. The negotiations eventually collapsed in part because the two countries came to perceive that their geopolitical differences with other powers were of lesser significance than their differences with one another, or of insufficiently greater significance to warrant compromise and accommodation. Germany, in the final analysis, had little to fear from France, her traditional adversary. Despite enduring bitterness over Alsace and Lorraine, the French evinced little interest in the notion of *revanche*, owing mainly to their inferior military capabilities. There existed some danger of a conflict with Russia over Constantinople and the Balkans resulting from Germany's alliance with Austria-Hungary, but German leaders did not view this prospect as imminent.[49] And American obstruction of German colonial ambitions, although frustrating, did not produce the level of irritation that British intransigence did. None of these difficulties could induce the Germans to consider renouncing their plans for a great fleet, which as Bülow informed Tirpitz and William, would be the price of any agreement with Britain.[50]

Britain likewise was not disposed to conciliate Germany out of concern over others' geopolitical ambitions. The United States was a force only in the Western Hemisphere, where British interests seemed less vital. France was principally a Mediterranean naval power and an imperial competitor. She represented a minimal threat to Britain's home defenses; in 1901 Salisbury noted that an invasion by France was *"a danger in whose existence we have no historical reason for believing."*[51] Russia constituted a more substantial problem. Menacing India, the jewel in Britain's imperial crown, she was regarded by some as a more dangerous opponent than Germany. But Germany, as we have seen, manifested no similar apprehension and had no desire to antagonize Russia unnecessarily. Eventually, Britain managed to counter Russia in other ways, first by concluding a defensive alliance with Japan and then by seeking an understanding with France.

The inability of Great Britain and Germany to conclude a defensive alliance was, therefore, partly a consequence of the relatively (compared to these and other states) low level of heterogeneity in the exercise of British and German power. But this was not the whole story. That the prospect of collaboration in security matters was discussed as seriously as it was indicates that, for a time anyway, persons on both sides perceived Anglo-German geopolitical interests to be more in harmony than the interests of these and other powers. Indeed, on this basis, at least a narrow window of opportunity for an agreement appears to have existed around 1898, when Britain in particular viewed France and Russia as her principal competitors. If geopolitics argued—albeit briefly—for an accommodation, however, other factors did not. As we shall see, by the late 1890s economic and ideological/cultural differences between the two countries had become so acute that in the absence of extremely compelling strategic motivations, which clearly did not exist, meaningful Anglo-German diplomatic cooperation was almost out of the question.[52] In any event, between 1896 and 1907, Britain succeeded in liquidating the bulk of her territorial disputes with other nations. A reconciliation with the United States was followed by a rapprochement with France and an entente with Russia. From 1907 to 1914, Germany remained Britain's sole rival in geopolitical affairs.

The case of Britain and Germany, like that of Britain and the United States, suggests that it is not so much the aggregate power possessed by states that affects their relations as it is the ways in which this power is employed. For some time following the Franco-Prussian War, Britain and Germany were indisputably the two strongest members of the European state system, yet they remained on reasonably good terms. Toward the end of the century they drifted apart, as the exercise of their power became increasingly homogeneous. This growing lack of heterogeneity was both functional and geographic and was manifested in a keen naval race as well as a series of imperial confrontations.

The declining heterogeneity in the exercise of British and German power militated strongly against any reconciliation. Within the confines of the bilateral Anglo-German relationship, imperial, naval, and continental competition constituted a formidable barrier to good relations. Seen from a multilateral perspective, its impact was little more favorable. For Britain and Germany were—for most of the prewar period—less heterogeneous with respect to one another than with respect to other of their potential adversaries. This was so particularly from the British standpoint. As indicated in the preceding chapter, American aims clashed with Britain's perceived vital interests to a lesser extent than did German ambitions. In the next chapter, it will become clear that by shortly after 1900 the same had come to be true of French objectives. Thus Britain, in a position of considerable strategic difficulty, was encouraged to resolve her differences with these countries while maintaining her staunch opposition to Germany.

Although geopolitical competition was certainly the most visible cause of the Anglo-German antagonism in the years before 1914, it was by no means the only one. Indeed, this rivalry might have been overcome, as in the case of Britain and the United States, had economic and ideological/cultural factors argued strongly for peace. But they did not. While some degree of interdependence existed between the British and German economies, its beneficent influence was outweighed by the pernicious effects of a rapidly growing commercial competition. At the same time, a profound political-cultural gulf came to separate the two nations, further contributing to their mutual antipathy. It is an examination of these aspects of the Anglo-German relationship to which we now turn.

Economic Activities

At first glance, the economic context in which Anglo-German relations developed would seem to have been considerably more conducive to peace and harmony than the geopolitical environment. Throughout the late nineteenth and early twentieth centuries, the value of commercial transactions between Great Britain and Germany increased steadily. Trade across the North Sea, which amounted to £35 million in 1870, rose to £45 million in 1890 and £66 million in 1905. This last figure represented roughly 7 percent of all English commerce and about 14 percent of the German total. Great Britain was consistently Germany's most important trading partner, and while Germany in 1905 still ranked but fourth on Britain's list of associates, behind the United States, France, and India, by 1910 she was firmly entrenched in second place.[53]

In addition to its large volume, Anglo-German commerce was characterized by a certain degree of structural complementarity. German wines, toys, and clocks, for example, were imported by England because they were not produced domestically, and the same was true of the British-made electrical machinery and fine textiles purchased by Germany. Moreover, specialization and product differentiation were such that in many cases German and English goods that appeared to compete with one another did not actually do so. For this reason, Britain in 1907 could export to Germany partly and fully manufactured steel items worth better than £3 million, while importing from Germany nearly £5 million of similar commodities in return.[54] All of this suggests a measure of mutual dependence and implies that many businessmen in Britain and Germany did have a major stake in the maintenance of stable and amicable relations between their respective countries. Indeed, the German ambassador to London, Metternich, reported in 1909, "In the course of time I have been in touch with many representatives of industry and trade in England and Scotland, and nowhere have I found in the same degree the sincere desire for the continuation of good relations between the two countries in trade and politics, and nowhere so strong a fear that they might be disrupted. If the relations between the two peoples could be regulated solely on the basis of commercial interests and by the whole body of representatives of those interests, mutual relations would today be excellent."[55]

Despite this positive dimension, however, the net impact of commercial activities on Anglo-German diplomacy of the prewar period was a negative one. The British and German economies were becoming increasingly homogeneous, and the unifying influence of interdependence was far outweighed by the divisive effects of a keen and emotionally charged trade rivalry.[56]

Competition in trade between Great Britain and Germany began to emerge during the 1880s and 1890s as the latter's economic development led her to manufacture rapidly increasing quantities of various industrial products that had long been the almost exclusive province of British firms. German output of such commodities as pig iron, steel, chemicals, and textiles approached or surpassed that of Britain, and exports of these items began to successfully challenge English goods in the markets of the world.[57] In Britain's own home market, imports of German cotton, iron, and steel manufactures quadrupled between 1890 and 1902, while purchases of German woolens more than doubled.[58] German exports to Belgium and Holland, roughly equal in value to British exports in 1894, were by 1912 more than twice as large; a more or less similar pattern prevailed in other continental markets.[59] Even in the territories of the British Empire, German goods made significant inroads at Britain's expense. An 1897 study commissioned by Colonial Secretary Joseph Chamberlain found forty-five instances in which German products were displacing those of the mother country.[60] It is important to recognize that in none of these third markets did British exports actually decline. Indeed, the value of English merchandise purchased abroad grew throughout the prewar period. But the rate of this increase did slow markedly, a fact which could be attributed to German competition. Furthermore, in relative terms, Britain's share of world trade was falling. Whereas in

1880 she had been involved in 23 percent of all global commerce, by 1913 she was taking part in only 17 percent. During this same time, Germany's portion had risen from 10 to 13 percent.[61]

Although concern over Germany's commercial advance had been evidenced by British observers as far back as 1891,[62] the first real alarm at these developments was sounded in 1896. In that year, E. E. Williams, with a well-publicized series of articles in the *New Review* entitled "Made in Germany," brought the enormous flow of German goods into the British market to the attention of the general population.[63] Williams, it must be noted, was worried but not particularly hostile to Germany. He believed that the problem could be solved by greater diligence and effort on the part of British companies and their workers. Within a brief span of time, however, others had decided that Germany and Britain were locked in a battle for the commercial supremacy of the world. The Conservative *Saturday Review*, in an infamous article of September 1897, wrote that

> in Europe there are two great, irreconcilable, opposing forces, two great nations who would make the whole world their province, and who would levy from it the tribute of commerce. England, with her long history of successful aggression, with her marvellous conviction that in pursuing her own interests she is spreading light among nations dwelling in darkness, and Germany, bone of the same bone, blood of the same blood, with a lesser will-force, but, perhaps, with a keener intelligence, compete in every corner of the globe. In the Transvaal, at the Cape, in Central Africa, in India and the East, in the islands of the Southern sea, and in the far North-West, wherever— and where has it not?—the flag has followed the Bible and trade has followed the flag, there the German bagman is struggling with the English pedlar. Is there a mine to exploit, a railway to build, a native to convert from breadfruit to tinned meat, from temperance to trade gin, the German and the Englishman are struggling to be first. A million petty disputes build up the greatest cause of war the world has ever seen. If Germany were extinguished to-morrow, the day after to-morrow there is not an Englishman in the world who would not be the richer. Nations have fought for years over a city or a right of succession; must they not fight for two hundred million pounds of commerce?[64]

The paper's position was clear: *Germaniam esse delendam*—Germany must be destroyed.[65]

Expressions of this sentiment continued to appear in British publications throughout the pre-1914 era. One author compared Britain and Germany to Rome and Carthage,[66] while another called upon the

British government to "[meet] force with force and violence with violence instead of meeting it with polite and perfectly useless remonstrances."[67]

If Englishmen were becoming agitated at the prospect of losing their economic mastery to Germany, Germans were equally worried about the measures London might take in order to prevent this from happening. Two possibilities seemed to them most dangerous. The first of these was a combination of tariff reform and imperial preference, a proposal widely discussed in Britain at the turn of the century. The prospect that Germany's hitherto almost free access to Britain's home, and particularly her colonial, markets might suddenly be restricted was a specter that haunted the German public mind. As Karl Rathgen explained in an essay, "On the Plan for a British Imperial Customs Union," "The meaning for Germany is very clear: the endangering of German trade and export interests. The commercial decomposition of the British empire is advantageous for us. The increase of German imports in the British colonies is greatly exaggerated in England. But it is present, and for the future the colonial markets offer great possibilities for development. That England's currently dominant position as middleman might be damaged would not be sufficient compensation for their loss."[68]

When the British government announced in July 1897 its intention to terminate its commercial treaty with the *Zollverein* (assumed by the Empire in 1871), an agreement which granted Germany the same trading rights in the British colonies as Britain herself possessed, a storm of protest erupted in Germany, and many nationalist newspapers claimed that their country was to be denied her most valuable export market.[69] Although England never did institute a high degree of protection, and the worst fears of German traders never materialized, German uneasiness continued so long as such measures were contemplated in Britain. As late as 1910, Albert Ballin was writing to William, "I am quite convinced that everything hangs on the future development of trade and traffic. To-day, as I have said before, Tariff Reform and a Zollverein with the Colonies are the catchwords that are on everybody's lips, and the anti-German feeling is so strong that it is scarcely possible to discuss matters with one's oldest friends, because the people over here have turned mad and talk of nothing but the next war and the protective policy of the near future."[70]

The second possibility that gravely concerned many Germans was that Britain might utilize her superior naval strength to deal a crush-

ing blow to German commerce. While this idea was not taken
seriously in London, inflammatory articles in the British press provided ample fuel for such apprehension. Citing the *Saturday Review*
diatribe of September 1897, the *Hamburger Nachrichten* warned that
the notion "that England will seize the first opportunity when circumstances are favorable to wage war against Germany is no idle
speculation."[71] Political leaders echoed this line. Tirpitz, in his
memoirs, adopted the same position he had advanced throughout the
prewar period: "The older and stronger firm inevitably seeks to stran-
gle the new and rising one before it is too late."[72] Bülow told the
Budget Committee of the Reichstag that an attack by England was
possible because "Germany is now a serious economic competitor in
world markets as a result of our tremendous industrial development,
our increasing trade, and our increasing overseas interests."[73] And
William II stated flatly that "after the recognition of the superiority
of German industry, England will soon set about its destruction, and
will undoubtedly succeed if we do not energetically and quickly prevent this disaster with a vigorous naval buildup."[74]

  As these last words suggest, the commercial competition between
Great Britain and Germany was closely connected to their rivalry for
maritime supremacy. The need to protect Germany's overseas trade
from the reprisals of a jealous England was easily the most potent
argument in the arsenal of German naval propagandists. A large German navy, it was commonly asserted, was the only means by which
Britain could be compelled to abandon her plans for imperial preference and the closing of her markets to German goods. Similarly,
naval power was the sole mechanism by which Britain could be deterred from going to war in order to destroy German commerce, or
could be defeated in the event that deterrence failed. Logic of this
nature was frequently employed by German navalists from Tirpitz
and William on down. Whether or not they truly believed what they
were saying can be debated, but its ultimate impact cannot. It was an
exceedingly effective tool in obtaining public support and arousing
popular enthusiasm for Germany's program of naval expansion.[75]

  One reason that commercial rivalry was such a salient issue, and
such a divisive factor, in the pre-1914 relations of Germany and Britain
is that its implications, in the eyes of many contemporary observers,
extended far beyond the realm of purely economic matters. To those
possessed of a mercantilist Weltanschauung, a healthy foreign trade
appeared vital to industrial growth and economic strength, which, in
turn, seemed essential to military power. From their perspective,

commercial competition was not merely economic competition but also geopolitical competition, and a threat to trade not simply that but a menace to national security and one's international strategic position as well.[76]

Nationalist elements in both countries employed arguments reflecting this point of view when analyzing the Anglo-German trade rivalry. The German professor and propagandist, Karl Rathgen, in an article on "The Denunciation of the English Commercial Treaty and its Danger for Germany in the Future," declared that "the fight for supremacy in the world must inevitably lead Germany into a conflict of interests with Greater Britain and to an extent which cannot occur with any other European Power. The vital struggle will be for the markets remaining open to the Germans; and the best of these markets are the colonies."[77] In a similar vein, Gerhard von Schulze-Gävernitz claimed:

> German industrial progress is overtaking that of England with giant strides. It has gradually amassed those stupendous aggregations of capital that first rivaled the individual capitalism of England and then grew to American dimensions. The day is now not far distant when the economic power of Germany will equal that of England, mistress of the world and still its leading banker and creditor. Then the two-power standard for her navy will have become financially impossible. With purely economic development British sea dominion must pass away,—melt under the veritable sunshine of peace. To-day, perhaps,—but not to-morrow,—New Germany, rising, can be struck to earth by a mailed fist. Thence comes for England, while she still has power in her hands, the great temptation to a "preventive war." By blockade and privateering they think that German trade,—70 to 80 per cent of it sea trade,—would be all but destroyed and German wares crowded out of the markets of the world.[78]

British patriots, for their part, were no less convinced of this relationship between economics and politics and its meaning for Anglo-German diplomacy. Lord Alfred Northcliffe, on a motor tour of Germany, wrote to H. W. Wilson, "Every one of these new factory chimneys is a gun pointed at England, and in many cases a very powerful one."[79] And C. C. P. Fitzgerald, a retired admiral, baldly asserted that "Germany's ambition now is, first to ruin our oversea trade, by any means, fair or foul, and then—having impoverished us until we can no longer afford to compete in warlike preparations—to attack us by force of arms upon the first suitable opportunity."[80]

It is necessary to point out that this mercantilist perspective, and the concomitant concern over commercial competition, was not uni-versal among British and German elites. This was true even among those on the right of the political spectrum. In Britain, for example, Lord Salisbury commented, "All that we hear, I think, of the Germans and their rivalry . . . must take its origin more from the fertile and inventive writers who have to produce adequate copy than from any real foundation in fact."[81] His successors in the Unionist government, Balfour and Lansdowne, although favorably disposed toward tariff reform, likewise refused to accept the notion that commercial jeal-ousy was a basis for the Anglo-German antagonism; Balfour termed the idea a "complete delusion."[82] On the German side, Holstein and Metternich agreed with this assessment, and there is some indica-tion that even Bülow may have been partly persuaded.[83] Moreover, the left-wing elements in both countries remained solidly commit-ted to free trade and firmly convinced that economic rivalry, to the degree it existed, did not constitute a fundamental conflict of interest between Germany and Great Britain.[84] In Germany, this fact was of limited importance because of the relative weakness of these groups, but in Great Britain, where the Liberals were in power after 1905, it was more worthy of note. It meant that the governing party, and particularly Foreign Secretary Edward Grey, was not influenced in its views nor motivated in its policies by considerations of German commercial competition.

All of this, of course, reduces the negative impact on Anglo-Ger-man political relations that can be attributed to trade rivalry. One must still take care, however, not to minimize the significance of this effect. Among important members of the British and German govern-ments, among influential sectors of the press, and among broad seg-ments of the population, commercial competition played a sub-stantial, and perhaps in some instances decisive, role in shaping attitudes and opinions. It spawned considerable suspicion, apprehen-sion, and ill feeling on both sides of the North Sea, and in certain corners, by no means isolated, provoked fears of war and even the belief that armed conflict between Great Britain and Germany was inevitable.

Declining heterogeneity in the economic activities of Britain and Germany seriously damaged Anglo-German diplomacy of the prewar era. Although elements of complementarity and interdependence were present, the two countries engaged in fierce competition in the British market and in foreign markets as well. As a consequence, while incentives to stable political relations were at best modest, deep fears and animosities were aroused. The net effect of economic factors was thus to reinforce and exacerbate rather than to mitigate conflicts of geopolitical interest between the two countries.

The contrast between the Anglo-German and Anglo-American cases in this regard may be apparent. Two points, however, should be stressed. First, Britain imported greater quantities of merchandise from Germany and the United States than from any other country and would seem to have had an interest in seeing that these flows continued unabated. The difference in the two cases lay in the composition of these imports. Whereas Britain depended heavily on the United States for supplies of foodstuffs and raw materials, her trade with Germany consisted mainly of manufactured articles. The latter, while providing a benefit to British consumers in terms of lower prices or increased availability, were not needed to feed the population or to maintain industrial health and stable employment. Indeed, because they competed to some extent with British production, they were actually held to be harmful. As a consequence, Britons generally, and the government in particular, were far less reluctant to contemplate closing the home and imperial markets to German manufactures than to American primary materials and far more concerned with avoiding an Anglo-American war than an Anglo-German one.

A second and related point concerns the opposite side of this equation. Both the United States and Germany exported more goods to Britain than to any other country and had therefore a substantial interest in seeing that the British market remained open to them. But the United States, recognizing Britain's reliance on her primary materials, anticipated the loss of this market only in the extreme event of war over some geopolitical difference (e.g., the Venezuelan boundary dispute), whereas Germany feared closure as a consequence of commercial competition. Thus, for American traders, it was important to ease tensions with Britain in order to avoid an armed conflict. For their German counterparts, on the other hand, a relaxation in the power-political sphere appeared to offer few advantages, since closure might well occur anyway. To the German mind, only a policy of pressure, involving the construction of a great fleet and the threat of war, could conceivably induce the British to keep their markets open. In the end, an apparently similar interest produced quite different results.

This further suggests that the harmful effects of economic competition between Britain and Germany were compounded by a
serious case of asymmetrical interdependence, itself partly reflective
of the homogeneous structure of Anglo-German trade. Generally
speaking, Germany depended on British export markets to a far
greater degree than Britain depended on German imports, since these
goods tended to duplicate what Britain herself already produced. The
Germans thus worried, and justifiably so, that the British might close
their markets to German goods, inflicting severe damage on the German economy while causing only minor inconvenience to their
own.[85] Americans, on the other hand, had little to be concerned
about in this regard. The British economy needed imports from the
United States as badly as American producers needed the British
market. Britain could not, therefore, with impunity close her markets to the bulk of American goods, a fact widely appreciated in both
countries.

Societal Attributes

If power politics and economics tended, on balance, to drive Great
Britain and Germany apart, ideological and cultural factors did little
or nothing to help bridge the widening chasm. This does not imply
that the two countries were entirely without ties in this regard.
Indeed, on the surface, Germany and England were similar in many
ways, perhaps more so than any other pair of European states. They
shared a common Teutonic heritage, a basically Protestant religious
orientation, and an interest in and appreciation for one another's art,
literature, music, and philosophy. Furthermore, their ruling houses
were closely related, William II being the grandson of Queen Victoria
and the nephew of Edward VII.

Nor does this imply, in either country, an absence of persons who
professed to be moved by such considerations. Dr. Theodor Harnack,
a well-known German historian and theologian believed to be close
to the throne, stated, "We Germans are bound to the English by blood
relationship, by culture essentially the same amidst all its differences, and for centuries past we are bound together by a vast interchange of thought and resources. You sent us Boniface. Your
Shakespeare has become our Shakespeare. Your political institutions
have educated us politically; and last, but not least, your literature,
flowing from a clear abundant spring, has been our intellectual nour-
ishment for more than 200 years."[86] His sovereign, the Emperor

William himself, once told his royal uncle that Britain and Germany "are of the same blood and they have the same creed and they belong to the great Teutonic race which Heaven has entrusted with the culture of the world. . . . that I think is grounds enough to keep Peace and to foster mutual recognition and reciprocity in all what [*sic*] draws us together and to sink everything which could part us!"[87]

In England, this sentiment was echoed by such groups as the Anglo-German Friendship Committee, which declared, "We know of no possible ground of serious quarrel between the two countries. On the contrary, we find in their history, their common faith and long friendship, their mutual indebtedness in literature, science and art, the strongest reasons for the maintenance of cordial and friendly relations."[88]

Allusions to racial and/or cultural brotherhood can also be found sprinkled throughout the British Parliamentary debates of the period. One M.P. in 1911 expressed his desire that "if we are to have special friends . . . the Great German Empire should be included. They are nearest to us in kindred, their thoughts, their literature, their life generally is nearer to that of our country than those of any other Continental power."[89] A second noted that the "Germans are our blood relations,"[90] and a third added that "even our Court speaks with a German accent."[91]

For the most part, however, the favorable impact of these connections on popular attitudes and official policy in England and Germany was quite limited. Although undeniably present, these links were, by any objective criteria, not nearly so strong as those that existed between Great Britain and the United States. When Joseph Chamberlain, in his famous Leicester speech of November 1899, asserted that the bonds that held Britain and the United States together could do the same for Britain and Germany, most Englishmen disagreed. The *Times* wrote, "Mr. Chamberlain knows the history and situation of the three peoples too well to imagine seriously that in any conditions we could possibly establish or maintain with Germany such relations as might be quite feasible in the case of America." "We are," the paper stated, "bound to the Americans and they to us by ties of blood and sentiment which do not exist between us and any other race."[92] Moreover, these links were also relatively weak in comparison to the serious economic and geopolitical issues dividing the two countries. A common Teutonic heritage was just not sufficient to mitigate a dispute over the maritime supremacy of the world. As the German ambassador to London, Lichnowsky, put it in 1912:

We must tell ourselves that the regard for our philosophers, poets, and musicians, and their influence on the intellectual upper classes in England, cannot be the decisive factor in the sympathies of a great power, that the friendship and unity of nations requires, rather, the similarity of their interests and particularly their antagonisms. This point of view is decisive compared to historical reminiscences, ties of blood, or even an affectionate "debt of gratitude which the entire world owes to German genius and science." Such considerations are quite effective at occasional speeches and after-dinner talks, but in hard fact they fail to work, and they prove themselves impotent when the necessities of life of a people and the legitimacy of human progress are at issue.[93]

Finally, and perhaps most importantly, the positive impact of these racial, religious, and cultural connections was offset and outweighed by the adverse effect of other, negative aspects of the Anglo-German relationship. In particular, the two countries differed radically with respect to basic political and social philosophy and organization. While turn-of-the-century Britain was an industrial-capitalist, liberal, parliamentary democracy, imperial Germany was an autocratic, bureaucratic, authoritarian state in which conservative feudal elements remained extremely powerful. These differences were appreciated, and even exaggerated, on both sides of the North Sea, and they colored the attitudes and perceptions of important segments of popular opinion as well as governmental leaders themselves.

Englishmen, who could agree on practically nothing else, were in fact almost unanimous in their distaste for the German political system, its ideology, and its methods. The pages of the British press were filled with harsh criticisms of Prussian militarism, discriminatory suffrage laws, prosecutions for lese majesty, and, more generally, royal absolutism and the suppression of the popular will. To some writers, indeed, the antagonism between Britain and Germany appeared to originate in a fundamental clash over political-cultural values. In his book, *The Anglo-German Problem,* Charles Sarolea, a professor at the University of Edinburgh, contended, *"The present conflict between England and Germany is the old conflict between Liberalism and despotism, between industrialism and militarism, between progress and reaction, between the masses and the classes. The conflict between England and Germany is a conflict, on the one hand, between a nation which believes in political liberty and national autonomy, where the Press is free and where the rulers are responsible to public opinion, and, on the other hand, a nation where public opinion is still muzzled or powerless and where the masses are* still under the heel of an absolute government, a reactionary party, a military Junkertum, and a despotic bureaucracy."[94]

Few others went quite this far, but there can be no question that dislike and distrust of German political ideals and techniques made many Britons hesitant to support a closer relationship with Berlin. The *Spectator* accurately captured the sentiment prevailing among the British population, and no doubt members of the government, too, when it wrote in 1905 that "it would make very greatly for a better understanding between the two countries if the German government were not to show themselves so opposed to liberal ideas. . . . We admit fully that in reality the autocratic and anti-liberal system of government that prevails in Germany is no business of ours, and that we have no sort of right to object to it. Still, we cannot ignore the fact that its existence does influence men's minds here unfavourably towards the German Empire. It makes men say, in effect: 'That is not the kind of government which we can feel confidence in, or with which we should care to ally ourselves.' "[95]

In this respect, the distinction made by Englishmen between Germany and the United States is most striking. Both of these nations were rising imperial powers with growing navies. Both threatened British interests in various regions of the globe. Yet Britons, while they detested and feared Germany, almost universally admired the United States and felt minimal apprehension at her ambitions. Part of this, of course, was purely geographic. The German menace was the more immediate, the North Sea being considerably narrower than the North Atlantic. But a large portion was ideological and cultural as well. Imbued as they were with a sense of Anglo-Saxon solidarity, the vast majority of Englishmen simply did not believe that America could wish or do them serious harm.[96]

The profoundly unfavorable view in Britain of Germany's social and political structures, processes, and norms was, by and large, reciprocated in German perceptions of England. It is true that German opinion in this regard was somewhat less unified than was British; sizable left-wing, especially social democratic, elements in Germany did look approvingly at Britain as an example worthy of emulation.[97] But these groups never attained a significant, not to mention preponderant, share of political power. And, ironically, the degree of influence that they did possess actually served to darken the attitude toward England among the remainder of the population. Because other segments of society hated and feared the left, they also despised, by association, the foreign country with which it was most closely identified. This tendency was, in fact, actively encouraged by Bismarck, who employed attacks on the British system as an integral component of his strategy to suppress social democratic forces and minimize domestic resistance to his conservative rule. Under the guidance of the Iron Chancellor, the German press directed a steady stream of abuse at English institutions and practices, particularly those of the Liberal administrations of William Gladstone. As Paul Kennedy writes, throughout his tenure in office, Bismarck waged "ideological warfare against what he considered to be dangerous political opponents, and the most suitable way to do this was to discredit their creed and their proposed policies by a continuous, one-sided assault upon the 'parliamentary model-state' itself."[98]

Except for the social democrats and a dwindling number of liberals, the great bulk of the German people—and especially the ruling classes—subscribed to what one historian has called a " 'Germanic ideology,' which defined itself, as it were negatively, by its dislike of a Liberal, free-trading, parliamentary democracy as symbolised by Britain."[99] Nowhere was this sentiment more strongly held than among the German agrarians. Remnants of a feudal past, the Junkers and peasants were easily the most reactionary elements of Wilhelmian society. Their antipathy toward Britain's social and political configuration was deeply rooted, and as much pragmatic as philosophical. More than anything else, they feared that England's present would become Germany's future. Britain was, after all, heavily industrial and primarily urban, controlled by bourgeois-capitalists and possessing a large and increasingly militant proletariat. Agricultural interests had played a declining role in British society since the repeal of the Corn Laws.[100] Despite the rapid modernization of Germany after 1871, the Junkers, and their peasant allies, still retained at the turn of the century a substantial measure of social, economic, and political power. But if Germany were to continue along the English path of industrialization and democratization, there was a real possibility that the rural classes would be largely eradicated. At best, their status and influence were sure to be drastically reduced.[101]

Because they hated England and all that she stood for, the Junkers and peasants could hardly have favored initiatives aimed at improving relations with that country. And because they were so powerful, in some instances their opposition was probably fatal to chances for diplomatic cooperation. On the specific issue of the proposed Anglo-German alliance of 1898–1901, for example, Pauline Anderson has argued that "the attitude of the German Agrarians was the greatest obstacle to such a tie. While this group exercised so large a measure of political and social control, a policy so antipathetic to it as alliance with England could not have been undertaken. The Agrarians could not have been reconciled to allying themselves with an industrialized state whose materialistic philosophy they despised. They would not have welcomed closer contact with the liberalism, cosmopolitanism and Trade Unionism characteristic of England."[102] The German historian, Friedrich Meinecke, has agreed, noting that "German statesmen must always have said to themselves that the conclusion of an alliance with England would result in a heated political dispute with the conservative element—which was at no time a mere faction of malcontents, but a group intimately connected to the entire political system."[103]

Great Britain and Germany were, during the late nineteenth and early twentieth centuries, broadly heterogeneous with respect to their societal attributes. The racial, religious, cultural, and dynastic ties occasionally alleged to bind them together were of little or no value during the immediate prewar period, and were, in fact, overshadowed by grave differences of a political-cultural nature. This "ideological gap," as one historian has termed it, was by itself almost certainly insufficient to precipitate open hostilities between the two countries.[104] But it contributed to animosity and mistrust on both sides, and gave many persons reason to believe—and even to hope—that England and Germany would never be friends. Here, perhaps, was the most crucial distinction between the Anglo-German case and the Anglo-American one. Whereas a high degree of ideological and cultural homogeneity cut across and mitigated the impact of potentially devastating geopolitical (and, later, economic) rivalry between Great Britain and the United States, the low level of homogeneity characteristic of Britain and Germany paralleled already serious conflicts in these areas and served to multiply their divisive effects.

Summary

Unlike Britain and the United States, England and Germany proved incapable of developing stable, friendly relations in the years

Table 2. Great Britain and Germany, 1898–1914

Exercise of Power	Very Low Heterogeneity: imperial competition and bitter naval rivalry; conflict over the European balance.
Economic Activities	Low Heterogeneity: some interdependence; intensive and extensive commerical competition.
Societal Attributes	Low Homogeneity: common Teutonic heritage; strong political-cultural differences along dimensions of liberalism/authoritarianism and industrialism/agrarianism.

immediately preceding the First World War. In this chapter, I have attempted to explain their unfortunate, and even disastrous, failure in this regard. My analysis is summarized in table 2.

The combination of geopolitical, economic, ideological, and cultural factors present in Anglo-German relations of the prewar period was insufficient for peace from a relative, multilateral, perspective, as well as an absolute, dyadic one. Compared to their quarrels with other countries, German and British differences with one another were more fundamental. This was true not only in geopolitical affairs, but also in the economic and societal spheres. For Britain in particular, this meant that should the international environment require her to engage in external balancing, accommodations with other of her potential adversaries—among them the United States and France—would come first, an understanding with Germany later or not at all.

It may also be worth noting that Anglo-German relations of the prewar period did not lack potentially catalytic events. But, because circumstances were so unfavorable, these did not precipitate a reconciliation. Instead, the First Moroccan Crisis, the Agadir Crisis, and other such disputes, to the extent they caused a thorough examination of the diplomatic relationship between the two countries, did not bring about a new appreciation of the value of friendship, but provided further confirmation of negative stereotypes and images and reinforced the belief that an armed struggle might be impossible to avoid.

4

England and France, 1900–1905

Narrative: The Rapprochement

The relations of Great Britain and France, so cordial today, have not always been peaceful. For over 800 years, the peoples of these two countries glared menacingly at one another across the English Channel, their uneasy coexistence punctuated by frequent episodes of open warfare. From the time of the Norman invasion to the end of the Napoleonic era, forces of France and England met in at least seven major conflicts as well as numerous lesser skirmishes. So ancient and abiding was the Anglo-French antagonism that by the nineteenth century it was accepted virtually without question as an axiom of international politics.[1]

The years after 1815 saw some limited improvement in the tenor of Anglo-French diplomacy.[2] Especially during the mid-1800s, relations were relatively friendly, and Britain and France engaged in a measure of military and economic cooperation. From 1854 to 1856 they fought as allies in the Crimean War, and in 1860 concluded the Cobden Treaty, which removed many of the barriers to trade between the two nations. By the decades of the 1880s and 1890s, however, France and England were at odds over colonial disputes in Asia and Africa.[3] Some of these issues were successfully liquidated without serious threat of war. In August 1889, for example, the two countries signed an agreement defining their respective holdings on the Gold and Ivory Coasts and in Senegal and Gambia. A year later, France agreed to recognize the British protectorate over Zanzibar and Pemba in exchange for Britain's promise of a free hand in Madagascar and recognition of French claims in the western and central Sudan. And in 1896, the two countries reached a settlement establishing the Mekong River as the dividing line between their possessions in Siam. Nevertheless, other items of contention were not so easily disposed of, and in the final years of the century it appeared that France and Britain might once again decide their differences on the field of battle.

Easily the most dangerous of these disputes was that involving Egypt.[4] In 1879, following a financial crisis that threatened disaster to holders of Egyptian bonds, France and England had instituted a system of "Dual Control" in the hope of setting Egypt's economic house in order. When, in 1881, a rebellion broke out, endangering the position of the khedive and threatening to plunge the country into chaos, the two powers plotted a joint intervention to suppress it. The French government, however, was unable to secure an appropriation for this purpose, and the British were left to act alone. This they did, and by the mid-1880s Egypt was effectively under British rule. While the government in London frequently professed its intention to eventually withdraw from Egypt, the government in Paris gradually became convinced that only a show of force could induce the British to retire.

With this in mind, the French in 1896 dispatched a small force under the command of Captain Jean-Baptiste Marchand to establish a presence on the Upper Nile. By July 1898, Marchand, his officers, and his troops had reached Fashoda. The British, who considered French control over the flow of Nile water downstream to constitute a menace to their position in Egypt, adopted a hard line. In September, an army under the leadership of Lord Kitchener arrived at Fashoda, and a stalemate ensued. London demanded the immediate and unconditional withdrawal of Marchand, while Paris pressed for a negotiated settlement. The outbreak of hostilities seemed imminent, but the French, faced with the marked superiority of British capabilities on both land and sea, finally capitulated in November. While the circumspection of the French foreign minister, Delcassé, thus defused the incident, the more general fear of war did not abate, particularly in France. Throughout the winter and spring of 1899 there was widespread expectation that Britain would soon attack, and defensive preparations were undertaken to meet this contingency.[5]

The opening of the South African conflict the following October further stretched Anglo-French relations toward the breaking point. Public opinion in France, as in most of Europe, sided wholeheartedly with the Boers, and the Paris press conducted a vicious campaign against British policy.[6] One French cartoonist, Charles Léandre, went so far as to pen a caricature of Joseph Chamberlain hiding behind Queen Victoria's skirts. The very nature of the drawing might have been considered insult enough, but when Léandre was decorated for his effort with the Legion of Honor, all Britain was incensed. Rumors of an impending intervention in the war by a coalition of European powers, including France, only increased the tension.[7] Many Britons were convinced that France intended to utilize the conflict as a cover, striking at England while her back was turned.[8] So agitated was British opinion that Paul Cambon, the French ambassador to London, feared an attack on France once the war in the Transvaal had been concluded.[9] Delcassé was sufficiently alarmed to establish a committee to consider the possibility of an armed struggle with Britain. This group, comprised of all the principal ministers as well as the chiefs of both the army and navy, produced a number of contingency plans, including those for such offensive operations as an expedition to Egypt, an attack on Burma in conjunction with a Russian march on India, and even an invasion of England itself.[10]

Although the winter of 1899–1900 thus proved nerve-wracking to both sides, war did not break out and emotions soon subsided. By March Cambon felt that he could detect the early signs of a coming détente.[11] With hindsight, it is evident that events in Africa, and the furor over them, had obscured developments that might have portended an improvement in Anglo-French relations. In 1895, for example, the Lord Mayor of London had been invited to visit the city of Bordeaux on the occasion of an international exhibition there. He had met with various political and commercial leaders of France, including the foreign minister, Hanotaux, and at his reception M. Hanotaux had even toasted the queen.[12] Throughout 1895 and 1896 there had appeared in publications on both sides of the Channel articles suggesting the possibility of a rapprochement.[13] The *Times*, noting that a permanent alliance would be "incompatible with the settled traditions of our foreign policy," nevertheless called for "the best possible relations with our French neighbours."[14] And, in 1896, an Entente Cordiale Society had been formed in England. The purpose of this organization, whose members were leading figures of the political and business communities, was

1. To cooperate in maintaining and perpetuating the friendly relations that now happily exist between the two Nations.
2. To use its influence to develop a better knowledge and higher appreciation of the French Nation in England, as also of the English Nation in France, by the organization of Public Meetings, Conferences, and the circulation of Literature, etc.
3. To promote friendly intercourse and common action between the representatives of the two peoples, socially and commercially.

4. To ensure a more accurate knowledge of the respective feelings and opinions of the two Nations in all questions affecting their common interests.[15]

The following year, in 1897, a branch of the Entente Cordiale Society had been founded in France.

This slow and not-so-steady movement toward an understanding was, of course, halted and even reversed by the Fashoda affair and the crisis over the war in South Africa. But after 1900, the pace of rapprochement began to accelerate once again. In January 1902, Delcassé was quoted on the floor of the British Parliament as stating that he believed the current relations of England and France to be "excellent,"[16] and by March 1903, Cambon noted that in order to be popular in England it was now necessary for one to appear friendly to France.[17]

The year 1903 saw, in fact, a number of events that both reflected and contributed to the growing amity of the two nations. The first, and perhaps most significant, was the visit of the new English king, Edward VII, to Paris during the month of May.[18] As Prince of Wales, Edward had been a frequent visitor to the city and had developed a genuine affection for the French people. His gracious demeanor and friendly utterances on this occasion had a seemingly magical effect on popular opinion. Whereas he had been greeted upon his arrival with jeers and cries of *"Vive Marchand!" "Vive Fashoda!"* and *"Vivent les Boers!,"*[19] by the time he left Paris the masses were shouting *"Vive Edouard!"* and *"Notre Bon Edouard!"* and the crowds were so dense that he had difficulty departing.[20] Paul Cambon summed up the entire event in rather hyperbolic fashion when he said that "[King Edward] won the hearts of the Parisians in a day. . . . Without him the Entente might never have been made."[21]

The visit of King Edward to Paris was reciprocated in July, when the president of the French Republic, Emile Loubet, accompanied by Delcassé, journeyed to London. This overture of goodwill was also a resounding success. The London papers were extremely favorable, and the general public voiced its approval as well.[22] As Cambon later wrote to Delcassé, the "indifference, the reserve, which ordinarily characterizes the English, had, for a moment, vanished. The people heartily endorsed the tributes and kind attention paid the president of the Republic by the monarch and all the important figures of England, showing by their cheers a genuine enthusiasm. Not for fifty years had a foreign head of state been the object in this country of such acclaim, and if the fact was striking in London, it seemed to me perhaps still more significant in a small, tranquil provincial town like Dover, where the entire population emerged from its habitual calm to demonstrate warm sympathy toward France and its representative."[23]

The reaction of the English people to the French president and his party did not go unnoticed across the Channel. On 11 July *Le Temps* declared, "The Franco-English 'rapprochement' is a *fait accompli*. France and Great Britain are able, unreservedly, to deal with one another as 'friendly nations.'"[24]

Later that same month, the growing harmony in Anglo-French relations was further exhibited, and its cause strengthened, by a visit to London of more than 150 members of the French Chamber of Deputies.[25] These men belonged to the so-called Arbitration Group, which, under the direction of Baron d'Estournelles de Constant, was actively promoting a treaty of arbitration between Britain and France. They had been invited to London for discussion of this idea by the Commercial Committee of the British House of Commons. The visit of the French deputies was the occasion for the exchange of numerous pleasantries revealing a depth of mutual affection that would have been unthinkable half a decade before.

In October 1903, the efforts of the Arbitration Group, the Commercial Committee, and especially of Thomas Barclay, onetime chairman of the British Chamber of Commerce in Paris, came to fruition.[26] On the fourteenth of that month, England and France concluded a treaty of arbitration for the settlement of their disputes. Under this agreement, differences that could not be resolved by diplomatic means were to be referred to the Permanent Court of Arbitration established at The Hague by the Convention of 29 July 1899, to which both countries were signatories. In practical terms, this accord was virtually meaningless, for issues affecting the "vital interests, the independence, or the honour of the two Contracting States" were specifically excluded from its application.[27] Symbolically, however, the treaty was of some importance, for it constituted the first legal statement of intent on the part of Great Britain and France to compose their differences without resorting to military action. This much was recognized by Lord Hylton, who, in addressing the House of Lords on 2 February 1904, stated, "With regard to the treaty signed between France and Great Britain, I think your Lordships will view with pleasure any extension of the system of arbitration as a means of arriving at a fair and peaceful solution of international disputes.

The class of questions which will call for solution under the new treaty may be of a limited scope, but the principle adopted appears easily capable of enlargement; and your satisfaction in this matter will, I feel, be the greater, inasmuch as it affords a further proof of the amicable relations which happily exist between ourselves and our neighbours across the Channel."[28] It is thus evident that by early 1904, substantial progress had been made toward a rapprochement between Britain and France. An optimistic observer might have concluded that an entente cordiale was already at hand. The more cautious person, however, would have reserved judgment, for a small number of colonial disputes still hung like the sword of Damocles over Anglo-French relations. Upon his visit to London in July 1903, Delcassé had held conversations with Lansdowne on these questions, and negotiations between Lansdowne and Cambon had opened shortly thereafter.

The talks bore fruit on 8 April 1904, with the signing in London of a set of agreements that effectively eliminated the last points of contention between the two powers.[29] There were three accords in all: one relating to Egypt and Morocco; a second concerning Newfoundland and West and Central Africa; and a third dealing with the New Hebrides, Madagascar, and Siam.[30] Under the terms of the first, and most important, declaration, France agreed not to obstruct the actions of Great Britain in Egypt, nor to require that any time limit be fixed for the British occupation there. In return, Britain allowed France a free hand in Morocco, to "preserve order in that country, and to provide assistance for the purpose of all administrative, economic, financial, and military reforms which it may require." The two governments also pledged to respect each other's commercial and trading rights in the territories under their control.

By the second convention, France agreed to renounce certain fishing privileges that she held in Newfoundland by virtue of the Treaty of Utrecht, including the right to use a French shore for such purposes as the drying of fish. In compensation, the French retained the right to fish in territorial waters off the Newfoundland coast, and Britain agreed to pay a pecuniary indemnity to French citizens who were forced to give up their establishments on the French shore or their occupations as fishermen as a consequence of the accord. Britain also granted to France some minor territorial concessions in Senegambia, accepted settlement of boundary questions in the Niger and Chad in accordance with French desires, and ceded to France the Iles de Los.

Under the terms of the third agreement, France and Great Britain fixed the River Menam as the line dividing their spheres of influence in Siam—the British zone to the west and the French zone to the east. In addition, the English government withdrew its objection to a customs tariff erected at Madagascar upon the annexation of that island by France. And the two countries pledged to arrive at a solution to their jurisdictional difficulties in the New Hebrides.

With the signing of these agreements on 8 April, the Anglo-French rapprochement was secure. Ratification by the respective legislatures of France and England was almost a foregone conclusion, and the votes were decidedly anticlimactic. In June, when the Balfour government brought its Anglo-French Convention Bill to the floor of the House of Commons, support was so overwhelming that it was not deemed necessary to divide the House, and the measure passed without a dissent. In France, where the agreements were put to a vote in November, approval was less unanimous, but the accords were still ratified by a wide margin—443 to 105 in the Chamber of Deputies and 215 to 37 in the Senate.

That the Entente Cordiale, or friendly understanding, embodied in the colonial pacts marked a fundamental transformation in the historical relations of Great Britain and France was widely accepted. There were, naturally, some expressions of doubt. In England, H. W. Wilson warned that "it would be dangerous to presume too much on the present *entente* which may go the way of many predecessors."[31] Across the Channel, Gabriel Louis-Jaray cautioned, "One year is hardly enough to know if the history of several centuries is dead."[32] And there were others who agreed.

But these voices were, generally speaking, lost in a veritable flood of optimism and approbation. A French senator, M. d'Aunay, exulted that ratification of the accords was a matter of "affirming the rapprochement of two great nations which were destined to get along, and of rendering impossible, in the future, the occurrence of a conflict which would be, for both, as for humanity, an utter catastrophe."[33] Alcide Ebray, in the journal *Débats*, stated that the signing of the agreements placed the relations between France and Britain on a "new and pacific basis." It was, he said, "the inauguration of a new era in Anglo-French relations and in the history of the world."[34] These sentiments were echoed by many Frenchmen, though perhaps none so eloquent as Paul Doumer, Chairman of the Budget Committee of the Chamber of Deputies, who wrote, "The settlement of April 8 may . . . be regarded as the inauguration of a new era. It affirms the existence of friendly relations between the two countries and shows that both alike are desirous to arrive at an understanding, and to put an end to the differences which unavoidably arise from the defence of their respective interests. It is the outward and visible sign and the first product of the *entente cordiale*. England and France, in fact, are now under a new *régime*, in which the significant features are good feeling and harmony, to which the name of *'entente cordiale'* has been applied."[35]

In Britain, the story was much the same. A leading article in the *Times* called the conclusion of the 8 April agreements "an event of high historic importance. No consummation," the paper claimed, ". . . has been more earnestly desired by the best public opinion of the two nations; none is more likely to cement in the future that sense of common aims and common interests which is the surest pledge of universal peace."[36] E. J. Dillon, in the *Contemporary Review*, was equally enthusiastic. Dillon wrote, "If every diplomatic act or international agreement which by removing the causes of misunderstandings lessens the chances of war is a gain to the world, the Anglo-French Convention may be characterised as the most auspicious event of the 20th century. . . . to pave the way for permanent peace was the aim pursued by the heads of both countries."[37] It was probably Sir Albert Rollit, a member of the British Parliament, however, who gave the most lofty expression to these feelings. In a speech before the House of Commons, Rollit proclaimed, "Not only have many differences been removed, but the means of preventing, at any rate, hostile action with regard to differences in the future has been achieved. Yes, the force of right will now supplant the right of force, the barriers will fall down between nation and nation and be set up only between right and wrong. . . . Whatever we may say as to the result of the passing of the Bill now before the House, permanent peaceful relations between the two countries have been accomplished."[38]

The years immediately after 1904 did nothing to diminish the significance attributed to the Anglo-French rapprochement by these observers. For the close and friendly relationship that had evolved between Great Britain and France continued to develop. By late 1905, the two countries were engaged in conversations aimed at military and naval cooperation. They demonstrated their solidarity in 1906 at Algeciras, when they joined together to frustrate German designs on Morocco. And, less than a decade later, French and British soldiers fought side by side in the First World War.

The same general diplomatic unity has persisted throughout the twentieth century. From 1939 to 1940 Britain and France stood together against the advances of Hitler's *Wehrmacht*. When France could no longer withstand the onslaught of the Nazi machine, Winston Churchill held out to Frenchmen the offer of British citizenship and pledged to fight on until France should be liberated.[39] In the years following the Second World War, France and England allied themselves in the North Atlantic Treaty Organization (NATO) and, after considerable aggravation and misunderstanding, in the European Community. Even today, at a time when France does not participate in NATO operations, when Britain's leaders discuss withdrawing from the Common Market, and when the governments of the two countries are as ideologically different as any in the Western democracies, the cordiality and friendship at the core of Anglo-French relations seems secure. The peace that emerged between these nations eight decades ago has become as axiomatic as the hostility that preceded it. And, although this very fact is reason for caution, it is difficult to conceive of conditions that might induce Great Britain and France to renew their ancient rivalry.

The Exercise of Power

The Entente Cordiale of 8 April 1904, which formally brought to an end the long and bitter colonial competition between England and France, was barely preceded by the informal termination of a closely related naval rivalry. Throughout the nineteenth century, as France and Britain contended for imperial possessions, they waged a similar battle for command of the seas. While the French navy always remained a distant second to that of Britain, the combined fleets of the Franco-Russian Alliance did near parity with England around 1900. This naval race aroused considerable suspicion and animosity on both sides of the Channel, and especially in Britain, which depended almost entirely upon her maritime supremacy for home and imperial defense. Beginning in 1901, however, the French navy deteriorated so rapidly that naval competition between England and France virtually ceased. Embarking upon what one historian has called "a scheme of retrenchment and reform which crippled French sea power," the naval minister, Pelletan, ordered a halt to the construction of battleships then in progress, cancelled fleet maneuvers, secured a reduction in the amount of coal voted for steaming pur-

poses, suspended work on the modernization of out-of-date battleships, cut the Mediterranean force from fourteen battleships to
nine, and politicized the service, seriously undermining discipline.[40]
French naval expenditures, which had risen steadily, approximately
doubling between 1870 and 1900, fell in 1902 and again in 1903.[41] "After
1902 the French naval bugaboo was an anachronism in England."[42]

French naval retrenchment and the willingness to compromise on
colonial issues flowed from imperatives of both imperial expansion
and national defense. The Fashoda incident had revealed France's
utter inability, alone or with the support of Russia, to extend her
influence in North Africa against British wishes. Delcassé's decision
to withdraw Marchand had been determined by the "necessity of
avoiding a naval war which we are absolutely incapable of carrying
on, even with Russian help."[43] But for some time, he and other French
leaders remained hopeful that German backing might be procured in
order to exact colonial gains at Britain's expense. Overtures to this
effect had, in fact, been made by the foreign minister, Hanotaux, as
part of his Fashoda strategy,[44] and were renewed around 1900, at
which time Delcassé sought to force the British out of Egypt by
means of a Franco-German intervention in the South African War.[45]
Ultimately, however, it was this proposed collaboration that shattered French illusions regarding German assistance in colonial
efforts. For the Germans, after initially appearing to favor the
scheme, refused to participate unless France accepted the Treaty of
Frankfurt and the loss of Alsace-Lorraine. This condition, of course,
could not be met. From this experience French officials concluded
that no meaningful support could be obtained from Berlin. The
ambassador to Russia, Montebello, wrote to Delcassé, "For our part
we now know that if there was any question of reaching agreement
with Germany on any diplomatic action whatsoever, it would first be
necessary for France to renounce all claim to the territories which
she lost in 1871."[46] To this view Delcassé also subscribed.[47]

Unable, for obvious political reasons, to write off their lost
provinces in order to purchase German assistance, French statesmen
realized that further colonial expansion could not be achieved in
opposition to Great Britain, but only through cooperation with her.
They thus began to seriously contemplate the idea of renouncing
their claim to Egypt in return for other considerations. One of these
was the opportunity to consolidate the French position in Morocco.
After Egypt, Morocco ranked highest among French imperial objectives. The country was alleged to be of great economic value, capable

of producing vast amounts of grain, endowed with prime grazing land, and teeming with minerals. Its strategic worth was substantial, as a consequence of its proximity to the Straits of Gibraltar and certain French possessions, especially Algeria.[48] French desires for a "preponderant influence" in Morocco were menaced from several directions. The British were, of course, interested in the territory, and an attempt by London to seize control could not be ruled out.[49] Moreover, an additional and increasingly aggressive contender had lately appeared on the scene. Through the Moroccan Association, founded in 1903, pan-German and colonialist elements in Germany were pressuring their government to stake a claim to Morocco. French imperialists took immediate alarm, and Delcassé was moved to warn, "The Moroccan question must be solved within three years, and given the way in which the Germans are talking and putting forward (through the Moroccan Association) the idea of a German seizure of Morocco, we must not allow them three years. In three years it would be too late; the German race, with its tendency to expand and overrun, would have given itself a historic and nationalist justification for what is still only the momentary demand of a minority."[50]

When British diplomats expressed a readiness to barter Morocco for Egypt, French officials were happy to oblige. Eugène Etienne, head of the powerful *parti colonial,* and other members of his group had been suggesting the exchange for several years, and Delcassé, too, had become convinced of the wisdom of the bargain.[51] By the terms of the Entente Cordiale, France secured her position in Morocco, for she received not only Britain's pledge to grant her a free hand in that country but also the promise to provide "diplomatic support" for French policy there. It was the London government's fulfillment of this promise that enabled France to resist German demands for a voice in Moroccan affairs at the Algeciras Conference of 1906.

In the pursuit of imperial consolidation, then, French statesmen opted to withdraw their opposition to Britain's colonial claims in order to continue in opposition to Germany's continental claims. Advancement of French interests, virtually impossible without some concession, could have been achieved by renouncing either Alsace-Lorraine or Egypt. Weighing the alternatives, Frenchmen and their leaders decided that their geopolitical disputes with Britain were less fundamental than those with Germany. Alsace and Lorraine, still considered French soil, could not be given up. But Egypt, while important, was expendable.[52]

Although the desire for imperial acquisition played a significant role in pushing France toward an accommodation with England, the colonial bargain was, from the French perspective, not merely an end in itself but the means to a larger strategic aim: the strengthening of France's position vis-à-vis Germany on the continent of Europe. Paris officials, it should be noted, did not intend a policy of *revanche*. France was militarily incapable of recovering her former provinces by fighting Germany single-handedly, and active British participation in such a scheme could never have been obtained. Rather, their motives were purely defensive and were grounded in a deeply rooted fear of further German aggression. There had been major war scares in both 1875 and 1887, and, as historian P. J. V. Rolo writes, "The loss of Alsace-Lorraine was no mere symbol of wounded pride but a nagging reminder of basic insecurity."[53]

A number of specific incidents served to reinforce and perpetuate French apprehensions. The most telling of these involved German machinations with respect to the Franco-Russian Alliance. Since 1894, her close association with Russia had been France's main source of protection against the German threat. And the German government had been engaged in what French officials perceived to be a systematic effort to destroy it.[54] In 1900, for example, Berlin had nominated Count Waldersee to head the force charged with suppressing the Boxer Rebellion in China. She told the French—falsely, according to the tsar—that Waldersee's appointment had been proposed by St. Petersburg. The following year, the German emperor invited the Russian ambassador in Berlin to attend a celebration in honor of the tsar's birthday. The festivities were scheduled to take place in Metz, in the former French province of Lorraine. Such events convinced French leaders that Germany was bent on sowing suspicion between France and Russia in order to break up their alliance. Delcassé wrote to Montebello, "I learn from a source whose reliability I have several times been able to put to the test that, in giving personal instructions to Prince Radolin on his departure for Paris [as the new German ambassador], the German Emperor said to him: 'I hope you will take less time to set France and Russia at odds than your predecessor took to set France and England at odds.' The invitation of the Russian ambassador to Metz is a manifestation of this design, which had already been revealed by the incident of the Waldersee nomination."[55] He later told his special assistant, Maurice Paléologue, that "German policy . . . has only one object, and it never varies—the disruption of the Franco-Russian alliance!"[56]

In light of the German threat, French officials saw compelling reasons for an accommodation with Britain. First, the extensive naval preparations for battle with England drained France of scarce strategic resources needed for continental defense. An astute British observer noted in 1903, "The nation's finances will not permit France to rival at one and the same time the huge army of Germany, which may menace her land frontier, and the powerful Fleet of Great Britain."[57] Second, if France were actually to become embroiled in a war with England, she would leave herself dangerously, perhaps fatally, exposed to German advances. It was imperative that this possibility be precluded. As Delcassé warned darkly in a speech before the French Senate, "If by mischance a conflict should break out between these two powers, it is not to the conqueror, whichever it might be, that would go to [sic] the principal benefits of the victory."[58] French leaders hoped for still more, however, than the passive advantages of benevolent neutrality. They wished to enlist Britain as an active participant in a defensive coalition—with France and Russia—against Germany. In a conversation with Lansdowne, Etienne openly expressed his belief "that the most serious menace to the peace of Europe lay in Germany," and "that a good understanding between France and England was the only means of holding German designs in check."[59] For his part, Delcassé had long harbored visions of an Anglo-French political alliance. As he exclaimed to Paléologue on one occasion, "What glorious prospects will open for us then, *cher ami*! If we had both Russia and England behind us, shouldn't we be strong against Germany!"[60]

The strategic imperatives of a reconciliation with Britain were strengthened by the chronic Russo-Japanese tension in the Far East and the eventual outbreak of war in February 1904. At the very least, Russia's involvement in Asia detracted substantially from her value as an alliance partner on the continent of Europe, weakening the position of France in the face of the German threat. Moreover, there was a real danger that France herself might be drawn into the conflict, either to prevent a Russian defeat (though this was not expected) or because of pressure from public opinion. If this were to occur, France would find herself at war not only with Japan, but with Great Britain, which would be required by the terms of the Anglo-Japanese Alliance of 1902 to come to the aid of her ally. France would then be even further exposed to German aggression, and all hope of friendship with Britain, and the benefits to be derived from it, would be irretrievably lost. It was, therefore, critical that France should cooperate with England in limiting the Far Eastern conflict. As early as December 1903, the French ambassador in London, Paul Cambon, told Lansdowne of his desire that the two countries should " 'pour as much cold water as possible' on the embers."[61] The extent to which the strategic implications of the Far Eastern situation actually intensified French yearnings for good relations with England is not entirely clear. Historians have written of their significance, but direct evidence is scanty.[62] It seems safe to assume, however, that the growing crisis in Asia and its potential consequences must have made the strategic advantages of a settlement with Britain appear greater and more crucial than ever.

In the quest for national security, as for imperial gain, the French approach to England reflected a decision to abandon an anti-British colonial policy in favor of opposing Germany on the continent of Europe. Here again the choice was based upon a conscious ordering of priorities and grounded in the fact that, at the most fundamental level, the exercise of French and British power was more highly differentiated than the exercise of French and German power. For most Frenchmen, the problem of national security was central, that of imperial expansion peripheral. Britain posed a minimal threat to France's home defense. She was almost exclusively a maritime power, possessed of a modest army that had performed without distinction in South Africa. Although capable of blockading and bombarding the French coast, she was ill equipped to undertake an invasion of France itself. Nor did Frenchmen, with good reason, suspect Britain of harboring any designs on French territory. They anticipated a British attack only in the event of some colonial confrontation. Germany, by contrast, was quite another matter. She was a land power, the dominant land power in Europe, and she was perched on France's eastern border. Her military forces, legendary for their prowess, appeared competent to invade and perhaps to conquer France, and the government in Berlin seemed disposed toward an attempt. Under these circumstances, it was logical that France should limit her visions of imperial grandeur and seek an accommodation with England. As Delcassé remarked shortly after the humiliation of Fashoda, "England is a rival and a competitor whose conduct is often harsh and extremely disagreeable. But England is not an enemy, and above all, England is not *the Enemy*. . . . if only Russia, England and France could conclude an alliance against Germany."[63]

As geopolitical incentives encouraged French statesmen to pursue an understanding with Britain, similar motivations were at work on

While war may be a political act in achieving national goals, it is not the only option, & some times never the best option

the British side. Much like their counterparts in Paris, London officials had come to see reconciliation as a mechanism for extending their nation's imperial influence. They were particularly desirous of doing so in Egypt. While Britain's political grip on that country was firm as a result of the military occupation, financial difficulties had hampered British efforts there for some time. The crux of the problem was the *Caisse de la dette publique,* an international body founded in 1876 to protect European holders of Egyptian bonds. The *Caisse* indirectly controlled the expenditures of the Egyptian government, and France, through its membership, had continually managed to obstruct British plans for financial reform and economic development. British leaders were anxious to remove this obstacle—Lansdowne said to do so would be an "immense thing"—and the proconsul in Egypt, Lord Cromer, repeatedly pressed for an accommodation with France that would abolish the *Caisse.*[64]

In isolation, Britain would not have needed French cooperation in carrying out her Egyptian policy. Fashoda had demonstrated that the British military was sufficiently strong to impose Britain's will regardless of French attitudes. But there were complicating factors. Legally speaking, the consent of all the Great Powers was required before London could implement its reforms. And British officials did not expect Berlin to give its blessing. "We are almost sure," remarked Cromer to Lansdowne, "to have much difficulty with Germany."[65] Lansdowne agreed that Germany would have to be reckoned with.[66] From this broader perspective, then, French approval appeared almost essential. Britain could not possibly take on both France and Germany in a war over Egyptian finances, and there is no reason to believe that such an idea was ever entertained in Whitehall. If, however, Germany could be given to understand that France would not back her in a challenge to British actions in Egypt, a challenge was not likely to be forthcoming. And if Britain could be certain of French assistance in the improbable event of a German military response, this small risk was worth running. By conceding her interest in Morocco, Britain secured each of these objectives. The public accord relating to Egypt and Morocco bound France to acquiesce to future British policy in Egypt, while a secret article pledged France to support Britain in overriding the objections of other powers after the year 1910.[67]

Although the advancement of her interests in Egypt was an attractive, and perhaps necessary *quid pro quo* for concessions in Morocco, for Britain, as for France, colonial gains did not constitute the most compelling reason for a compromise. Rather, the imperatives of national and imperial defense were preeminent, as Britons came increasingly to believe that an accommodation with France was vital to British security.

The difficulty of Britain's strategic position around the turn of the century has been described in the second chapter. By 1903 there had, in fact, been an improvement in several respects. Relations with the United States had grown sufficiently cordial that America was no longer considered a potential foe, and in 1902 Britain had gained a measure of protection against Russia in the Far East by concluding a defensive alliance with Japan. In British eyes, however, these achievements were still inadequate to solve the problems of defense. There were two main reasons for this. The first, and more recent in evolution, was the rising danger from Germany.

The development of Germanophobia in Britain has received extensive treatment in chapter 3 and requires but brief consideration here. British suspicion of Germany had its origins in the mid-1880s, when Bismarck's quest for colonies led his country to become Britain's imperial rival. It gained reinforcement from later colonial confrontations, especially over South Africa, where the Kruger Telegram and other expressions of German support for the Boers greatly excited British opinion. And it took on added momentum during the late 1890s as Germany emerged as a vigorous commercial competitor. The perception of Germany as a tireless, unrelenting adversary finally became fixed in British minds after 1900, when the rapid expansion of German maritime power menaced Britain's traditional command of the seas. By 1902, in the words of Paul Kennedy, there was among Englishmen the "conviction that there existed a 'German threat' or 'German challenge' which had to be countered. Furthermore, this was a view which was held not merely by certain right-wing journalists, but also by influential figures in the navy, the army and the Foreign Office; by the Crown; by significant members of the Liberal Party; and, last but not least, by a part of the Cabinet, although not by the new prime minister, Balfour, nor by Lansdowne. Although the latter attempted a conciliatory policy towards Berlin, they neither felt willing nor able fully to counter this fast-growing germanophobic sentiment."[68]

That the rising fear of Germany in Britain helped propel her into better relations with France seems clear. The French ambassador in London, Cambon, reported, "The English draw nearer to us in proportion as they feel the hostility between their country and Germany grow and become more acute."[69] Among the general public this was certainly the case. The *Spectator* echoed the feelings of many Britons when it wrote in 1902 that "nothing would keep Germany in such perfect order and so absolutely spoil her dreams as an understanding between us and France."[70] A more sophisticated analysis in the *Fortnightly Review* of that year explained that, in light of the German menace, cordiality with her neighbors across the Channel was essential to Britain. J. L. Garvin, writing under the pseudonym "Calchas," argued that a war with France, even should Britain win, would mean catastrophe: "Our maritime strength would be immensely reduced even by the wear and tear of triumph, and Germany would be brought nearer the naval equality with this country which, above all things, her people desire. . . . In one word, the *contrecoup* of another conflict with France would be profoundly disastrous to ultimate British interests even if our fleet asserted its ascendency upon the seas."[71] Garvin closed his article with an appeal for an Anglo-French rapprochement. It is doubtful whether many Englishmen saw a value in reconciliation with France beyond this kind of benevolent neutrality or reinsurance—whether they anticipated active French assistance in any future Anglo-German confrontation. What is certain is that when friendly relations with France were finally established, they were welcomed in Britain as a means of ensuring Germany's diplomatic and military isolation.[72]

There were also those within the British government who looked to an understanding with France primarily to check German ambitions. Joseph Chamberlain, until his resignation in 1903, was perhaps the most influential, and his views were shared by many at the Foreign Office.[73] "What an effect it will have in Europe and how the Germans will hate it!" wrote Charles Hardinge in March 1904.[74] Louis Mallet agreed that "a close understanding with France is a great safeguard for us—and that our object ought to be to keep Germany isolated."[75] And Francis Bertie, the leader of the anti-German faction among the diplomats, also believed that "we have nothing to fear from Germany if we remain on good terms with France."[76]

However, these voices, strong though they were, did not reflect the main current of thought among those in positions of greatest authority, specifically the British cabinet. In particular, Lansdowne, the foreign secretary, and Balfour, the prime minister, did not regard the German menace as being of paramount importance. Rather, they and their colleagues were more concerned with a second, and what they perceived to be a graver, threat to British security—that of Russia.[77]

The Anglo-Russian imperial rivalry was not a recent phenomenon. For a great many years Britain had found herself at odds with Russia over questions of territory and influence at the perimeter of her empire. But around the turn of the century the situation became more acute. The projection of tsarist domination into Afghanistan appeared to compromise British interests in Persia and the Persian Gulf, and as the railway from Orenburg to Tashkent neared completion, British officials became increasingly uneasy about the prospect of a Russian advance on India. In 1903, Balfour noted that "the chief military problem which this country has to face is that of Indian, rather than of Home, Defence."[78]

What made the Russian problem so worrisome was that British leaders felt almost impotent to halt the apparently inexorable process of Russian expansion. Balfour commented mournfully in 1903 that "the most fundamental fact is that the troops at our disposal are relatively few, the troops of Russia practically unlimited."[79] He was seconded in this opinion by the secretary of state for India, Hamilton, who wrote, "I do not believe our position in Persia or even on the Persian Gulf is such as would enable us successfully to have recourse to force to prevent the further advance of Russia."[80] The Russian Empire, he felt, was "practically impenetrable to attack."[81] At the Admiralty, Lord Selborne also concurred with this general assessment.[82] As historian George Monger has put it, these men "had a feeling almost of helplessness as [they] watched the advance of the Russian colossus across Asia."[83]

The pessimism of the British cabinet regarding Russia was in large part a reflection of doubts about the adequacy of Britain's imperial resources. Since before 1900, chancellors of the exchequer had been warning of the dangers of grossly inflated military expenditures. By 1903 the government had become well aware of the immense burden of defending India even in peacetime, and Austen Chamberlain stated flatly that it would be "impossible to finance a great war, except at an absolutely ruinous cost."[84] The sudden emergence of the German menace, of course, gravely compounded Britain's difficulty in this respect. It was, as Selborne noted, essential "to have something in hand against Germany," but it would be "a terrific task to remain the greatest naval Power . . . and at the same time to be a military Power strong enough to meet the greatest military Power in Asia."[85]

For a combination of interrelated military and financial reasons, then, the British cabinet determined that a conflict with Russia must be avoided and an accommodation with St. Petersburg achieved. Reconciliation with France, Russia's ally, was seen as a means by which this objective might be obtained. Lord Cromer wrote to Balfour in October 1903, "I cannot help regarding an understanding upon all pending questions with France as possibly a stepping-stone to a general understanding with Russia."[86] Lansdowne was also urging this idea upon his cabinet colleagues. "A good understanding with France," he argued in a September 1903 memorandum, "would not improbably be the precursor of a better understanding with Russia, and I need not insist upon the improvement which would result in our international position, which, in view of our present relations with Germany as well as Russia, I cannot regard with satisfaction."[87]

The importance of a rapprochement with France as a mechanism for defusing the Russian problem became ever greater as hostilities between Russia and Japan neared and then erupted in early 1904. When the British government had, in 1902, concluded a treaty of mutual defense with Tokyo, it had done so for the purpose of securing Japanese support for British policy in the Far East. The other side of the coin, the chance that Britain might one day be called upon to assist Japan, was largely ignored in the rush to agreement.[88] Now, however, the chickens were coming home to roost, and the prospect that Britain would be dragged by her ally into a war with Russia appeared quite real. There were two possibilities feared by British statesmen. The first was that Japan would be overwhelmed by a Russian onslaught; then it might be necessary to become involved in order to rescue a valued defense partner, or the force of public opinion might make neutrality exceedingly difficult.[89] The second, and far more dangerous, was that France, as Russia's ally, might also enter the conflict. If this were to occur, Britain would be legally required, under the terms of the Anglo-Japanese Alliance, to come to the aid of Japan. She would then find herself embroiled with both Russia and with France. It was thus crucial for Britain to gain assurance that France would remain on the sidelines. And, if French leaders could be persuaded to exercise a moderating influence on the Russians, Britain would feel no pressure to abandon her neutral stance.[90] As events developed, it became apparent that France was no less eager than Britain to stay out of the Russo-Japanese imbroglio, and Japan was so successful on the battlefield that restraining Russia was hardly necessary. But this could not be foreseen by the British cabinet, and negotiations toward a reconciliation with France took on added urgency during 1903 and 1904.[91]

Britain's decision to come to terms with France was, from a strategic perspective, a continuation of the policy of cautious consolidation previously manifested in her approach to the United States. Again the London government sought an understanding with the adversary whose exercise of power seemed to clash least with its own, in order to relieve the strain on imperial defense. It is impossible to know, of course, just how far the British would have been willing to go in this regard had the French adopted a less conciliatory attitude.[92] But British statesmen were clearly prepared to compromise. And once French leaders showed themselves disposed to renounce Egypt and began to withdraw their challenge to Britain's naval mastery, the road to accommodation lay open. In view of the relatively more significant conflict of geopolitical interests with Germany, and with Russia, satisfying French demands in Morocco and other minor areas of contention appeared a most reasonable course.

The late nineteenth century witnessed a considerable measure of geopolitical competition between Great Britain and France. These two countries possessed overlapping territorial aims in Asia and Africa, and they engaged in a spirited contest for control of the Mediterranean Sea. In neither geographic nor in functional terms was the exercise of their power characterized by a substantial degree of differentiation.

However, by the first decade of the twentieth century it had become apparent that Britain and France were more heterogeneous in this regard with respect to one another than with respect to other states, especially Germany. And this relative heterogeneity was an important factor in their reconciliation. Germany, the dominant military power in Europe, menaced French security in a way that Britain, with her modest army and her preoccupation with naval affairs, never could. Moreover, the price for German cooperation in the colonial field—formal renunciation of Alsace and Lorraine—involved a sacrifice of vital interests that could not be made. Abandoning Egypt, a painful but clearly lesser concession, enabled France to advance her imperial interests and at the same time to strengthen her position on the continent. Similarly, the rapid expansion of German maritime power and pressing problems with Russia led Britons to see an understanding with France as a means of obtaining maximum strategic benefits at the minimum cost. Germany threatened Britain's naval preeminence; Russia, India and her spheres of influence in the Near East. France seemed less a danger, and an accommodation that promised to bolster Britain's position vis-à-vis Germany and to put a brake to Russian ambitions while requiring nothing more than the cession of her interests in Morocco appeared a very attractive arrangement indeed.

Economic Activities

While considerations related to the exercise of power played a leading role in bringing about the Anglo-French rapprochement, a favorable economic context contributed as well. At the beginning of the twentieth century, Great Britain and France possessed strong, and increasingly important, material ties. Anglo-French commerce, particularly since the signing of the Cobden Treaty in 1860, had been growing steadily if not spectacularly. In 1865, France exported to Britain goods and services valued at £32 million, while French imports from Britain amounted to £9.1 million. By 1880, total trade between the two countries had risen to £58 million, and by 1900 to £74 million. For England, commercial intercourse with France accounted for approximately 6 percent of all exports and 10 percent of all imports. For France, these same transactions represented roughly 14 percent of imports and 30 percent of exports. The trade between France and Britain was, for France, greater than that with any other nation; for Britain it was second only to trade with the United States.[93]

This commerce exercised a pacific influence upon the political relations of France and England because it reflected a fundamental heterogeneity in the economic activities of the two countries. France, lacking the necessary resource base—especially coal—possessed by Britain (and, not incidentally, Germany) failed to develop the heavy manufacturing that dominated the British economy. As a result, Anglo-French trade was, with few exceptions, highly complementary. French and English goods did not compete seriously in one another's home markets, nor were they rivals in third markets. Instead, each country produced and sold commodities that the other did not. British exports to France consisted mainly of finished manufactures and some industrial raw materials (especially coal), while French exports to England were composed primarily of agricultural products and certain luxury items. This pattern of commerce meant that Britain and France were dependent on one another for a variety of imported goods and for export markets. At the same time, their relationship was not poisoned by any sort of meaningful competition.[94]

The Anglo-French commercial connection led important segments of public opinion in France and Britain to favor, and to push actively for, a reconciliation. Powerful support for the Arbitration Treaty of October 1903, for example, came from the business sectors. As Joseph Mathews has written, "Chambers of commerce in both countries found the idea singularly appealing. It fitted well with their hopes for peace and for better trade relations. . . . By the time of King Edward's visit to Paris (May 1903), twenty-seven British chambers of commerce, forty-one French chambers, [and] thirty-five trade unions in England representing 2,000,000 workers . . . had given their support to the movement."[95] By the time the treaty was actually signed, each of these figures was considerably higher.[96]

The arguments advanced by these groups in their letters and petitions promoting an accommodation found further expression in the presses of the two countries. In France, the primary consideration was the interdependence of the two economies and especially the reliance of the French export trade on British purchases. Here the principal gain from good relations was perceived to be the assurance that the English market would remain open to French products. While closure was most often seen as the likely consequence of an Anglo-French war, concern over such a prospect was heightened as the campaign for tariff reform in England gained momentum. Many in French business circles believed a political rapprochement with Britain to be the best method of forestalling any imposition of higher import duties on French goods.[97] Thus, during the years from 1902 to 1904, a number of articles appeared in French journals declaring the economic value of harmony with England. The influential opposition newspaper *Gaulois*, for example, gave its approval to the government's policy of reconciliation because "the ever-increasing importance of our mutual commercial relations would, even if there were no other reasons, sufficiently justify the necessity of maintaining all desirable courtesy in the relations between the two countries."[98] A writer in the *Revue des deux mondes* agreed, arguing that "from the commercial point of view, France and England have the most obvious interest in each other's prosperity and in the maintenance of friendly relations."[99]

In Britain, where reliance on Anglo-French trade was not so great, the noncompetitive nature of cross-Channel commerce was more frequently stressed. Here the dominant theme was not so much that a reconciliation was necessary to preserve and protect a vital commercial connection, but that the absence of an Anglo-French trade rivalry should enable an accommodation to be achieved. Thus J. L. Garvin, in a *Fortnightly Review* article of May 1902, contended that a rapprochement with France was possible because "the Republic is more our commercial complement than our commercial rival."[100] The *Spectator* concurred in this assessment, noting that "French commerce, again, does not compete seriously with ours. Where it is most important it is least competitive. We are no more able to supply the world with wines than France is able to supply it with coal, iron, and cotton."[101]

These commercial arguments in favor of reconciliation, while most influential among the business classes, were not overlooked by political leaders in Britain and France. Within the French government, neither Cambon nor Delcassé put much stock in them, but each clearly appreciated their attraction to important segments of public opinion. For this reason, the French ambassador, in his speeches in England, often emphasized "the increasing importance" of the "commercial and financial relations" between the two countries.[102] The foreign minister employed a similar strategy when addressing the French parliament. In a speech urging his colleagues to ratify the Entente Cordiale agreements, Delcassé stressed that "in the economic field, luckily, France and England are not rivals at all. That which we demand from England are raw materials which we do not produce or which we do not produce in sufficient quantity, and manufactured goods which we cannot ourselves produce as cheaply. And England, for her part, purchases from us foodstuffs which she lacks and luxury items in which we must scrupulously protect our superiority. It follows, gentlemen, that our commercial prosperity poses no threat to England, and that we ourselves have an obvious interest in her prosperity, since it is in France that England spends a good part of the profits which she realizes elsewhere."[103] During this same debate, French senators and deputies also cited the protection and enhancement of French trade with Britain as a factor leading them to favor the accords.[104]

Across the Channel, members of the British government, too, recognized the role of commercial interests, and the persons associated with them, in rallying public support for a policy of rapprochement. The correspondence between Monson, the British ambassador to

Paris, and Lansdowne contains numerous references to the activities of Thomas Barclay and the Baron d'Estournelles de Constant. These men were particularly prominent advocates of Anglo-French arbitration, and they conducted a formidable campaign on its behalf, organizing groups of merchants and business-minded parliamentarians in France and England and arranging for goodwill visits between them. Their efforts met with considerable success and were not unnoticed. Monson described one visit to Paris by representatives of the British chambers of commerce in 1900 as "the occasion of an interchange of cordiality very advantageous to friendly feeling on both sides of the Channel."[105]

While Lansdowne and other members of the British cabinet rarely, if ever, utilized commercial arguments to justify an understanding with France, lesser British officials did so. Earl Fitzwilliam, speaking before Parliament in favor of the Anglo-French Arbitration Treaty, echoed a statement of Paul Cambon, saying, "The business relations of the two countries are so important that it would be absurd to allow anything to cause a rupture of them."[106] And Sir Albert Rollit, during the Commons debate on the 8 April Agreements, offered this rationale for rapprochement: "Not only are France and England close neighbours, but in trade they stand more largely in the relation of mutual customers rather than competitors. . . . even if we lose something in Morocco or Madagascar we open a wider commercial horizon in greater commercial union and unity between France and England by this great plan for the improvement of international relations."[107]

On the financial side of the economic ledger, Britain and France also possessed incentives to reconciliation. Beginning in 1888, the Russian government had floated a series of loans on the Paris market. By 1904, the amount of French capital tied up in Russian bonds was at least 11 and possibly as much as 12 billion francs. This figure represented more than one-quarter of all French foreign investment and, since upwards of one-half of French savings at the time were invested abroad, it may have represented an eighth of total French savings. Russian securities held in France during the first years of the twentieth century yielded an annual income of as much as 450 million francs.[108]

To a substantial extent, then, the French financial sector, and perhaps even the whole of the French economy, was dependent upon the continued health and stability of the tsarist regime. It was also, in fact, dependent upon the actions of Great Britain, for policy formulated in London could greatly influence the operation of Russia's economic system. The most immediate concern was probably the Russo-Japanese conflict. Even if Britain should choose not to intervene, extended fighting would weaken the Russian economy and jeopardize the ability of the government to pay its debts. If Britain should become involved, or if an Anglo-Russian war should for some other reason break out, the likelihood of deferral or default could only increase. It was therefore vital to France that Britain be persuaded to refrain from engaging in any hostilities with Russia and, if possible, that she be convinced to impose some measure of restraint upon her Japanese ally in order to limit the crisis in the Far East.[109]

Even without this threat of war, however, France had reason to be gravely concerned about the state of the Russian economy. The tsarist government had, in the years immediately preceding 1904, spent an overwhelming proportion of its loan procurements on military equipment and technology rather than the development of a badly needed industrial infrastructure. The inevitable consequence of this diversion of resources into such nonproductive areas had been stagnation and an ever-increasing demand for more funds. Paris financial circles, already heavily committed in Russian bonds, were reluctant to extend themselves further, but at the same time they feared a crisis unless additional credit were given. The path out of this dilemma seemed to lie with Britain. If France could improve her relations with that country, and those between London and St. Petersburg, she might find in Britain a strong financial partner willing to relieve her of her burden and deliver her from impending disaster.[110]

On the British side of the Channel, this prospect was viewed with considerable favor. The English economy was recovering from the effects of the war in South Africa, and there would soon be capital available for lending. Given the huge Russian appetite for funds, the opportunity appeared an excellent one. Even the London Rothschilds, at one point quite anti-Russian, were by 1904 interested in such a venture. In April 1906, the dreams of the British financial world came true. A loan of 2.225 billion francs from France to Russia was floated almost exclusively in London, marking the first English subscription to a Russian loan in more than thirty years.[111]

Besides their "Russian connection," Britain and France were also linked by significant bilateral financial ties. A French government investigation in 1902 estimated French holdings of British securities at about 900 million francs. Most of this amount was in government bonds, bank credits, and continuations. The study also found that French nationals had invested upwards of 150 million francs in various British colonies and 1.5 billion francs in gold mines in British South Africa.[112] Compared to the quantities of French capital placed in Russian securities, these figures were relatively small. But the protection of these investments was occasionally advanced in the French press as a reason for improving relations with England.[113]

The bilateral financial relationship between Britain and France was probably more crucial to the former, however, than to the latter. In large measure, the London market depended upon French funds. It was estimated by the *Economist* in the spring of 1904 that French creditors held up to £40 million in English bills.[114] Their holdings of other short-term assets may have been still larger.[115] Even more than the French capital placed in longer-term securities (see above), these investments represented a vulnerability in the British economy. If, in the event of a Far Eastern war or some other cause of Anglo-French estrangement, French money were suddenly withdrawn from England, the price of sterling would fall, interest rates would have to be raised, and there might even be some danger of financial collapse.[116] On the other hand, if close relations with Paris could be established this threat could be averted, and British financiers might find France willing to support the pound in times of weakness. This, in fact, occurred in both 1906 and 1907. Upon heavy withdrawals of gold from London, the Bank of France came to the rescue, loaning the Bank of England reserves and discounting English paper.[117]

In the first years of the twentieth century, Great Britain and France were closely linked in matters of trade and finance. These connections exercised a positive influence upon Anglo-French diplomacy because they reflected a fundamental complementarity between the French and British economies, especially in the commercial sphere. The high level of heterogeneity characteristic of the economic activities of these nations during this period contributed to their political understanding in two ways. First, a substantial measure of mutual dependence on the exchange of goods and capital for continued prosperity provided an incentive for the maintenance of cordial relations. Second, and perhaps equally vital, the absence of competition for markets meant that a potentially damaging source of animosity, and a serious barrier to reconciliation, was lacking. The significance of this is more forcefully revealed when one remembers the role of trade rivalry in the deterioration of Anglo-German relations.

The commercial and financial rationale for a reconciliation carried limited weight with political leaders in France and Britain. Alone it could not have persuaded either government of the need for peace. But the value attached to the economic advantages of an understanding by powerful segments of French and British society was of considerable importance. While not dictating policy, these groups and their successful mobilization of public opinion provided critical support for the potentially controversial colonial concessions made by statesmen in pursuit of the rapprochement. This fact was appreciated by the two governments, and officials in both countries therefore employed economic arguments in seeking to justify their sacrifices.[118]

Societal Attributes

Great Britain and France did not, of course, possess either the variety or the intensity of the ideological and cultural ties that so intimately linked England and the United States. No phenomenon like Anglo-Saxonism was present in Anglo-French diplomacy. On a purely racial basis such nationalist sentiment could not exist between the French and the English, for the former were a Latin people while the latter were of Anglo-Saxon stock. Generally speaking, the bonds of common language, literature, religious orientation, and culture broadly defined, which proved so powerful in the relations of England and the United States, were absent from the relations of Great Britain and France.

Nevertheless—and this becomes more evident when one compares the Anglo-French relationship to those of Great Britain and Germany and Germany and the United States—France and England did share certain attitudes and attributes that encouraged a rapprochement. For the most part, these lay in the realm of social and political philosophy. Both Britain and France possessed a commitment to liberalism and representative government and were opposed to autocracy and absolutism. During the period of reconciliation, numerous references were made to this effect, and to the role of this similarity in drawing the two countries together. Among British politicians, the lead was taken by members of the Liberal Party. H. C. G. Matthew writes, "Most Liberals regarded the Entente with France as the natural result of common democratic impulses."[119] As Sir Henry Campbell-Bannerman, who became prime minister in 1905, remarked, "Friendship with France is, to the Liberal party, something more than a cherished ideal or an historical tradition. . . . to Liberals it has been given to a special degree to appreciate the incalculable benefits which the great nation of France has bestowed upon mankind."[120]

In the British press, such thoughts were voiced by a number of publications. In December 1903, the *Spectator* wrote of the "very positive inducements" to good relations with France. It commented upon the liberal tendencies of both countries and claimed that "Britain was the original model for reforming France; and . . . British Constitutionalism still remains as a guiding force in her domestic politics."[121] After the conclusion of the Entente Cordiale, the *Spectator* assured its readers that the era of Anglo-French harmony would be a lasting one. The "strongest reason" for this, asserted the paper, was that "the two nations . . . hold one far-reaching idea in common. They both believe in liberty as essential to the progress and happiness of mankind. . . . Both hate to hear of oppression, whether defended in the name of religion, or of security, or of the 'Monarchical principle.' . . . They, and they alone, of the Great Powers of Europe wish what is broadly called 'Liberalism' to prevail."[122]

Across the Channel in France, similar sentiments were expressed. A 1903 article in the *Siècle* argued that friendship "ought to exist between the French and English, both of whom are devoted to liberty under different forms. It is our natural alliance."[123] Statements by various politicians also reflected this view. Paul Deschanel, a French deputy, claimed, for example, "Thinking people of both nations are agreed that a hostile policy between the two great liberal nations, between the country of the *Habeus Corpus* and the country of the Declaration of the Rights of Man would be a crime against civilization."[124] His fellow legislator in the French Senate, M. d'Aunay, concurred, saying that "material interests are not the only ones which have brought France and England closer together. There is also a community of tendencies and of civilization which has made possible the union of these two peoples of liberty, democracy, and representative regimes."[125]

France and Britain, at the time of their rapprochement, possessed at best a medium level of homogeneity in their societal attributes.

Having no language or heritage in common, they did share a basic belief in liberal principles and institutions of representative government. This probably exerted some favorable influence on the threat assessments of the two countries, helping them to see one another as less dangerous than other states with whom they shared fewer characteristics. It does not seem to have provided a strong independent incentive for a rapprochement. The French and British had little feeling that a war between them would be civil or fratricidal and hence little reason to avoid conflict for that reason. Expressions of a sense of common identity that began to surface around 1900 did so largely after the strategic benefits of a reconciliation had become evident, and can be interpreted as attempts to justify an understanding rather than reflective of any motivation to achieve one. Still, this in itself suggests that the level of societal homogeneity that existed between Britain and France served at least some function as a psychological prop that permitted imperial concessions to be accepted by both countries. Whether Britain and Germany, or Germany and the United States, could have done similarly is at least questionable given the degree of ideological and cultural alienation present in the relations of those countries.

Crisis as Catalyst

As noted in chapter 2, the Anglo-American reconciliation was set in motion by a single dramatic event, the crisis of 1895–96 over the boundary between Venezuela and the colony of British Guiana. The same cannot be said of the Anglo-French rapprochement. In this case, sentiment favoring an accommodation did not erupt suddenly in the wake of an acute confrontation, but developed gradually during a period of several years. Nevertheless, the Fashoda Crisis of 1898 must be viewed as at least a partial catalyst for the Entente Cordiale. A brief account of this incident has been given above.

The impact of Fashoda was felt principally by the French, who, as has been noted, found themselves in an inferior position and were forced to capitulate. Their inability to stand up to Britain in this instance shattered the cherished myth that France could pursue an effective anti-British colonial strategy alone or even with the support of Russia. An appreciation of this situation did not, it is true, drive French leaders directly into the arms of the British. Instead, they flirted briefly with the idea of procuring diplomatic assistance from

Berlin. However, it quickly became apparent that the price of German aid—formal renunciation of Alsace and Lorraine—was too high. Finally, Frenchmen realized that a choice would have to be made between Egypt and their former provinces. The decision, though painful, was not difficult. Andrew and Kanya-Forstner write:

> The failure of the Fashoda strategy threw into sharp relief the contradictions inherent in the international position of the Third Republic. . . . Her great enemy in Europe was Germany; her great rival outside Europe was Britain. As a European power, she needed British support against Germany; as a colonial power, she needed German support against Britain. She could not reasonably hope to challenge Germany's right to remain in Alsace-Lorraine while at the same time challenging Britain's right to remain in Egypt. *And the fact that the Lost Provinces were always, in the last resort, more important than the Nile would always make genuine co-operation with Germany—and hence a serious challenge to Britain—impossible.*[126]

Fashoda, then, was instrumental in disabusing Frenchmen of several key illusions. Once the situation had become clear, they began to explore the possibility of an understanding with Britain. This perceptual shift was accentuated by a change in the balance of power within the French government, a development also precipitated by the crisis. Ned Lebow explains:

> From 1871 on, two rival perspectives, one continentalist and the other colonialist, vied for control over the foreign policy of the Third Republic. The continentalists saw France as a Europe-oriented power for whom Germany's rise to great power status constituted a serious threat. They were wary of colonial expansion, as it diverted resources from the nation's most important foreign objective, the containment of Germany. It also courted conflict with Great Britain with whom the continentalists favored rapprochement, for they viewed her together with Russia as a counterweight to German power. The colonialists advocated very different foreign policy objectives. They aspired to make France a world power, for they viewed colonial empire as the *sine qua non* of national greatness. Because French expansion overseas often encountered British opposition, many among the colonialists favored an understanding with Germany as a means of strengthening France's position vis-à-vis her traditional rival.[127]

Until Fashoda, the colonialists, centered around the Colonial Ministry, held the upper hand over the continentalists, centered around the Foreign Ministry.[128] But the abject failure of the Fashoda strategy produced a reversal of fortunes. Within the Colonial Ministry, those who favored a combative stance toward Britain were discredited and were supplanted by those who advocated a more conciliatory approach. The latter, including Etienne and Lanessan, were more concerned with the economic benefits of imperialism than with the accumulation of territory and national grandeur. They saw French commercial and financial interests in Egypt as safe under British rule and were not anxious to challenge it. They were, however, eager to secure Morocco, which they deemed to be a source of great potential wealth, and they believed that an exchange with Britain might enable them to do so.[129] This change brought the policy preferences of the Pavillon de Flore into congruence with those of the Quai d'Orsay, whose position had already been strengthened by the fact that the Colonial Ministry bore primary responsibility for the Fashoda debacle. The net result was that the continentalists in the Foreign Ministry could, after 1898, pursue their dream of an accommodation with England free from the determined opposition of a colonialist faction.[130]

The path from Fashoda to the Entente Cordiale was neither rapid nor direct. Movement toward a reconciliation gathered momentum slowly and not always steadily. Moreover, the episode seems to have exerted little or no influence on British policy. Probably the closest approximation to a catalytic event for Britain was the South African War, which demonstrated the danger of Britain's isolation and prompted fears that she could not endure alone.[131] Still, the revolution in French attitudes precipitated by Fashoda seems to have been a necessary precondition for an understanding. For this reason, the Fashoda Crisis can rightly be regarded as a catalyst for the Anglo-French rapprochement.[132]

Summary

This chapter has offered an explanation for the dramatic and unexpected reconciliation between England and France that began shortly after the Fashoda Crisis and culminated in the famed Entente Cordiale. Table 3 summarizes the Anglo-French relationship at the beginning of the process.

In contrast to the case of Great Britain and the United States, discussed in chapter 2, conditions necessary for an understanding did not exist in an absolute sense, within the bilateral confines of the

Table 3. England and France, 1900

Exercise of Power	Low Heterogeneity: strong imperial and related naval rivalry.
Economic Activities	High Heterogeneity: complementarity in trade and finance; considerable interdependence.
Societal Attributes	Medium Homogeneity: many differences; some similarity in commitment to representative government and the rule of law.

Anglo-French relationship. Rather, their presence was relative, and the reconciliation of England and France can only be explained by taking the international situation into account. Compared to their conflicts of geopolitical interest with certain other powers, French and English differences with one another were less fundamental. The balancing of external threats, grounded mainly in such calculations, constituted the principal motivation for the rapprochement. Commercial and financial ties provided important, but secondary, incentives, while the absence of economic competition and lack of ideological antagonism were significant facilitating factors.

5

Germany and the
United States,
1898–1914

Introduction

The common history of Germany and the United States may be
said to have commenced with the founding of the German Empire in
1871. It was an auspicious beginning, for this event was greeted with
great enthusiasm in the United States. Americans viewed the Franco-
Prussian War as a struggle for liberty and national unification not
unlike their own, and they eagerly anticipated the development of
Germany into a federal republic on the American model. Their
encouragement and support were welcomed by the Germans, many
of whom expressed their appreciation in return. Buoyed by this initial surge of mutual admiration, harmony and goodwill prevailed
between the two countries for almost twenty years.

Unfortunately, this happy state of affairs was not destined to endure forever. Toward the end of the century, dark clouds began to
appear on the horizon of German-American relations. In 1889, a
squabble arose over control of the Samoan Islands in the South Pacific. Although a negotiated settlement was reached, the episode left a
legacy of suspicion and animosity that never entirely disappeared. A
second storm erupted over the Philippines in 1898, when American
and German naval forces confronted one another in Manila Bay. And
a year later, Samoa re-emerged as an object of controversy between
the two countries. These disputes were, like the first, resolved
without violence, but not before further inflaming already heated
passions.

After about 1900, the principal locus of tension between Germany
and the United States shifted from the Pacific to Latin America and
the Caribbean. Americans became increasingly concerned over
alleged German territorial ambitions in these regions, while Ger-

mans grew ever more resentful of the Monroe Doctrine. Disagreements, both real and imagined, over Haiti, the Danish West Indies, Venezuela, and Brazil, among others, caused relations to continue to deteriorate. Throughout this era, tariff battles and commercial competition in various markets of the world also served to heighten the German-American antagonism. So, too, did a deepening awareness of the fundamental philosophical and ideological differences between the two societies.

As early as the winter of 1897–98, German strategists began to seriously consider the prospect of war with the United States. Reciprocal planning in Washington did not lag far behind. Although they ultimately found it necessary to concentrate the bulk of their attention on Great Britain rather than America, between 1898 and 1905 German naval leaders looked upon the United States as their most probable adversary. American planners, for their part, consistently viewed Germany as the most likely, or even the only, future opponent. If it is true that in 1917 Germany was forced by the particular circumstances of her fight with England and France to attack American shipping, thereby drawing the United States into battle, it is also true that by 1914 a credible threat of German-American conflict had already existed for nearly two decades.[1]

The diplomacy of Germany and the United States in the last years of the nineteenth century and the early years of the twentieth thus evolved in a manner similar to that of Anglo-German affairs. For a while, the portents appeared favorable, and the two governments and their respective peoples stood on polite, even cordial, terms. As time passed, however, friendship faded, and well before hostilities actually broke out, relations between Washington and Berlin had become sufficiently strained that armed conflict seemed likely, if not inevitable. Here, again, was a peace that might have been, but tragically, was not to be.[2]

The Exercise of Power

The leading causes of German-American estrangement during the prewar period lay in the realm of geopolitics. Foremost among these was a keen and emotionally charged imperial rivalry, centered first upon the South Pacific and the Far East and then upon Latin America and the Caribbean. Germany and the United States emerged as major world powers at approximately the same point in time. Both were young, full of energy, and eager to expand their spheres of influence. Although the extent of their competition was often greatly exaggerated by contemporary observers, and their clash of interests frequently more apparent than real, the contacts between the two countries in various regions of the globe did prove a source of considerable controversy and irritation in the conduct of their mutual relations.

The first imperial dispute between Germany and the United States occurred in 1889 over the Samoan Islands.[3] Since the days of the Civil War, Americans had been interested in Samoa as a potential site for a coaling station and as a trading outpost on the route to Australia and New Zealand. In 1878, the United States secured the rights to a harbor at Pago Pago in return for a promise to assist in the resolution of any differences between Samoa and a foreign power. The following year, Germany and Great Britain also obtained treaty rights in the islands. Each of the countries dispatched missionaries, naval officers, commercial agents, and consuls to the area as a struggle for predominance ensued. The contest came to a head in late 1888 and early 1889 when the Germans staged a coup, deporting the Samoan king and installing a puppet ruler in his place. Several thousand of the king's followers fled to the jungle to begin a guerrilla campaign, and in December 1888 they ambushed a group of German sailors, killing and beheading a number of them. Enraged German officials, convinced that Americans and Britons in Samoa had been aiding the rebels, declared martial law, stated that ships of every nationality would be searched for weapons, and announced that permanent German control over the islands would have to be established.

At this point, the American public, which had been following the events in far-off Samoa with a certain fascination, became thoroughly aroused. Tales of German brutality and intrigue, reports that American lives and property were in danger, and a determination not to appear fainthearted spurred the most vocal jingoes to heights of impassioned oratory. The prospect of a battle with Germany was seriously discussed in leading newspapers.[4] In Washington, Congress quickly appropriated $500,000 for the protection of American lives and property and an additional $100,000 for the improvement of Pago Pago harbor and the construction of a coaling station there.[5] Senator John H. Reagan of Texas spoke for millions of his fellow countrymen when he belligerently declared, "I do not want to see this country engaged in war with Germany or with any other government. . . . but, Sir, there is something worse than the calamities of war, and that is the sacrifice of the honor of a great nation. The sacrifice of the rights of its citizens, the humiliation of its officers in the face of an arrogant power, is worse than war; and I would not submit to it."[6]

Reaction in Germany was rather more muted. The government, in particular, was not anxious for a rupture with the United States, and Bismarck sought to ease tensions by expressing his willingness to resume negotiations over the future of the islands. Still, the situation was considered dangerous enough that in February 1889, Baron Max von der Goltz, acting chief of the German Admiralty, requested that his staff prepare a memorandum detailing how a war with the United States might be waged. In what was to become for Germans an all-too-familiar refrain, the report noted that the German fleet was not powerful enough to confront the American navy directly; thus, its activities would have to be confined to commerce raiding.[7]

The most acute stage of the Samoan Crisis was brought to a close by a violent hurricane that struck the islands in March 1889, sinking or driving aground all of the German and American ships in Apia harbor. In the aftermath of this tragedy, in which scores of men were drowned, even the most hotheaded nationalists adopted a concil-iatory tone. As the *New York World* reflected soberly, "How small and unworthy seem the passions of men, their bickerings, their jeal-ousies, their taunts and threats, in the light of that universal compas-sion which thrills humanity when brave men perish beneath the pitiless power of winds and storms and hungry seas! Surely the awful devastation wrought in the harbor of Apia makes our recent quarrel with Germany appear petty and unnatural. Can it not be confidently predicted that the bonds which now join us to Germany as together we mourn the fate of those who perished in their duty will make the coming diplomatic conference at Berlin a council of friends, not a quarrel of restless rivals?"[8] And, indeed, at the Berlin Conference of 1889, the three powers did manage to arrive at a temporary accom-modation, agreeing to a joint protectorate over the islands with the native Samoan dynasty ostensibly remaining in control.

Although the mutual suspicion and animosity engendered by this controversy lingered on and never completely vanished, for the better part of a decade following the Samoan episode relations between Germany and the United States continued free from further imperial incidents. The new German chancellor, Caprivi, and the American president, Cleveland, were both more concerned with domestic issues than foreign policy, and neither manifested any real desire for overseas expansion. By 1898, however, Caprivi had been succeeded by

Bülow, and Cleveland by McKinley, and a second round of imperial competition began.

The spark that ignited this renewed rivalry was the Spanish-American War, which began in April of that year. For some time, German naval enthusiasts had been eagerly anticipating the disintegration of the Spanish Empire. In 1897, Tirpitz, heading the German cruiser squadron in East Asia, had notified Berlin that Spain's grip on the Philippines was weakening and that the islands might soon be available.[9] The Emperor William was excited by this prospect, writing several months later, "I am determined, when the opportunity arises, to purchase or simply to take the Philippines from Spain, when her 'liquidation' approaches."[10] And Germany's ambitions were not limited to the Philippines. In June 1898, Bülow sent Hatzfeldt a shopping list of desired possessions in the Pacific, which also included the Sulu Archipelago and the Caroline Islands.[11]

Given these aims, German officials looked upon the Spanish-American conflict with a certain schizophrenia. On the one hand, they were intensely displeased by the prospect that the United States, should she emerge victorious, might acquire a substantial portion of the Spanish Empire, particularly the Philippines. William, when told of American plans to seize the islands, exclaimed angrily, "The Yankees cannot do that! Because one day we will require Manila."[12] On the other hand, German leaders hoped that the United States, being deeply involved in Cuba and the Far East, could be pressured into granting Germany major concessions in the Caribbean and the Pacific in exchange for promises of noninterference. Naval men especially believed the time propitious for obtaining naval bases and coaling stations in these areas. Eduard von Knorr, commanding admiral of the German navy, sent William two memoranda in which he argued for territorial acquisitions during the war. In the first, dated 20 April 1898, Knorr called for the taking of a naval base in the West Indies. In the second, dated 1 July, he requested that Germany seek a base in the Far East, preferably on Mindanao, Palawan, or one of the Sulu Islands.[13] Tirpitz likewise pressed for an aggressive policy in the Caribbean, telling Bülow, "The *last moment* has come for us to acquire Curaçao and St. Thomas. North America cannot object or oppose us, because she is for the present satisfied with Cuba and has much to occupy her there."[14]

When the German government attempted to wrest such concessions from the United States, however, it met with almost total failure. On 10 July 1898, Baron Oswald von Richthofen, acting foreign minister, told the American ambassador in Berlin, Andrew White, that America would have to choose between the friendship of Germany and that of Great Britain. Opting for the latter would, he warned, result in the formation of a continental coalition against the Anglo-Saxon powers. German goodwill was much more to America's advantage and could be purchased at a modest price: Samoa, the Carolines, parts of the Philippines, and the Sulu Archipelago.[15] White, who was generally sympathetic to his German hosts, indicated his readiness to discuss the matter further, but when he reported the conversation to Washington he was severely chastised by Secretary of State Day and ordered to adopt a much firmer stance.[16] The United States government, reasonably confident of its strategic position and, perhaps more importantly, too proud to bow to such blatant coercion, refused to negotiate the German demands.

For the Germans, American intransigence was a bitter pill to swallow. Their bluff had been called, and they were virtually impotent to compel the United States into a more accommodating attitude. German naval power in the summer of 1898 was simply inadequate to challenge American maritime might in either the Caribbean or the Far East. Even Tirpitz reluctantly admitted that the day of decision for the Spanish Empire had come too soon.[17] While William raged on about the need for a great fleet and railed against the imbeciles in the Reichstag who would deny him one, officials in Berlin could do little but watch, hoping that fate might yet allow them some spoils.[18]

It was with this in mind that the Germans dispatched a squadron under the command of Vice-Admiral Otto von Diederichs to the Philippines in July. Although the stated purpose of this expedition was to observe the American assault on Manila and, if necessary, protect the rights of German nationals in the city, its real motive was to be on hand to take the islands should the United States decide to withdraw.[19] The arrival of the German force, which was larger than the American fleet, rendered the Americans exceedingly nervous, and a confrontation soon erupted between the American commander, Admiral Dewey, and Diederichs over the latter's alleged failure to comply with blockade regulations. On more than one occasion, German ships halted for inspection only after warning shots were fired across their bows, and when Dewey and Diederich's flag lieutenant, Paul von Hintze, met to discuss the situation, the former lost his temper and told the German that "if Germany wants war, all right, we are ready."[20]

The danger inherent in this incident was greatly exaggerated in the

United States. German records indicate that neither Diederichs nor his superiors in Berlin were prepared to push matters to the point of open hostilities.[21] But Americans assumed the worst, and the episode had a profound effect on popular opinion. In its wake the *Morning Oregonian* called Germany a "bitter, relentless, uncompromising enemy."[22] The *Washington Post* saw the German government as a "sleepless and insatiable" foe.[23] And the *Chicago Daily Tribune* trumpeted: "MAY HAVE WAR WITH GERMANY. CONFLICT WITH UNITED STATES IS THOUGHT IN BERLIN OFFICIAL CIRCLES TO BE NEAR."[24] These and other newspapers kept the prospect of a German-American war alive in the public mind for the better part of a year, and the mistrust of Germany caused by the events in Manila Bay colored American attitudes toward that country for a generation.

In 1899, the Samoan problem emerged again as a bone of considerable contention. The three-power protectorate established a decade before had proved unworkable as each nation schemed and plotted in pursuit of predominance. This time, however, the dispute was largely an Anglo-German one, and the United States played mainly the role of an interested spectator. The islands were finally partitioned between America and Germany, with Great Britain receiving compensation elsewhere.[25] While this episode was not especially damaging to German-American relations, it did serve to reaffirm the determination of the German government to seek territorial acquisitions and demonstrated the pressure placed on Berlin, in light of prior failures, to secure such gains. A statement issued by the Berlin Section of the German Colonial Society illustrates the frustration felt by a large segment of popular opinion at both America's imperial expansion and the insufficiently aggressive (in their minds) policies of their own leaders:

> A favourable opportunity to establish themselves at Samoa has been seized—by the Americans. Not by us Germans, whose interests in these splendid islands are by far the greatest, and whose sailors have shed their blood! We look quietly on, and when America and England share the booty, and perhaps magnanimously give us a crumb or two, we rejoice at the success! . . . Is that the position which is due to us in the world? Does no one realise the extent of the humiliations to the great German Empire if we are compelled to recede here where our rights are the greatest?
>
> We cannot bring ourselves to believe this, or to give up the hope that we will eventually claim our rights. But why this delay, why are fears and apprehension allowed to spread, why does no word come from an authoritative source?[26]

If Germans generally were displeased with the meagerness of their territorial acquisitions in the Pacific and the Far East, they were no less disappointed by their lack of success in Latin America and the Caribbean. Here, even more clearly than in other regions, the United States stood out as the chief obstacle to the fulfillment of their desires. The Monroe Doctrine, indeed, was a veritable red flag waving in front of German faces. Bismarck, in 1898, called it an "insolent dogma" and "a species of arrogance peculiarly American and inexcusable,"[27] while a writer in the *Münchner Allgemeine Zeitung* asked bitterly, "Who gives the Yankees the right to say: America belongs to us!? What principle of natural or divine law can they cite? Or can they claim only the law of might for their monstrous pretensions? . . . Germany's next task will be to do away with the Monroe Doctrine, amicably or by force."[28]

German aims in Latin America and the Caribbean were basically two. The navy and its supporters, as has been seen, hoped for the construction of naval bases and coaling stations that would enable them to project German maritime power deep into the Western Hemisphere. Colonialist elements, on the other hand, sought to erect a German empire in the New World, utilizing Brazil, where many Germans had settled, as a springboard for further expansion. These objectives were, of course, complementary, as the *Grenzboten*, a navalist publication, demonstrated in proposing this plan: "As soon as Germany has drawn South Brazil within her sphere of interest, she can offer emigrants an absolute guarantee that their interests will be safe guarded. A colonial army should be organized among the settlers so that they need not return to Germany to perform their military service. Then in a few years a young German colonial empire will grow up there as mighty as, if not mightier than, any other that ever emanated from Europe."[29]

Although the Emperor William himself shared in these ambitions, writing of South America, "*We* must be paramount there,"[30] the *Wilhelmstrasse* took only the most minimal steps to bring about their realization. Restraint on the part of German foreign policymakers was not, of course, founded upon any sort of sympathy for the American position, but on the hardheaded recognition that any perceived violation of the Monroe Doctrine would almost certainly provoke the United States into war and that Germany was not capable of winning such a contest. When Holleben, the ambassador in Washington, warned the Foreign Office in response to an inquiry regarding the possibility of purchasing a naval base or coaling station at Santo

Domingo that "the impression would surely be most unfavorable" and that he could not predict "the extent to which the hostility of public opinion and the government would be unleashed upon us," the whole idea was dropped like a hot potato.[31] Indeed, German ambassadors to the United States went to great lengths to dispel American anxiety. In 1901, Holleben declared in an official interview that "reports that Germany seeks to acquire coaling stations or even naval bases in South America and the West Indies" were totally unfounded, and that they had "been spread by enemies who do not wish to see Germany have friendly relations with the United States."[32] In 1906, his successor, Baron Speck von Sternberg, published a widely read article on "The Phantom Peril of German Emigration and South-American Settlements" in which he emphatically disavowed any intent on the part of Germany to seek a colonial empire in the Western Hemisphere.[33]

Despite these repeated assurances, however, Americans remained fearful, and in some cases almost paranoid, of German aims in the New World. As far back as 1896, Charles de Kay, the American consul-general in Berlin, had warned that "the United States must be prepared for an 'aggressive' colonial policy in Germany and this aggression points towards South America."[34] German colonialist agitation, faithfully reported in the American press, helped spread this apprehension among the broader public, as did a subsequent series of incidents involving real or suspected German intrigues in such places as the Danish West Indies, Venezuela, and Haiti. In 1898, Theodore Roosevelt expressed his concern that "with Germany . . . we may at any time have trouble if she seeks to acquire territory in South America,"[35] a "nightmare" which continued to haunt him during his tenure as president.[36] Henry Cabot Lodge, the influential senator from Massachusetts, believed that Germany intended to smash the Monroe Doctrine and establish colonial rule in Brazil,[37] while *Harper's Weekly* noted a longing in Germany to "blow the Monroe Doctrine sky-high," claiming that "among well-informed and far-seeing Germans, there is a deep-rooted conviction that a collision between the United States and the German Empire is inevitable . . . because, through our Monroe Doctrine, we forbid the fruition of Germany's expansionist aspirations, which can only be satisfied in South America."[38] Most Americans, it is probably safe to say, would have agreed with the General Board of the United States Navy when it reported in 1906, "Germany is desirous of extending her colonial possessions. Especially is it thought that she is desirous of obtaining a foothold in the Western Hemisphere, and many things indicate that she has her eyes on localities in the West Indies, on the shores of the Caribbean, and in parts of South America. It is believed in many quarters that she is planning to test the Monroe Doctrine by the annexation or by the establishment of a protectorate over a portion of South America, even going to the extent of war with the United States when her fleet is ready."[39] And, indeed, as the British ambassador in Washington informed London, suspicion of German designs was "shared by the Administration, the press, and the public alike."[40]

It is true that after 1905 or 1906, these anxieties began to dissipate somewhat. Even Roosevelt proclaimed himself less concerned than before,[41] and William Howard Taft told the cabinet in 1909 that a letter detailing German aggression in Latin America was "absurd."[42] John B. Jackson, an American diplomat in Havana, echoed this view when he notified the State Department two years later that from his vantage point there appeared "nothing of an aggressive character and nothing to indicate the survival of any possible pan-German, political ambitions."[43] Generally speaking, however, American apprehension of German aspirations in the Western Hemisphere remained strong throughout the prewar period.

Imperial jousting between Germany and the United States in the years before 1914 was accompanied by a related naval rivalry. Unlike the Anglo-German competition, this contest never captured the public imagination nor assumed an independent identity or momentum. Still, as the two countries expanded their fleets during the late nineteenth and early twentieth centuries, they did so with a keen regard for one another. The rapid growth of American maritime power was, in fact, sparked by the controversy with Germany over Samoa in 1889. William McAdoo of New Jersey spoke for Congress and for millions of Americans when he said, "The lesson of it all is this . . . give us sufficient naval power to protect us from these insults. If the United States were a naval power—if the United States had powerful ships— Bismarck would never have allowed the landing of a single German soldier on the Samoan Islands."[44] Alleged German intrigues in Latin America and the Caribbean prompted Theodore Roosevelt to write in 1897 that the United States must keep its navy "at a pitch that will enable us to interfere promptly if Germany ventures to touch a foot of American soil."[45] The confrontation between Dewey and Diede-richs in Manila Bay a year later provided further evidence of the importance of building against Germany.[46] With the improvement in relations between the United States and Great Britain, America's naval needs came to be calculated almost exclusively on the basis of German strength.

For Berlin, of course, the American fleet was usually a consideration secondary to the fleet of Great Britain. But the German naval program nevertheless reflected the desire and the intent to compete with the United States. William himself raged at Germany's impotence in Samoa and the Philippines, hopeful that "once our navy has passed through the transition period perhaps the moment will come to reckon with the U.S."[47] And a British diplomat stationed in Munich reported to London in 1906 that the growing German fleet was not intended primarily for a war with Britain, but rather for a possible collision with the United States over Latin America.[48]

The imperial and naval competition between Germany and the United States in the several decades before World War I was indicative of a sharply declining heterogeneity in the exercise of German and American power. In functional terms, each country constructed a large fleet to enable it to defend or extend its possessions and spheres of influence. In geographic terms, vital, or at least important, interests began to overlap in the Pacific, in the Caribbean, and in Latin America. This growing homogeneity in both the means and ends of power constituted a serious obstacle to cordial relations. Indeed, historian Alfred Vagts entitled the summary chapter of his great work on German-American relations of this period "The Futility of Diplomatic Harmonization in [an Era of] Imperial Rivalry."[49]

While the increasing lack of heterogeneity in the exercise of German and American power was clearly a formidable barrier to pacific relations from a bilateral perspective, it might be supposed that it was less substantial from a multilateral balance-of-power/threat perspective. In fact, Germany and the United States were certainly more heterogeneous in this regard than Germany and Great Britain. Did this not favor an understanding between the two countries? The answer, for the most part, was no. In the first place, the Germans, for whatever reasons, never really acknowledged the need for or the possibility of American goodwill in countering the British. Although some halfhearted attempts to improve the climate of American opinion were made, no major initiatives—such as public and formal acceptance of the Monroe Doctrine—were forthcoming. This sug-

gests that,in some absolute sense, the level of power-political competition between the two countries, reinforced by economic rivalry
and ideological alienation, was simply too high to be overcome even
if, in relative terms, it argued for an accommodation. Second, and
perhaps more importantly, no reciprocal motivation existed on the
American side. For the United States, Germany was the main, and
after about 1898 the only, enemy. The need to obtain German support
in the face of more compelling threats was absent, and thus, too, the
incentive to make concessions in pursuit of a rapprochement.

Naval and imperial rivalry symptomatic of homogeneity in the
exercise of power was clearly the most dangerous source of German-
American discord in the years before 1914. In its absence, the chances
of war between Germany and the United States would have been
small indeed. Nevertheless, this factor alone cannot explain the
failure of the two countries to achieve a rapprochement. For such
difficulties might have been overcome, as in the case of Britain and
the United States, had economic and ideological/cultural factors
exercised an ameliorating influence. But, as in Anglo-German diplomacy of the period, they did not. Instead, a growing commercial
competition and a deepening ideological alienation only served to
further inflame the passions aroused by geopolitical differences.
These aspects of the German-American relationship are examined in
the following sections.

Economic Activities

Over the course of the late nineteenth century and into the twentieth, commercial transactions between Germany and the United
States expanded steadily. The value of goods and services flowing
from America to Germany, which averaged $50.2 million per year
from 1871 to 1875, rose to an annual figure of $93.4 million from 1891 to
1895 and $193.6 million from 1901 to 1905. During this last period,
German-American trade accounted for more than 7 percent of all
U.S. exports and over 15 percent of total German imports. At the
same time, the value of merchandise shipped from Germany to the
United States also increased substantially, from an annual average of
$43.2 million in 1871–75, to $81.8 million in 1886–90, and $109.8 million
in 1901–5. During this last half decade, commodities exchanged
between Germany and the United States accounted for about 9 percent of total German exports and approximately 11 percent of all

American imports. By the turn of the century, Germany and America each traded more with one another than with any other nation save England.[50]

This trade tended, however, to be as much harmful as beneficial to relations between the two countries because of the generally homogeneous nature of their economies. First in agricultural commodities and then in manufactured items, German and American producers found themselves increasingly in competition with one another. Their rivalry was most intense within the German home market, but it extended to the American market as well. The most bitter bone of contention was the importation into Germany, especially after about 1890, of vast quantities of American foodstuffs. In 1892, for example, almost half of German wheat imports, and roughly 15 percent of all the wheat consumed in that country, came from the United States. In 1896, 68 percent of the foreign corn purchased by Germany was grown in America. Germany also imported, at various times, large amounts of rye and oats from the United States.[51] American grains, particularly wheat, were plentiful and relatively inexpensive, the consequence of better farming methods and improvements in transportation. Competition from cheap American crops helped drive German wheat prices sharply down. Between 1871 and 1901 the price of Prussian wheat fell by 30 percent, and during one period from 1873 to 1894 by 50 percent.[52] This drastic decline proved a boon to German consumers, but it threatened the existence of the powerful Junkers. Among Germany's landed classes, America was the country most feared. The Agrarian League reserved its harshest attacks for the United States, and its official organ, the *Korrespondenz des Bundes der Landwirte*, warned more than once that Germany was being reduced to the status of an American province.[53]

Given the Junkers' political clout and their central role in German society, it is not surprising that the German government never accepted the proposition, so long held in England, that reliance on foreign foodstuffs was both necessary and desirable. Rather, self-sufficiency was deemed to be far preferable and was in some quarters believed to be possible.[54] Beginning in 1879, Berlin imposed a series of tariffs on grain, designed to support prices, restrict imports, and stimulate domestic production. The reasons for doing so were explained by an American commercial agent who wrote in 1891 that Germany could not allow her grain to be "depreciated in value and rendered unprofitable by excessive importations. The men thus threatened were for the most part of noble lineage and pillars of the monarchy, with sons constituting the flower of the German army, and the State could not idly view their demoralization. It had to make an effort to shield them from acute foreign competition, especially when that competition threatened to destroy their standing as a class by driving them into bankruptcy and forcing the sale of their lands or reducing them to inferior ways of living that would ill comport with their standing."[55]

In addition to the duties aimed at American grains, the German government also erected barriers against other American agricultural products that competed with Germany's domestic suppliers.[56] A ban on all imports of American pork except hams and bacon was proclaimed in 1890; a complete ban was imposed three years later. In 1894, live cattle and fresh meats from the United States were prohibited from entering the German market, and a like prohibition against fresh and dried fruits was enacted in 1898.[57]

For its part, the American government acted to restrict the flow of German sugar into the United States. The McKinley Tariff of 1890, which repealed an existing duty on raw sugar, added a bounty of two cents per pound on domestic output. The Wilson Tariff of 1894 reimposed a 40 percent *ad valorem* tax, and the Dingley Tariff of 1897 further increased the duty, eliminating the *ad valorem* rate and making it specific. As sugar was Germany's single largest export, these measures were far from popular there.[58]

Competition between American and German agricultural items began to be accompanied in the 1890s by a growing rivalry in manufactured goods. Here too, the main locus of conflict was the German market, where American merchandise made inroads at the expense of German industries.[59] In 1898, an American consul reported that "German iron manufacturers are very much alarmed at America's capacity to compete with them in the German market."[60] By 1901, "the financial and daily press were filled with dissertations on 'The American danger,'"[61] and a "general panic" existed among the German population and the government.[62] The 1904 issue of the State Department's publication, *Commercial Relations of the United States with Foreign Countries*, remarked upon the "very unfriendly disposition, to call it by its mildest name, displayed at the appearance, in even the smallest quantities, of American manufactures in the German market," and stated that "the first appearance of an American shoe, machine, agricultural implement, etc., creates such industrial excitement among German manufacturers as would lead to the belief that their industries were immediately threatened." In assessing the breadth of American competition, the publication provided a list of American manufactured products exported to Germany in 1904, noting that "every article . . . finds its counterpart in German manufactures."[63]

The consequence of the commercial competition between Germany and the United States in one another's home markets, and the repeated attempts at protection that this competition engendered, was an almost continual tension in the relations of the two countries. A tariff war appeared imminent on more than one occasion when the process of retaliation and counter-retaliation threatened to get out of hand.[64] On the whole, the animosity created by this rivalry was more severe in Germany, which was more seriously affected, and where the traditionally antagonistic industrial and agricultural interests were united in their antipathy toward America. As Andrew White, the American ambassador to Berlin, noted, by 1897, "German feeling toward [the United States] had become generally adverse and, in some parts of the empire, bitterly hostile. . . . we finally had against us two of the great influential classes in the empire: the manufacturers and the landowners."[65]

If German-American industrial competition in home markets was divisive, the impact of rivalry in third markets was perhaps stronger still. As early as 1895, the American consul in Cologne reported that "the United States seems to be looming up in the German mind as the country most to be feared in the future as their competitor in the world's markets."[66] The consul-general in Berlin wrote in 1899 that "the enormous growth of American manufactured exports, [and] the aggressive competition of American metal and other products in South American and Eastern markets . . . weigh heavily on the hearts of the people here."[67] Another consular report in 1903 enclosed an article from a German newspaper that bitterly and systematically surveyed the gains made by America at Germany's expense. The agent believed the article to be representative of German opinion, and he noted that "American competition" and "The American danger" were frequent headlines in the German press.[68]

Not all Germans, of course, were convinced of the reality of this menace. The Liberal *Die Nation* argued in 1902 that "the ability of the United States to compete in industrial sectors is almost universally overrated," noting that "the sale of German industrial products in neutral markets has remained stable in spite of American competition."[69] The German consul-general in New York called the assertion that "American industry threatens to devour the German" "outrageous" and "pure rubbish."[70] And historian Alfred Vagts, upon reviewing the reports of the various German consuls in Latin America and the Far East, concluded that, in fact, German-American competition was "neither very general nor very acute."[71]

Nevertheless, the "American menace" was accepted as real by most Germans, from the ministerial bureaucrats to the emperor himself.[72] In 1897, the Naval Ministry's economist declared that America posed a greater threat than Britain to Germany's economic health.[73] Ernst von Halle, in a 1901 memorandum, claimed that the United States was determined "to replace the old continent as the supplier of every type of product in world markets."[74] Perhaps German fears were best summarized in a book published by the Central Bureau for the Preparation of Commercial Treaties, which saw the situation as follows: "After the Americans had established their supremacy as exporters of agricultural products, which export they have organized in such a masterly manner as to defy all competition, they immediately turned to exportation of industrial products . . . at so low a price that they will in a very little while conquer the world markets. . . . Our chief danger lies in the probable eventuality that America's wholesale production of manufactured articles will drive us out of the foreign markets by underbidding us in price. In short, the Americans are the sole commercial-political opponents whom we must earnestly dread. . . . the United States is—in an economical sense— our enemy."[75]

The apprehension felt in Germany at the German-American trade rivalry was reciprocated in the United States. Melvin Small has noted that during the years before the outbreak of war "the public media spent more space on economic difficulties than on any other facet of German-American relations" and that "the business community was constantly concerned not only with specific problems, but with the general threat of German competition."[76] Reports sent back to Germany by the ambassador in Washington, Holleben, were filled with accounts of American hostility. In 1898, Holleben wrote, "Since the great upswing, which took Germany to a position as an economic power, there has been a sharper and sharper conflict in economic questions between Germany and the United States, so that the mood within the latter concerning us has recently entered an acute phase. Germany is now in daily conversation and in the press the most hated country. This hatred is naturally directed mainly at the bothersome competitors, but it carries over into purely political areas. A situation has arisen here such that with the daily evidence of the operation of this Germanophobia, one must take comfort in the aphorism: many enemies, much honor."⁷⁷ This description was confirmed by a reasonably impartial observer, the French chargé d'affaires in Washington, in a 1901 dispatch to the French Foreign Office: "One cannot really say that relations between Germany and the United States are bad. They are worse than bad. They eye each other suspiciously; they are jealous of each other; they know that they are fighting for the commercial supremacy of the world. No agreement is possible in this area, and it is sufficient that some lieutenant of the Berlin Guard occupies his spare time in organizing on paper an invasion of American territory by German troops to lend new credence to the words of Admiral Dewey that America's first war would be with Germany."⁷⁸

German commercial competition was a matter of such grave concern in the United States partly because many Americans perceived it to be inextricably linked to Germany's colonial ambitions. Some worried that economic penetration would serve as a means for gaining political control. One author warned his readers that Germany was "engaged in the peaceful conquest of Spanish America."⁷⁹ Still others, more numerous, believed the causality to be reversed and that Germany, in her drive to secure export markets, would seek to establish colonies. This view was most prevalent within the American navy. The Black War Plan of 1913 envisioned a conflict with Germany over the Monroe Doctrine based upon her "expanding population, her need for a protected overseas market, and German-American 'trade competition.' A battle is on throughout the world for commercial supremacy," the Plan stated, "wherever German and American goods are brought into competition."⁸⁰

For the most part, government officials in the United States were more sanguine about German commercial competition than the general public. In Berlin, however, it was widely supposed that economic considerations determined Washington's policy toward Germany and that chances for good relations were therefore almost nil. Holleben wrote in one dispatch, "Economic interests are in international relations by their nature decisive, where border issues and such questions of power are not of immediate consideration. It follows that for Europe, and especially for Germany, future relations with the United States will depend not so much on whether the Republicans or the Democrats are in power, but on which economic trend holds sway."⁸¹ The emperor noted his agreement in the margin.⁸² Later, in a letter to Hohenlohe, the German ambassador suggested that "a permanent rapprochement with America is thinkable only as the result of Germany's economic demise."[83]

The commercial differences between Germany and the United States aroused "animosities and heated sentiments" on both sides of the Atlantic.[84] They reinforced, and were themselves reinforced by, the geopolitical issues that divided the two countries. Among broad segments of the populations, and to a lesser extent in official circles in Washington and Berlin, trade rivalry helped foster antipathy and mistrust, and the idea that German-American friendship was neither desirable nor possible.

It is important to note that the pernicious effects of commercial competition were not offset, to any measurable degree, by the salutary influence of a close financial relationship.[85] Prior to 1900, American investments in German concerns were virtually nonexistent, and the purchase by a New York banking syndicate in September of that year of 80 million marks of German treasury bills caused outrage and consternation in Germany.[86] German holdings of American securities were more substantial, an estimated $200 million in 1899, mainly in railroad stocks.[87] However, this figure represented a decline from previous levels as German capital found more lucrative investments at home. The relative dearth of German-American financial connections—and the political implication of this absence—appears most striking when contrasted to the network of ties between Britain and the United States during this same era. As Vagts explains: "In the year 1900, German capital investment in the United States was lower than it had been for a long time. The diplomatic and commercial-political differences between Germany and the United States thus fall into a period when German capital involvement, and the personal relationships connected with it, were at the lowest point. . . . Anglo-American linkages of this type were, to all appearances, much better maintained and as a consequence—directly or indirectly—their diplomatic relationship in this era of the 'Anglo-Saxon Alliance.' "[88]

In the last years of the nineteenth century and the first years of the twentieth, Germany and the United States suffered from a decreasing level of heterogeneity in their economic activities. Initially in agricultural commodities and then in manufactured articles, German and American producers competed fiercely in one another's home markets and in world markets. This trade rivalry over-shadowed elements of complementarity and interdependence that undoubtedly did exist, and paralleled rather than cut across the geopolitical differences between the two countries, thus exacerbating their divisive effects. It represented a serious impediment to friendly relations, for it implied that strong incentives to stability were lacking while heated animosities were being aroused. Nor was the overall impact of the economic dimension on the Anglo-German relationship much improved by close connections in the financial sphere. Flows of capital between Germany and the United States were small and had little or no political salience.

Societal Attributes

The geopolitical and economic rivalries that divided Germany and the United States around the turn of the century coincided with an increasingly profound ideological and cultural estrangement. This alienation strongly resembled that between Germany and Great Britain during the same period and was rooted in the heterogeneous societal attributes—particularly the social and political philosophies and institutions—of the two countries. As one analyst has summarized the situation, the German and American systems reflected "two essentially different conceptions of the state: that of the economically-liberal laissez-faire state, in which one from the German side saw only disorder, egoism, and corruption, and the half-absolutist, neofeudalistic, bureaucratic state, which in American eyes destroyed the freedom of the individual and lacked democratic legitimation through the 'voice of the people.'"[89]

Within German society, it was the conservative ruling elements who were most virulently antipathetic toward the American system, for they saw in it a model for the future development of Germany that was entirely inimical to their interests. Their distaste found expression in a number of right-wing newspapers. Wrote the American consul-general in Berlin: "[The editors of these papers] take their cue from the upper class, who are now, as they were in our Civil War, bitterly resentful of republican institutions. They have a strong influence even on the liberal press. They fear beyond everything that the people will contrast our government and methods with their own to the disadvantage of the latter and systematically print articles derogatory to the United States and our people."[90]

These articles, which portrayed the American political system in the most unflattering light, were not confronted with any serious, scholarly study of the United States. In the fifty years (100 volumes) prior to 1914, the *Historische Zeitschrift* published a mere five essays dealing with America. During the last quarter century before the war, this journal printed not one such article. The *Historische Taschenbuch*, between 1830 and 1892, compiled an equally dismal record.[91] German animosity and ignorance combined to produce a biased view of America, one which omitted the best aspects and accentuated the worst, and which inspired an acute lack of sympathy for the United States among the broader part of the German population. The patronage that pervaded American party politics, the spoils system, the prevalence of bosses and machines, and the general ferment that followed the Civil War all contributed to the belief that the political system of the United States was both irrational and corrupt.[92] Except for a few democrats who clung tenaciously to an admiration for America, most Germans came to see the United States as "evidence against the [alleged] desirability and advantages of mass democracy." In their preoccupation with reason and order, the American system appeared to them "more like an apparition out of the 'Wild West' than a seriously-taken (let alone imitable) form of political organization."[93]

Not surprisingly, this rather jaundiced view of the American political system contributed to—and was accompanied by—an unfavorable and somewhat unjustified stereotype of the average American citizen. The American, or "Yankee" as he was popularly known, was a creature both different from and inferior to the typical German. According to one description, he was a "boorish fellow, who condoned corruption in public life and approved of every swindle in economic life; who pursued the dollar and sensation, a barbarian in science and art, a bigotted, sanctimonious hypocrite who chewed tobacco and whose chief amusement was found in lynchings."[94]

If Germans generally rejected American political philosophy and its institutional and procedural manifestations, Americans, for the most part, gladly returned the favor. At the time of the Franco-Prussian War, the political-cultural differences between the two nations had been apparent to few in the United States. Indeed, the German battle against France was widely interpreted as a struggle for liberty and independence much like the fight waged by America against Britain barely a century before. Most Americans believed that the unification of Germany marked the first step in the evolution of that country into a federal republic founded upon American ideals of liberal and representative government.[95] In a special message to Congress, President Ulysses S. Grant said, "The union of the States of Germany into a form of government similar in many respects to that of the American Union is an event that cannot fail to touch deeply the sympathies of the people of the United States. This union has been brought about by the long-continued, persistent efforts of the people, with the deliberate approval of the governments and people of twenty-four of the German States, through their regularly constituted representatives. In it the American people see an attempt to reproduce in Europe some of the best features of our own Constitution, with such modifications as the history and condition of Germany seem to require."[96]

Over the next four decades or so, however, this rosy vision of a "United States of Germany" was replaced by the picture of an increasingly repressive, militaristic, authoritarian, and autocratic society. American papers regularly attacked Germany's compulsory military service, her inequitable electoral systems, her suppression of free speech through imprisonments for lese majesty, and the emperor himself, who proved a particularly inviting target whenever he made a proclamation regarding the divine right of kings.[97] Although some authors were careful to maintain a distinction between the German people, whom they believed to be basically good, and the government, which they saw as inherently evil, others held that the German political system reflected badly upon the entire nation. One writer was disgusted that "the German people have no aspiration after political liberty, no desire for self-government,"[98] and a second agreed that it was "impossible . . . to respect a people who act like wards, not like free men, who are bullied and who let their Government bully."[99]

America's ideological alienation from Germany reached new heights after 1914, when Germany went to war with Britain, by that time firmly established in American minds as a nation of fellow Anglo-Saxons committed to liberalism and representative government. Many in the United States viewed or came to view the conflict as a struggle between competing political systems. Upon the outbreak of hostilities, the *New York World* ran the editorial headline, "Autocracy or Democracy," a theme repeated in numerous other papers.[100] The *New York Times* wrote, "It is significant that in the confusion in which Europe has been plunged the two great representative democracies of England and France have borne themselves with the greatest calm and dignity and sense of international responsibility. Observing in letter and in spirit the neutrality to which the United States is bound, it is still open to us to expect and to wish that the sway of autocracy shall not, in the end, be strengthened."[101]

While the *Times* thus called upon Americans to maintain a strictly neutral stance, others did not agree that their country could take the position of a largely disinterested spectator. Within the Wilson administration and without, many believed that the same hatred of liberal democracy that (they alleged) led Germany to attack France and Britain would impel her to turn upon the United States should those adversaries be defeated. The *New York World* cautioned, "The issue is now joined. Either German autocracy must be crushed, or European democracy will be obliterated. There is no middle course. If the forces that the Kaiser has loosed are victorious, the map of European republicanism may as well be rolled up, and the American people prepare to make the last great stand for democracy."[102] Wilson's close friend and trusted advisor, Colonel House, warned the president in 1916 that, were Germany to win the war, "democratic governments will be imperilled throughout the world."[103] This concern was reiterated again and again by Secretary of State Robert Lansing, who worked diligently to persuade Wilson of its validity.[104] In a memorandum of July 1915, Lansing drew the logical conclusion: that her interest in seeing that Germany did not emerge victorious might compel the United States to enter the European conflict. Wrote Lansing, "I have come to the conclusion that the German Government is utterly hostile to all nations with democratic institutions because those who compose it see in democracy a menace to absolutism and the defeat of the German ambition for world domination. . . . The remedy seems to me to be plain. It is that Germany must not be permitted to win this war and to break even, though to prevent it this country is forced to take an active part."[105]

Ultimately, of course, Germany's decision to resume unrestricted submarine warfare against American shipping, rather than fear of German victory, provoked the United States to action in 1917. But it is at least conceivable that under other conditions, had Germany appeared truly likely to win, such apprehensions, springing largely from ideological suspicion and animosity, might have been sufficient to draw America into the fray.

At any rate, well before 1914 the gulf separating the German and American political systems seemed from both sides to be virtually unbridgeable. Close and amicable relations between the two countries appeared next to impossible, and some segments of the populations, especially on the German right, judged them to be undesirable as well. In this atmosphere of antipathy and mistrust, disputes over commercial and geopolitical issues assumed an almost artificial significance. Indeed, one student of the period has concluded that "American and German differences, in the final analysis, were ideological as much as practical."[106]

The ideological antagonism between the United States and Germany was not—contrary to what one might suppose—mitigated to any appreciable degree by a sense of solidarity produced by the great number of German expatriates and their descendents living in America. It was, of course, true that the German-American element was very large. Albert Faust has estimated that in 1900, out of a total American population of 76 million, 18 million were of German origin, while only a slightly higher figure, 20 million, were of English stock.[107] As late as 1914, there existed between 500 and 750 German language newspapers in the United States, including 53 dailies.[108] For several reasons, however, this superficially important bond between the two countries exercised only the most minimal effect on their political relations.

In the first place, the Germans themselves harbored but limited feelings of kinship for their countrymen who emigrated to America. Bismarck, in a Reichstag speech in 1884, commented that "a German who discards his fatherland like an old coat is for me no longer a German."[109] A similar attitude prevailed among other German leaders, and among the upper classes, who generally believed that those Germans who left the country were only those "incompetent to succeed at home."[110] The American consul-general in Berlin noted in 1896 that the German papers exhibited "more ill-will toward their emigrated brethren than toward Americans of a different descent."[111]

Moreover, and this constituted the basis for much of the German resentment, German-Americans retained little allegiance—culturally or otherwise—to their mother country. Instead, they rapidly became assimilated into American society, adopting the language, customs, and beliefs of the new land.[112] These were predominantly Anglo-Saxon, for the United States had taken shape in its early years under the direction of men who were almost exclusively English in origin. As one author explains, "Everywhere the first-comers were Anglo-Saxons. . . . the economic prosperity attendant on the superior techniques of the immigrants did not give them the power to mold the cultural and political life of the state. Again and again, it can be seen how the first few thousand settlers in an area had far more weight in this respect than hundreds of thousands who came later. They set up the school system; the legal system; they wrote the state constitution; they had the most political experience; they had the prestige which led the later-coming majority—or at least their children—to conform to *their* standards, rather than vice versa."[113]

Thirdly, many, if not most, German-Americans shared the ideological predispositions of Americans more generally in their affinity for representative democracy and their distaste for authoritarian and autocratic government. A substantial portion had entered the United States following the failure of liberal revolutions in 1848, while others had left Germany after her unification under Prussian rule. Even the German language newspapers in the United States expressed revulsion at the German political system. The *Indianapolis Tägliche Telegraph* wrote in 1884 of "the caricature that is presented by the alleged parliamentary system over there" and claimed that "the Germans are languishing under the guardianship of a dictator who received his training in Russia."[114] The *Philadelphia Neue Presse* contended that "all German-Americans no doubt are of the opinion that a republican system would stand the test in Germany as well as in the United States," adding, "if it were ours to say, Germany would be a republic."[115]

Finally, despite their great numbers, German-Americans were largely unrepresented in the halls of power, especially within the American government. Men such as Carl Schurz were the exception rather than the rule. Most of those in positions of authority, capable of making and influencing policy, were Anglo-Americans or at least considered themselves to be so. Under such circumstances, the favorable impact of even ardently pro-German German-Americans on political relations between the two countries was bound to be severely circumscribed.

The prewar period in German-American relations was marked on both sides by a pervasive sense of ideological estrangement. This feeling reflected the different political and social philosophies of the two countries as well as more concrete institutions and processes. Contrary to what one might have expected, this alienation was not ameliorated to any significant extent by the fact that a large percentage of Americans was actually of German descent. As in the case of Britain and Germany, then, a fundamental absence of homogeneity in the societal attributes of Germany and the United States seriously damaged prospects for a reconciliation. It reinforced the geopolitical and economic antagonisms that divided the two countries, helping to harden and solidify their negative images of one another. And it meant that any real incentive to avoid a conflict, out of a regard for shared attributes and a sense of common identity, was almost utterly lacking.

Summary

This chapter has furnished an account of the inability of Germany and the United States to establish stable, amicable relations in the critical years from 1898 to 1914. The analysis is summarized in table 4.

In German-American relations, as in Anglo-German diplomacy of the same period, a combination of geopolitical, economic, and ideo-logical/cultural elements necessary for peace was lacking from both an absolute, dyadic, and a relative, multilateral point of view. While Germany's disputes with America were less fundamental than those with Britain, this did not lead her to actively pursue an accommodation with America, perhaps because she could not overlook, even under such circumstances, her disagreements with that country. Moreover, from the perspective of the United States, no such incentive to an understanding existed, for American differences with Germany exceeded, in both breadth and depth, those with any other power.

Table 4. Germany and the United States, 1898–1914

Exercise of Power	Low Heterogeneity: imperial competition and related naval rivalry.
Economic Activities	Low Heterogeneity: commercial competition in home and third markets; weak financial ties.
Societal Attributes	Low Homogeneity: superficially linked by German-Americans, deep ideological and political-cultural differences.

6

Conclusion

Why Peace Breaks Out

This study has sought to answer the question, "Why does peace break out?" Under what circumstances will states end a period of mutual hostility and enter into a stable, amicable relationship with one another? My examination of four historical cases has revealed three conditions conducive to great power rapprochement: heterogeneity in the exercise of national power, heterogeneity of economic activities, and homogeneity of societal attributes. If two states' situation in these respects is sufficiently favorable, then a catalytic crisis may set the process of reconciliation in motion.[1]

The essential logic of this explanation and the exact nature of the causal connections involved have been discussed, in theoretical terms, in chapter 1. The empirical validity of these linkages in specific historical instances has been established through the within-case analyses that occupy the greater portion of this book. Additional evidence for the argument can be seen in a "cross-case" comparison (see table 5).[2]

Table 5. Summary of the Cases

	Great Britain/ United States	England/ France	Great Britain/ Germany	Germany/ United States
Exercise of Power (Heterogeneity)	Medium/Low	Low	Very Low	Low
Economic Activities (Heterogeneity)	Medium/High	High	Low	Low
Societal Attributes (Homogeneity)	High	Medium	Low	Low
Outcome	Peace	Peace	War	War

It is, unfortunately, not possible to make a general statement regarding the precise levels of heterogeneity or homogeneity along each of the three dimensions—individually and combined—necessary for a reconciliation. To do so would require, as noted in the opening chapter, accurate, reliable measures of each concept and a formula for constructing an index, as well as the consideration of a far greater number of cases. This problem is rendered more complex by the fact that the necessary levels may exist in either a relative sense, in view of two states' relations with other powers, or an absolute sense, within the context of their own bilateral relationship.

These difficulties mean that we cannot determine, in advance, the exact point at which two particular states will become capable of achieving a rapprochement. Nevertheless, the framework presented here possesses predictive value. As I shall argue below with respect to Soviet-American relations, it can provide us with clues as to whether or not a reconciliation is probable, and to the kinds of developments that would make one more (or less) likely in the future.

A "Realistic" Approach to International Politics

An inquiry into the origins of great power rapprochement is, by its very nature, an investigation of the most fundamental sources of states' attitudes and actions. In this regard, a significant aspect of the study is the doubt it casts upon a narrow realist interpretation of international politics. Realism holds that the international power structure, and each state's position therein, determines the course of interstate relations. Yet even among the world's strongest states, where considerations of power would be expected to dominate, other factors have in the past proved crucial. Indeed, the cases examined here indicate that any "realistic" conception of international politics and of foreign policy behavior requires, at a minimum, some means of taking the ways states exercise their power, their economic activities, and their societal attributes into account.

A Soviet-American Rapprochement?

If the analytic framework developed in this study can help to explain the past, it may also enable us to better understand contem-

porary, and predict future, international politics. What of the prospects for a Soviet-American rapprochement?—the issue with which
this study began. It requires no genius to recognize that, until recently at least, conditions have not been especially favorable.[3] Since 1945,
relations between the United States and Soviet Union have been
characterized by a low and decreasing level of heterogeneity in the
exercise of power. With worldwide interests, the two countries have
contended for influence, directly or through the services of proxy
states, in Europe, Asia, Africa, Latin America, and the Middle East.[4]
This rivalry has grown as the expansion of the once small Soviet navy
has enabled the USSR to project her power into every region of the
globe. Confrontations of varying seriousness over Berlin, Korea, Vietnam, Cuba, Ethiopia, Afghanistan, and Nicaragua, among others,
have appeared as manifestations of this competition.

During this same period, Soviet-American relations have suffered
from pervasive ideological and political-cultural mistrust. Because
their doctrine postulates the irreconcilability of socialism and capitalism and the former's inevitable triumph around the world, the
Soviets either believe or act as though they believe that the United
States is determined to destroy systems such as theirs,[5] while many
Americans perceive the USSR to be committed to global revolution
and the overthrow of every democratic government.[6] Under these
circumstances, it is not surprising that apparently minor geopolitical
disputes (e.g., Nicaragua) have been transformed into symbolic
battles for national survival. No sense of common identity exists
between the Soviet and American peoples, no feeling that a war
between them would be fratricidal.[7] This minimal homogeneity of
societal attributes has had a clear and adverse effect on Soviet-American diplomacy.

The economic dimension of the relationship between the United
States and the Soviet Union has occasionally shown signs of promise.
This promise has, however, remained largely unfulfilled. Although
the two countries do not compete to any real extent in either home or
third markets, neither do they engage in much mutually advantageous commercial exchange. In 1980, for example, Soviet imports
from the United States accounted for less than 3 percent of all Soviet
imports, while these same goods accounted for less than 1 percent of
all American exports. Similarly, merchandise purchased by the
United States from the Soviet Union made up a tiny fraction of
American imports, while the amount was equally insignificant as a
percentage of Soviet exports.[8] Elements of complementarity, espe-

cially with respect to trade in grains and in advanced technology, have not been exploited and have, in fact, been employed by the United States for purposes of coercion, though without great success.[9] Much the same has been true in the financial sphere. While the Soviets have accepted some American investment in the form of joint ventures and coproduction arrangements, and they would certainly benefit from additional capital, currency regulations, proscriptions against equity investments, and other restrictions related to the need of the government to control economic life, have had the effect of severely limiting the flow of American funds. In sum, the Soviet Union and the United States possess a reasonable level of heterogeneity in the economic sphere, but the potential benefits of this situation have not been realized.[10]

The Soviet-American relationship as it currently stands—and has stood since 1945—is summarized in table 6. Intense geopolitical competition, a keen sense of ideological estrangement and mistrust, potentially strong but actually weak economic connections: this combination of factors has, as one would expect, proved insufficient to bring about a state of peace between the two countries. Nor does any fundamental improvement in Soviet-American relations seem likely without some alteration in these conditions. It may be instructive in this regard that the Cuban Missile Crisis, which appears on the surface to have had a catalytic potential equal to that of the Venezuelan boundary episode or Fashoda, did not produce anything remotely resembling a genuine superpower reconciliation.[11]

To claim that changes conducive to a far-reaching transformation of the Soviet-American relationship are probable or that a rapprochement could be easily effected would, of course, be naive. At the same time, however, the situation should not be judged completely hope-

Table 6. United States and Soviet Union, 1987

Exercise of Power	Very Low Heterogeneity: competition for power and influence in all regions of the world.
Economic Activities	Medium/High Heterogeneity: no major competition; potential for important ties in trade and finance.
Societal Attributes	Very Low Homogeneity: no basis for common identity; lack of mutual knowledge and understanding; strong ideological and political-cultural differences.

less. For within the context of the framework presented here, a number of promising developments can be imagined.

In terms of the exercise of power, perhaps the most likely scenario involves the rise of a third nation, possibly China, whose aims and ambitions would clash with those of both the United States and the Soviet Union, making them appear relatively more heterogeneous with respect to one another. While China (or any other nation) does not seem ready to assume this role in the near future, the prospect could become a reality at some later point in time.[12]

A second, somewhat similar, possibility is that a long-term decline in Soviet and/or American military capabilities could force a strategic retrenchment on the part of one or both superpowers, reducing the extent to which their interests overlap. This decline might come about through the increasing strength of others in the international system, especially in the Third World. The American experience in Vietnam and the Soviet experience in Afghanistan have demonstrated that the capacity of the superpowers to intervene successfully in places beyond their borders is already quite limited. As lesser states continue to develop, it will, in all probability, become still more difficult for the United States and Soviet Union to exercise power in many regions of the globe.

A deterioration in the strategic positions of the United States and/ or USSR might also result from a loss of economic vitality in the two societies.[13] The Soviet Union has yet to solve the problems associated with a command economy and faces a growing energy shortage.[14] For its part, the United States has had considerable difficulty competing in foreign trade, and the national debt is now assuming epic proportions. Although the correlation between a nation's economic strength and its military capabilities is not perfect, there is clearly a relationship between the two factors. The virtually unchallenged Soviet-American condominium in global geopolitical affairs has existed for but forty years. It is unlikely that it will endure forever.[15]

Prospects for a favorable change in the ideological/cultural dimension of Soviet-American relations also vary with one's time horizon. In the short term, of course, things look rather dim. The United States cannot be expected to abandon its commitment to representative government and liberal principles. Nor can one expect the Soviet Union to renounce socialism, particularly since Marxist-Leninist doctrine serves to legitimize the existing Soviet regime.[16] Moreover, Russian and American history, language, tradition, and culture are vastly different and will surely remain so. For the near future, perhaps the best for which we can hope is an end to the shrill ideological rhetoric that has permeated the diplomatic exchanges between the two countries as well as their domestic political discourse. This might bring about a substantial relaxation of tensions and should not prove too difficult to achieve, for while the gulf separating the United States and the Soviet Union is large, its significance can be exaggerated.

Over the long run, more fundamental changes may be possible. Although the American polity has moved well to the right in recent years, the pendulum is bound at some point to swing back. The welfare state liberalism—or "creeping socialism," depending upon one's perspective—of Roosevelt's New Deal and Johnson's Great Society may yet return as the dominant view regarding the proper role of government in political, social, and economic life. With respect to the Soviet Union, there are those who argue that communist ideology is dead, that official adherence to Marxist-Leninist dogma is little more than lip service to a set of ideas no longer believed valid. Should this be so, it is conceivable that some, if not all, of current orthodoxy will be jettisoned. In fact, Mikhail Gorbachev's current campaign for certain political and economic reforms might be taken as evidence of movement in this direction. Similar, but more far-reaching, changes have already taken place in the People's Republic of China, where the leadership has discarded or modified tenets of the socialist faith with a fervor unthinkable a scant decade ago.[17] While it would be foolish to pretend that convergence between the Soviet Union and the United States on matters of social and political philosophy and organization will ever be complete, potential for a significant narrowing of the present gap clearly does exist.

The best chances for a positive alteration of the Soviet-American relationship have usually been deemed to lie in the economic sphere. Indeed, commercial motivations played a major role in Washington's decision to recognize the Moscow government in 1933 and in the pursuit of détente during the 1970s. This assessment remains an accurate one, at least for the short term, though neither recognition nor détente produced important changes, cautioning us, perhaps, not to expect too much. As noted previously, the United States and the Soviet Union possess a reasonable measure of economic heterogeneity and considerable potential complementarity in both trade and finance. The Soviets could find continued supplies of American grain to be increasingly valuable, as well as imports of advanced technology, especially in the field of energy production. Investment by American companies could put a spark to the sluggish Russian economy. On the other side of the coin, Americans could come to view the Soviet Union as an attractive market for goods and capital, particularly as competition in other markets becomes fiercer. There are, of course, formidable obstacles to such developments, chief among them restrictions imposed by the dictates of Russia's command economy. In addition, the American government has hindered efforts to establish closer economic ties by attempting to manipulate commercial activities for political purposes. Still, if—as seems possible—the rationale for exchange becomes more compelling, and the United States and Soviet Union expand their contacts so that each possesses a meaningful stake in the other's prosperity and goodwill, some improvement in relations would be likely to result.

International Politics: Pre-1914 and Post-1945

At this point, it may be necessary to address the argument that contemporary international politics generally and Soviet-American politics more specifically are so different from those of the pre-1914 era that it is fruitless to compare them.[18] In particular, one might claim that nuclear weapons, and the fear of nuclear war, have been of such profound consequence that a study of the traditional sources of interstate hostility and friendship is almost beside the point. Interestingly, the two principal claims that may be advanced in this regard are, at least on the surface, contradictory.

The first is that nuclear weapons have acted as a kind of a "great pacifier," rendering warfare so terrible that nations simply will not fight. It is true, of course, that the avoidance of a potentially devastating nuclear conflict represents a new and important incentive to stable relations lacked by the major powers of the prewar, prenuclear period. It is further likely—though this cannot be proved—that a balance of terror has dissuaded the United States and the Soviet Union from engaging in open hostilities during the years since 1945. At the same time, however, there is no guarantee that it will continue to do so forever. Clearly, the prospect of nuclear destruction has not prevented either side from seriously considering the possibility of armed conflict or from preparing assiduously for it. In fact, although nuclear weapons may well make nations less eager to do battle with one another, the presence of such awesome arsenals with such enormous potential for destruction almost certainly increases the level of

[handwritten marginal note: Presence of nuclear weapon can only make the risk higher, it will never remove the threat of war.]

suspicion, hatred, and fear (see below). And in an atmosphere of intense antipathy and mistrust, there will always be the danger of war escalating out of some crisis or incident, even though such escalation may appear highly irrational.[19] Furthermore, there have been instances in which a nonnuclear power attacked a nuclear power despite the latter's immense capacity for retaliation. Most recently, the Falklands conflict between Britain and Argentina has shown that the existence of nuclear weapons does not necessarily preclude the outbreak of violence.[20]

The second argument is that nuclear weapons are the real, or at least the principal, source of hostility between those countries that possess them. Reduce or dismantle the arsenals of the superpowers, and conflict between them will cease. Such logic appears to motivate some—though by no means all or even a majority—of the most fervent advocates of arms control and disarmament. This claim is difficult, if not impossible, to sustain. It seems only too obvious that nuclear arms, and the nuclear arms race, have greatly exacerbated tensions between the United States and the Soviet Union. That they are the root cause of such tensions is by no means as clear. The Soviet Union and the United States were hardly on good terms between 1917 and 1941, when neither side possessed nuclear weapons. Moreover, were the possession of nuclear weapons a primary source of international antagonism, one would expect Britain, France, and the United States, all nuclear powers, to be at odds with one another.

As a general rule, one can probably say that nations do not normally seek to acquire arms in the absence of some adversary against which they might be used. While it may well be true that animosities between states are sometimes exaggerated or even encouraged by those with a bureaucratic or economic interest in the production of weapons and weapons systems, it seems a bit far-fetched to suggest that a military-industrial complex in the United States (and/or the Soviet Union) has somehow manufactured the cold war between the superpowers. Ultimately, arms races—including the nuclear arms race—appear as much or more a consequence of interstate hostility as its cause.

In sum, it is important to recognize that nuclear weapons, and the fear they inspire, have exercised, and will continue to exercise, a considerable and even profound impact on the relations between states. But their presence has not eliminated the need to analyze and to understand other, more fundamental, sources of states' attitudes and behaviors toward one another.

How Peace Breaks Out, and the Role of the Statesman

As noted in the opening chapter, the outbreak of peace between formerly hostile states may be viewed as a process consisting of at least two parts. In the first, the states—or, more accurately, those within them who make and influence policy—determine that war is not an acceptable mechanism for resolving their disputes and that some reconciliation must be achieved. In the second, this belief is acted upon, policies designed to promote a rapprochement are undertaken, and an expectation of nonviolent relations develops. The distinction between these two stages may be conceptualized as the difference between "why peace breaks out" and "how peace breaks out."

How peace breaks out—whether there is some optimal (or even necessary) strategy of reconciliation, and if so, what it might be—is an issue largely beyond the scope of this study. It does appear that one important element is the successful liquidation of all or nearly all outstanding geopolitical differences, which occurred in both the Anglo-French and Anglo-American cases. Such resolution not only removes as a source of tension the concrete issues over which conflict might erupt, but also generates good feelings between the two sides, convincing each that the other is serious in its desire to settle disputes in a nonviolent fashion.

Recognition that the outbreak of peace is a process that involves activities and policies directed toward its attainment, as well as a set of underlying incentives and obstacles to it, may lead one to wonder whether the factors that have been identified in this work as causal are really determining. A diplomatic historian of traditional bent might, for example, ask: what is the role of individuals in this framework? Is it not possible that highly motivated and especially imaginative leaders could achieve a reconciliation when geopolitical, economic, and ideological/cultural conditions are less than optimal? Conversely, is it not conceivable that disinterested or particularly incompetent diplomats could fail to achieve a rapprochement under apparently favorable circumstances?

The evidence suggests that capable statesmanship is indeed valuable in the pursuit of peace. Lansdowne, the British foreign secretary, and Delcassé, the French foreign minister, conducted the negotiations that culminated in the Entente Cordiale with considerable persistence and skill. So did their respective ambassadors, Monson and Cambon. King Edward's visit to Paris in May 1903 and the gracious and friendly spirit manifested by the British monarch on that occasion had a profoundly positive effect on French public opinion. Had these men failed to act as they did, the path of Anglo-French peace might have been a far more difficult one.

Much the same point can be made with respect to the reconciliation between Great Britain and the United States. Although Cleveland and Olney on the American side, and Salisbury on the British, showed limited tact and flexibility, their successors, including Hay and Balfour, proved more impressive. Britain's patience with sometimes crude American diplomatic behavior, as when she accepted without complaint Roosevelt's nominations to the binational commission that arbitrated the Alaskan boundary question, was instrumental in achieving the rapprochement.

On a more negative note, German diplomacy during the last years of the prewar period was almost uniformly poor. Those who led Germany after Bismarck managed to alienate most of Europe as well as the United States with their arrogant manner and duplicitous tactics. Had Holstein, Bülow, and William possessed the acumen of the Iron Chancellor, Germany's relations with other states might not have deteriorated so markedly. In particular, had Germany refrained from rapid and massive naval expansion, her association with Britain might have remained at least cordial, while the abandonment of intrigues in Latin America and the Caribbean could have saved her from so grievously offending the United States.

The construction of a great fleet and the refusal to renounce ambitions in the Western Hemisphere reflected, of course, conscious decisions by German leaders. This suggests that statesmen can directly influence at least one of the variables examined in this study. The growth of the German navy in waters close to British shores constituted a sharp decline in heterogeneity in the exercise of German and British power. Similarly, active German interest in territorial acquisitions in regions near the United States meant a low level of heterogeneity in the exercise of German and American power. Generally speaking, geopolitical objectives, and the strategies used to secure them, appear open to some manipulation by political leaders.

This said, it seems doubtful that even the most talented statesmen could effect a state of peace without the proper conditions. Economic, ideological, and cultural relationships may be far more difficult to alter than geopolitical ones, and the reflection of all three elements in popular opinion may be impossible to ignore.[21] The German navy, built in part to satisfy the whims of William II, was also a response to British commercial competition and received substantial public support on that basis. Trade rivalry, and the almost pathological distaste for Britain's sociopolitical system among Germany's ruling classes, would have rendered German leaders unlikely to make concessions to Britain on naval questions even had they been otherwise disposed to do so. Likewise, no German government could have appeased America by abandoning the quest for possessions in the Western Hemisphere without risking the alienation of powerful naval and colonial interests whose support was vital to its continued rule and whose antipathy toward the United States was grounded in economic and ideological antagonisms as well as geopolitical differences.[22]

On the other side of the coin, it would appear that even statesmen of limited competence might find it hard to fail when conditions for peace are sufficiently favorable. Cleveland, Olney, and Salisbury handled things badly enough, and while those who followed did better, the Senate's refusal to ratify the Olney-Pauncefote Arbitration Treaty and Roosevelt's packing of the Alaskan Boundary Commission were hardly examples of sterling diplomacy. It might be argued, in fact, that the Anglo-American reconciliation went forward despite, rather than because of, American statesmen. If this was true, it was due in large measure to the forbearance of British policymakers. Yet these men did not act without reason. Indeed, the geopolitical, economic, and ideological/cultural arguments in favor of an accommodation with the United States were so persuasive, and the popular enthusiasm for an understanding so strong, that exceptional patience and flexibility were virtually demanded.

This narrowing of options can also be seen in the Anglo-French case. Given the state of public sentiment and the prominence of the *parti colonial*, no French government could have abandoned the search for colonial gains. At the same time, German support for French colonial policy would, it had been amply demonstrated, require the formal renunciation of Alsace-Lorraine, an action equally unacceptable. Under these circumstances, an accommodation with Britain, involving an exchange of imperial interests, stood out as the only feasible course to take. Meanwhile, across the Channel, British leaders confronted similar restrictions. National and imperial security had to be guaranteed, but previous efforts to approach Germany had failed and renewed attempts were out of the question because of naval rivalry, economic competition, ideological antagonism, and the popular hatred these had inspired. An understanding with France, demanding relatively minor sacrifices, appeared the logical way to proceed.

It seems, then, that statesmen are both motivated and constrained by the domestic and international contexts in which they operate.[23] While certain aspects of their environment can be manipulated, others may be more resistant to change. The role of the statesman thus appears greatest at the margin. When environmental pressures are fairly weak or cut across one another, an unusually brilliant leader or an especially inept one may have a considerable impact on the course of events.[24] However, when these pressures point strongly in a particular direction, idiosyncratic personal influence is much less likely to occur.

marvelous grasp of the obvious

Notes

Preface

1. Hardy, *The Dynasts*, 87.

Chapter 1

1. Kenneth Boulding uses the term "stable peace," which he defines as "a situation in which the probability of war is so small that it does not really enter into the calculations of any of the people involved" (Boulding, *Stable Peace*, 13). Similarly, Bruce Russett and Harvey Starr conceive of stable peace as "the absence of preparation for war or the serious expectation of war" (Russett and Starr, *World Politics*, 410, original emphasis omitted).

2. Hobbes, *Leviathan*, 106–7.

3. Locke, *The Second Treatise of Government*, 12–13. See also Bull, *The Anarchical Society*, esp. 48.

4. See, for example, Robert J. Art and Robert Jervis, "The Meaning of Anarchy," in *International Politics: Anarchy, Force, Imperialism*, ed. Robert J. Art and Robert Jervis (Boston: Little, Brown & Co., 1973), 3.

5. See, for example, Boulding, *Conflict and Defense*, 253; Boulding, *Stable Peace*.

6. Deutsch et al., *Political Community and the North Atlantic Area*.

7. Ibid., 5. These concepts were originally developed in Van Wagenen, *Research in the International Organization Field*.

8. Deutsch et al., 6.

9. Ibid., 66–67.

10. Ibid., 133–58. Some of these conditions were considered essential for amalgamated security-communities.

11. It should be noted that two of the scholars working on the project did publish volumes devoted to the detailed analysis of individual cases. See Robert A. Kann, *The Habsburg Empire: A Study in Integration and Disintegration* (New York: Praeger, 1957); Raymond E. Lindgren, *Norway-Sweden: Union, Disunion, and Scandinavian Integration* (Princeton: Princeton University Press, 1959). In addition, two students of Deutsch later published case studies in which they applied some of the methods and concepts developed at Princeton. See Peter J. Katzenstein, *Disjoined Partners: Austria and Germany Since 1815* (Berkeley: University of California Press, 1976); Russett, *Community and Contention*.

12. Craig and George identify five stages in the improvement of relations between previously hostile states: détente, rapprochement, entente, appeasement, and/or alliance. Each successive stage is characterized by heightened efforts to eliminate the sources of antagonism and find a basis for cooperation. Rapprochement, in which the desire for agreement is first expressed, marks the actual beginning of conflict reduction, while appeasement, in which the prin-

cipal causes of animosity are methodically removed, represents its culmination. See Craig and George, *Force and Statecraft*, 238–52.

13. Wight, *Power Politics*; Morgenthau, *Politics among Nations*; Spykman, *America's Strategy in World Politics*; Waltz, *Theory of International Politics*. The term "balance of power," it should be noted, has not been used with consistent meaning by either statesmen or scholars. See Haas, "The Balance of Power," 442–77.

14. For historical analyses of the balance of power in theory and in practice see Gulick, *Europe's Classical Balance of Power*; Hinsley, *Power and the Pursuit of Peace*. Some balance-of-power theorists, it should be admitted, do not argue that a balance of power prevents war, but that war is in fact a mechanism that must sometimes be resorted to by states in order to maintain a balance of power. However, as Inis Claude notes, insofar as these theorists favor the preservation of a balance—if necessary through war—they do so because they believe, at least implicitly, that it contributes to the prospects for peace. See Claude, *Power and International Relations*, 54–55.

15. Organski, *World Politics*; Gilpin, *War and Change in World Politics*.

16. Similar to power transition theory (though with important differences) is "long cycle theory," developed most fully in the writings of George Modelski. See Modelski, "The Long Cycle of Global Politics," 214–35; Modelski, *Long Cycles in World Politics*. For good analyses of these and other related works see Levy, "Theories of General War," 344–74; Rosecrance, "Long Cycle Theory," 283–301.

17. On "internal" vs. "external" balancing see Waltz, *Theory of International Politics*, 168.

18. This form of balancing underlies the "Cardinal Principles Model" of foreign policy developed by Hartmann in *The Conservation of Enemies*. Hartmann contends that there is a limit to the total amount of enmity that a state can confront effectively. When this limit is exceeded, intelligent statesmen will seek to reduce the enmity they face by improving relations with one or more adversaries, sacrificing or compromising less important interests in order to preserve truly vital ones.

19. Popular or casual statements of balance-of-power theory usually have states being drawn together by the presence of a common external threat. But commonality is not a requirement. Balancing is a policy undertaken by the individual state in response to its own particular circumstances. Two or more states seeking to improve relations with one another may be doing so out of concern over contemporaneous, but different, dangers. Thus Morgenthau, for example, distinguishes between alliances based on identical interests and those based on complementary interests (Morgenthau, *Politics among Nations*, 177).

20. Walt, "Alliance Formation," 8–9, original emphasis omitted. The best-known statement that balancing behavior is determined solely by the distribution of capabilities is found in Waltz, *Theory of International Politics*, esp. 116–28. Though Waltz notes in passing that other factors may sometimes influence the actions of states, his theory makes no allowance for them.

21. Walt, *The Origins of Alliances*, 263–66.

22. Walt, "Alliance Formation," 18.

23. Richard Rosecrance has noted previously that the peaceful transition from the *Pax Britannica* to the *Pax Americana* runs counter to the predictions of the realist model. See Rosecrance, "International Theory Revisited," 707–8. Similarly,

Rosecrance and Raymond Dawson have suggested that the continuation of a strong alliance between Britain and the United States after 1949 cannot be explained by geopolitical calculations and balance-of-power principles. Rather, ideology, cultural ties, and common historical traditions were critical. The authors conclude, "between friends the balance of power does not mean very much." See Dawson and Rosecrance, "Theory and Reality," 21–51.

24. Claude, *Power and International Relations*, 64. See also Walt, "Alliance Formation," 8–13; Walt, *The Origins of Alliances*, 21–26.

25. Lenin, *Imperialism*.

26. The label "Marxist" is not entirely accurate. While Lenin's work clearly falls within the Marxist tradition, non-Marxist theorists have offered quite similar—and earlier—analyses of imperialism. See, for example, J. A. Hobson, *Imperialism: A Study*.

27. Marxist theorists have split on the question of whether imperialism and war result from competition for capital markets or for goods markets. The majority view, represented by Lenin, has emphasized the financial aspects of rivalry, while a minority view, advanced in particular by Rosa Luxemburg, has stressed the commercial elements. For a comparison of the two perspectives, see Cohen, *The Question of Imperialism*, 42–49. There is also a "mercantilist" perspective that is like the Marxist in that it views economic competition as a source of interstate conflict. However, while Marxists emphasize the primacy of economic interests, holding economic gains to be ends in and of themselves, mercantilists see the pursuit of economic objectives as a means to political and military power. Because it affirms power to be the principal factor motivating states and affecting their relations, mercantilism is basically a variation on the realist theme.

28. Keohane and Nye, *Transnational Relations*; Keohane and Nye, *Power and Interdependence*.

29. See Walt, *The Origins of Alliances*, 33–40, 181–217.

30. Burke, "First Letter on a Regicide Peace," 5:317.

31. Ibid., 318.

32. Morgenthau goes on to say, however, that "a *purely* ideological alliance, unrelated to material interests, cannot but be stillborn" (Morgenthau, *Politics among Nations*, 177–78; emphasis added).

33. Deutsch et al., *Political Community and the North Atlantic Area*, 123–37.

34. Ibid., 154–56.

35. Walt, "Alliance Formation," 20.

36. Doyle, "Kant, Liberal Legacies, and Foreign Affairs," 325.

37. Of course, any attempt was unlikely to be reciprocated by the United States, which perceived Germany to be its greatest threat. See chapter 5.

38. Craig and George, *Force and Statecraft*, 88.

39. Quoted in Craig and George, *Force and Statecraft*, 92.

40. In some fundamental sense, of course, the exercise of power is related to aggregate power. A state must possess power in order to exercise it. And the more powerful a state, the more extensive its geopolitical interests and ambitions are likely to be.

41. Generally, one state may be said to depend on another state to the extent that it relies on the other to provide goods and/or services that (1) it cannot produce domestically, (2) it cannot obtain elsewhere, and (3) it cannot do without. Thus, some heterogeneity of production is a necessary, although not a sufficient,

condition for dependence. The earliest, and probably best, analyses of the conditions of dependence, independence, and interdependence come not from students of international politics, but from theorists of social power. See esp. Peter M. Blau, *Exchange and Power in Social Life* (New York: John Wiley & Sons, 1964), chap. 5.

42. The idea of interdependence as "mutual reliance" is like the notion of interdependence as "mutual vulnerability," especially as the latter term is employed by Waltz. (Vulnerability is, of course, the flip side of reliance.) Interdependence has also sometimes been defined as "mutual sensitivity." On the concept of interdependence and the distinction between vulnerability and sensitivity see Waltz, *Theory of International Politics*, 139–46; Keohane and Nye, *Power and Interdependence*, 11–19; Baldwin, "Power Analysis and World Politics," 161–94; Baldwin, "Interdependence and Power," 471–506. Baldwin makes a very convincing case for "mutual vulnerability" as the traditional and proper definition of interdependence.

43. An explanation of the law of comparative advantage and of the gains from trade can be found in virtually any international economics textbook. A particularly good one is Caves and Jones, *World Trade and Payments*.

44. According to international trade theory, when states produce the same goods, trade occurs as the result of differing price levels in the countries involved. In reality, other factors may be important, including the quality of the items and minor variations in their characteristics. As this suggests, commodities need not be absolutely identical to compete; they need only be substitutes for one another. However, substitutability is itself to some extent a function of price. Consumers may be unwilling to substitute one good for another when their prices are fairly equal, and quite willing to do so when the price of one of the goods is substantially higher.

45. This may get at the distinction between "sensitivity" interdependence and "vulnerability" interdependence; see n. 42 above.

46. See, for example, Waltz, *Theory of International Politics*, 138.

47. See Keohane and Nye, *Power and Interdependence*, 16–18.

48. See Angell, *Peace on the March*. Angell's definition of what constitutes transnational participation is somewhat limited and does not include all transnational contacts. A good review of Angell's work is Warwick, "Transnational Participation," 305–24. A useful survey of some empirical evidence is Kelman, "International Interchanges," 205–18.

49. As Russett and Starr argue, "Contacts between highly disparate cultures are also as likely to arouse conflict as to bring the cultures together. . . . Ties between nations that are culturally similar and perhaps geographically close are more likely to be favorable" (*World Politics*, 423). Similarly, Warwick contends that "the outcome of transnational interactions will depend on the congruity of the cultures involved" ("Transnational Participation," 311).

50. See Ideological Solidarity above.

51. Walt, *The Origins of Alliances*, 35–37.

52. Lebow, *Between Peace and War*, 332. Lebow's analysis is based principally on an examination of the Fashoda Crisis and the Cuban Missile Crisis, although he briefly mentions other similar events, including the Anglo-American crisis over the Venezuelan boundary, in support of his arguments.

53. According to Lebow, "Images are resistant to change because critical information is often misunderstood, twisted in meaning to make it consistent, ex-

plained away, or ignored" (*Between Peace and War*, 333). In other words, when evidence and image conflict, the evidence is usually reinterpreted to fit the image rather than the other way around. Scholars differ on the psychological origins of misperceptions. Robert Jervis, adopting a cognitive approach, suggests that they are caused by states seeing what they expect to see, based largely on their past experiences (*Perception and Misperception*). Irving L. Janis and Leon Mann, by contrast, take a motivational perspective and propose that misperceptions are the consequence of states seeing what they want to see (*Decision-Making*). Lebow, *Between Peace and War*, esp. 102–12, provides an excellent discussion of these two viewpoints.

54. Lebow, *Between Peace and War*, 309.

55. Ibid., 326–33.

56. The logic of the comparative method was initially laid out by John Stuart Mill in *A System of Logic*, 1:448–71. Recent literature on the subject is extensive. See, among others, Lijphart, "Comparative Politics," 682–93; Lijphart, "The Comparable-Cases Strategy," 158–77; Przeworski and Teune, *The Logic of Comparative Social Inquiry*; Skocpol and Somers, "The Uses of Comparative History," 174–97; George, "Case Studies and Theory Development: The Method of Structured, Focused Comparison," 43–68. The best single treatment of the comparative method is an unpublished paper by George, "Case Studies and Theory Development."

57. This problem is not, of course, unique to the comparative method. It occurs in statistical procedures as well. However, in statistical procedures the probability of error can be reduced through proper sampling techniques to a minimal level, typically between 1 and 5 percent.

58. See chapter 6, n. 2.

59. The importance of within-case explanation as an integral part of comparative analysis is explained by George in his paper, "Case Studies and Theory Development."

60. One might well argue that post–World War II relations between the United States, France, and Britain and their former foes, Germany and Japan, have approximated a state of peace. The process by which this peace emerged was, however, hardly ideal, and in an age of vast nuclear arsenals could probably not be replicated. For this reason, these cases seem somewhat less worthy of examination than those considered in this study.

61. Similarly, military planning may indicate a breakdown of a state of peace when popular and elite attitudes do not, since fairly modest conflicts of interest can provide the impetus for extensive preparations. While strains in the Anglo-American relationship during the 1920s and 1930s could not reasonably be described as minor, it is clear that the American military establishment, especially the navy, thought a war between Britain and the United States much more likely than did civilian political leaders or the general public.

Chapter 2

1. The most comprehensive history, narrative and interpretive, of the Anglo-American relationship is Allen, *Great Britain and the United States*.

2. Charles S. Campbell, *Anglo-American Understanding*, 4.

3. Charles S. Campbell, *From Revolution to Rapprochement*, x.

4. For accounts of the crisis see Allen, *Great Britain and the United States*, 532–41; A. E. Campbell, *Great Britain and the United States*, 11–47; Charles S. Campbell, *American Foreign Relations*, 194–221.

5. Olney to Bayard, 20 July 1895, *Congressional Record*, 54th Cong., 1st sess., 28:191–96.

6. Salisbury to Pauncefote, 26 November 1895, *Congressional Record*, 54th Cong., 1st sess., 28:196–99.

7. *Congressional Record*, 54th Cong., 1st sess., 28:191.

8. Allen, *Great Britain and the United States*, 537.

9. A well-known British observer explained to his American readers that "the British people had not cared about the Venezuelan question because they had not known about it. It would be well within the mark to say that not one man out of ten thousand was aware that there was a Venezuelan question at all. Even in the House of Commons I doubt whether one member out of ten had heard of the matter. . . . Nobody had the least idea that your government considered the matter to be one of immediate and primary importance to America, justifying an ultimatum. That the Monroe Doctrine could be deemed involved had not occurred to our minds." See Bryce, "British Feeling on the Venezuelan Question," 145–46.

10. Nicholas, *The United States and Britain*, 52.

11. Charles S. Campbell, *From Revolution to Rapprochement*, 183.

12. Roosevelt to Lodge, 27 December 1895, Roosevelt and Lodge, *Selections from the Correspondence*, 1:205.

13. An excellent account is Blake, "The Olney-Pauncefote Treaty," 228–43.

14. *Economist*, 16 January 1897, 75.

15. *St. Louis Republic*, quoted in *Public Opinion*, 21 January 1897, 70.

16. Blake, "The Olney-Pauncefote Treaty," 237.

17. *Economist*, 20 February 1897, 271.

18. *Rochester Herald*, quoted in *Public Opinion*, 11 February 1897, 167.

19. *Times* (London), 23 April 1898, 11.

20. For a good account see Charles S. Campbell, *Anglo-American Understanding*, 25–55. See also A. E. Campbell, *Great Britain and the United States*, 127–55.

21. Pauncefote to Salisbury, 26 May 1898, quoted in Charles S. Campbell, *Anglo-American Understanding*, 49.

22. Memo by Tower, Pauncefote to Salisbury, 27 May 1898, quoted in Charles S. Campbell, *Anglo-American Understanding*, 50.

23. Charles S. Campbell, *Anglo-American Understanding*, 47. See *Public Opinion*, 24 March 1898, 360–61; 19 May 1898, 613–16; 26 May 1898, 643–46, for a survey of press comment.

24. 10 June 1898, *Parliamentary Debates*, 4th ser., 58 (1898): 1347–48.

25. See, for example, his famous Birmingham speech of 13 May 1898, quoted in Garvin, *The Life of Joseph Chamberlain*, 3:301–2; and his Commons speech of 10 June 1898, *Parliamentary Debates*, 4th ser., 58 (1898): 1438.

26. Olney, "International Isolation of the United States," 577–88; delivered as a speech at Harvard College, 2 March 1898.

27. A good account is in A. E. Campbell, *Great Britain and the United States*, 48–88. See also Charles S. Campbell, *Anglo-American Understanding*, 213–39.

28. See A. E. Campbell, *Great Britain and the United States*, 89–126, and Bradford Perkins, *The Great Rapprochement*, 162–72.

29. *Parliamentary Papers*, 1909, 167–73; Bureau of the Census, *Historical Statistics*, 139; Kendrick, *Productivity Trends*, 290–95; Mitchell, *European Historical Statistics*, 34, 818, 826. Where necessary, comparability of British and American statistics has been established by converting sterling into dollars (or vice versa) at the rate of £1.00 to $5.00. For a justification of this conversion ratio see Allen, *Great Britain and the United States*, 44.

30. Davis, *A Navy Second to None*, 168–71; Marder, *The Anatomy of British Sea Power*, 442n.

31. Davis, *A Navy Second to None*, 175.

32. Richmond Pearson Hobson, "America Must be Mistress of the Seas," 554–56.

33. Marder, *The Anatomy of British Sea Power*, 442.

34. Selborne to Curzon, 19 April 1901, quoted in Monger, *The End of Isolation*, 72n.

35. Marder, *The Anatomy of British Sea Power*, 442–43.

36. An index of "major-power capabilities" developed by researchers of the Correlates of War (COW) Project at the University of Michigan indicated that the United States had become more powerful than Britain by the year 1900. This index was based on six separate factors: total population, urban population, energy consumption, iron/steel production, military expenditures, and military personnel. See Sabrosky, "From Bosnia to Sarajevo," 10. According to the same index, by 1905 Germany had also surpassed Britain, but she remained far behind the United States.

37. Speech at Liverpool, 13 February 1903, quoted in *Times* (London), 14 February 1903, 9.

38. For a description of these see Monger, *The End of Isolation*, 1–7; Seaman, *From Vienna to Versailles*, 136–37.

39. Chamberlain to Milner, 16 March 1898, quoted in Garvin, *The Life of Joseph Chamberlain*, 3:367–68.

40. The following discussion draws heavily on Monger, *The End of Isolation*, 8–14.

41. Kennedy, *British Naval Mastery*, 209.

42. Monger, *The End of Isolation*, 8–9.

43. Brodrick to Chamberlain, 10 September 1901, cited in Monger, *The End of Isolation*, 10.

44. Memo by Selborne, 17 January 1901, cited in Monger, *The End of Isolation*, 10.

45. Woodward, *Great Britain and the German Navy*, app. 1.

46. Monger, *The End of Isolation*, 12.

47. War Office Memo, 15 August 1901, cited in Monger, *The End of Isolation*, 12.

48. Goschen to Curzon, 17 September 1900, quoted in Monger, *The End of Isolation*, 13; Brodrick to Curzon, 8 August 1901, quoted in Ronaldshay, *The Life of Lord Curzon*, 2:207.

49. Hamilton to Curzon, 4 July 1901, quoted in Monger, *The End of Isolation*, 13.

50. Lansdowne to Lascelles, 18 March 1901, quoted in Monger, *The End of Isolation*, 13.

51. Campbell-Bannerman to Bryce, 1903, quoted in Bradford Perkins, *The Great Rapprochement*, 156.

52. Memo by Bertie, 9 November 1901, Great Britain, Foreign Office, *British Documents*, 2:75.

53. Bourne, *Britain and the Balance of Power*, 341.
54. Grenville, *Lord Salisbury and Foreign Policy*, 68.
55. Bourne, *Britain and the Balance of Power*, 369–70.
56. Kennedy, *British Naval Mastery*, 211.
57. Admiralty memo, "Defence of Canada," 24 February 1905, quoted in Bourne, *Britain and the Balance of Power*, 382, 385. The Admiralty had been moving, reluctantly, toward this position for some time. A memo of 5 January 1901 noted that "Great Britain unaided can hardly expect to be able to maintain in the West Indies, the Pacific, and in the North America Stations, squadrons sufficiently powerful to dominate those of the United States and at the same time to hold the command of the sea in home waters, the Mediterranean, and the Eastern seas, *where it is essential that she should remain predominant.*" The Admiralty believed that naval superiority in American waters could still be achieved, but only if "the neutrality of the European Powers [were] absolutely assured," and it refused to speculate as to whether this condition could actually be fulfilled. Quoted in Charles S. Campbell, *Anglo-American Understanding*, 357–58; emphasis added.
58. Of those who have sought to explain British policy toward America during this period, Kenneth Bourne assigns the greatest weight to strategic considerations. Bourne writes that while trading interests and Anglo-Saxonist sentiment did play important roles, "security dictated Britain's decision to appease the United States" (Bourne, *Britain and the Balance of Power*, 410).
59. Osgood, *Ideals and Self-Interest*, 80.
60. Memo by Charles de Kay, 1 February 1896, quoted in Vagts, *Deutschland und die Vereinigten Staaten*, 1:619.
61. Stuart Anderson, *Race and Rapprochement*, 67.
62. *Harper's Weekly*, 3 January 1903, 16.
63. Herbert to Lansdowne, 29 December 1902, Great Britain, Foreign Office, *British Documents*, 2:164.
64. Sprout and Sprout, *American Naval Power*, 253. There is ample evidence in many of Roosevelt's letters to support this contention. See, for example, Roosevelt to Moore, 5 February 1898, Roosevelt, *The Letters of Theodore Roosevelt*, 1:768–69; Roosevelt to Lyman, 12 April 1901, Roosevelt, *The Letters of Theodore Roosevelt*, 3:52; and Roosevelt to Lodge, 27 March 1901, Roosevelt and Lodge, *Selections from the Correspondence*, 1:484–85.
65. Roosevelt to Lodge, 27 March 1901, Roosevelt and Lodge, *Selections from the Correspondence*, 1:485.
66. Brooks Adams, "The Spanish War," 645.
67. Bruce, "American Feeling Toward England," 462.
68. Memo by Dechair, January 1905, quoted in Marder, *The Anatomy of British Sea Power*, 444–45.
69. U.S. Navy, General Board, report to the secretary of the navy, 1906, quoted in Charles Carlisle Taylor, *The Life of Admiral Mahan*, 151–52. However, by 1913 the navy was no longer confident of British assistance, and by 1919 some navy men believed that an Anglo-American war over trade was not only possible, but even likely. See Schilling, "Admirals and Foreign Policy," 242–49.
70. See chapter 5.
71. Bureau of the Census, *Historical Statistics*, 550–53; Mitchell, *European His-*

torical Statistics, 512, 517, 599–600. Anglo-American trade in 1905 was more than twice the size of Anglo-German, Anglo-French, or German-American trade.

72. Mitchell, *European Historical Statistics,* 449–52; Bureau of Foreign and Domestic Commerce, *Statistical Abstract,* 418, 426–29, 465–66; *Parliamentary Papers,* 1903, 9.

73. Charles S. Campbell, *American Foreign Relations,* 211.

74. Atkinson, "The Cost of an Anglo-American War," 88.

75. Harvey, "The United States and Great Britain," 533.

76. Whelpley, "England's Food Supply," 804–5.

77. Angell, *Daily Mail* (London), quoted in *Literary Digest,* 14 September 1912, 411. For similar statements see Clarke, "England and America," 193; Gleig, "British Food Supply in War," 161–62.

78. See, for example, the statement of Gerald Balfour, president of the Board of Trade, 8 February 1904, *Parliamentary Debates,* 4th ser., 129 (1904): 661–63.

79. It was generally agreed that shipments of grain from Argentina, Australia, and New Zealand could not be increased sufficiently to cover more than a small fraction of the shortfall. See Gleig, "British Food Supply in War," 161–62; Harvey, "The United States and Great Britain," 532–33.

80. 6 April 1897, *Parliamentary Debates,* 4th ser., 48 (1897): 642–76.

81. War Office, "Memorandum on the standards of defence for the naval bases of Halifax, Bermuda, Jamaica, and St. Lucia," 17 September 1903, quoted in Bourne, *Britain and the Balance of Power,* 361–62.

82. Bacon, "American International Indebtedness," 276; National Monetary Commission, *The Trade Balance,* 174; Lewis, *America's Stake in International Investments,* 530, 546. American holdings of British and other foreign securities were negligible. See Bacon, "American International Indebtedness," 276.

83. Holleben to German Foreign Office, 7 December 1900, quoted in Vagts, *Deutschland und die Vereinigten Staaten,* 1:469.

84. LaFeber, "The American Business Community," 396–97. LaFeber argues that the crash was really fairly minor and that domestic American capital quickly filled the vacuum left by British withdrawals.

85. *Economist,* 4 January 1896, 15.

86. LaFeber, "The American Business Community," 397–98.

87. See, for example, "The Improvement in American Opinion," *Spectator,* 28 December 1895, 920; *Harper's Weekly,* 4 January 1896, 2.

88. Pauncefote to Salisbury, 24 December 1895, quoted in Mowat, *The Life of Lord Pauncefote,* 186.

89. Hay to Reid, 24 December 1895, Hay Papers.

90. Bradford Perkins, *The Great Rapprochement,* 124–25. See also Heindel, *The American Impact on Great Britain,* 138–75.

91. *Parliamentary Papers,* 1909, 79–80.

92. Heindel, *The American Impact on Great Britain,* 152.

93. Ernest E. Williams, "Made in Germany—Five Years After," 143.

94. J. A. Hobson, "The Approaching Abandonment of Free Trade," 435.

95. Heindel, *The American Impact on Great Britain,* 152.

96. *Parliamentary Papers,* 1897, 5–6.

97. See, for example, *Harper's Weekly,* 13 June 1903, 995; and 20 June 1903, 1046.

98. Stuart Anderson, *Race and Rapprochement,* 11–13.

99. On the "English Attack," see Mencken, *The American Language,* 12–23.

100. *Annual Review*, 241. The complaint was registered in a review of John Marshall's *Life of George Washington*.

101. *Edinburgh Review*, 185.

102. Mencken, *The American Language*, 79–81.

103. Charles S. Campbell, *American Foreign Relations*, 333–34.

104. For a discussion of Canada's ideological significance for Americans see Gardner, "Ideology and American Foreign Policy," 136–38.

105. Charles S. Campbell, *Anglo-American Understanding*, 9.

106. Stuart Anderson, *Race and Rapprochement*, 26–61. It is important to understand that while expressions of nationalist sentiment were frequently couched in terms of race, the concept of race was not a narrow biological one based purely upon ethnic origins or physical characteristics. Rather, notions of race were grounded in a much broader consideration of a whole range of cultural attributes as well.

107. Ibid., 95.

108. "American Dislike for England," *Spectator*, 25 January 1896, 128.

109. Waldstein, "The English-Speaking Brotherhood," 229.

110. Speech in Toronto, December 1887, quoted in Garvin, *The Life of Joseph Chamberlain*, 2:334.

111. Chamberlain to Olney, 29 September 1896, quoted in Garvin, *The Life of Joseph Chamberlain*, 3:168.

112. Quoted in Garvin, *The Life of Joseph Chamberlain*, 3:301–2.

113. Balfour to White, 12 December 1900, quoted in Judd, *Balfour and the British Empire*, 314.

114. Stuart Anderson, *Race and Rapprochement*, 91–94.

115. Statement of purpose of the Anglo-American League, 1898, quoted in Charles S. Campbell, *Anglo-American Understanding*, 46.

116. Quoted in Dennett, *John Hay*, 218.

117. Hay, *Addresses of John Hay*, 69.

118. Ibid., 78.

119. Mahan to Clarke, 5 November 1892, Mahan, *Letters and Papers*, 2:84.

120. Mahan to Thursfield, 10 January 1896, Mahan, *Letters and Papers*, 2:441–42.

121. Mahan to Sterling, 13 February 1896, Mahan, *Letters and Papers*, 2:445.

122. Olney to Chamberlain, 28 September 1896, quoted in Stuart Anderson, *Race and Rapprochement*, 105.

123. Olney to White, 8 May 1897, quoted in Stuart Anderson, *Race and Rapprochement*, 110.

124. Lodge to Hay, 21 April 1898, quoted in Stuart Anderson, *Race and Rapprochement*, 118.

125. Roosevelt to White, 30 March 1896, Roosevelt, *The Letters of Theodore Roosevelt*, 1:523.

126. Roosevelt to Lowell, 4 December 1897, Roosevelt, *The Letters of Theodore Roosevelt*, 1:724.

127. [Kerr], "Foreign Affairs," 26–27. Similarly, Archibald Hurd, in discussing the threat posed to Britain by the navies of the United States and Germany, argued, "The former may be dismissed. Americans are one with us in blood, language, and political ideals, but Germany constitutes a menace which the British naval authorities have been unable to ignore" ("Naval Concentration—and a Moral," 695).

128. "American Competition," *Saturday Review,* 8 June 1901, 730.

129. Stuart Anderson, *Race and Rapprochement,* 126. See also Seed, "British Reactions to American Imperialism," 254–72.

130. Edward Dicey, "The New American Imperialism," 501. For similar sentiments see Clowes, "American Expansion," 884–92.

131. Quoted in Blanche E. C. Dugdale, *Arthur James Balfour,* 1:164.

132. See Epilogue below.

133. May, *Imperial Democracy,* 267.

134. Stuart Anderson, *Race and Rapprochement,* 111.

135. Charles S. Campbell, *American Foreign Relations,* 221.

136. See House to Wilson, 30 July 1919, House, *The Intimate Papers,* 4:495; R. C. Wallhead, 14 March 1929, *Parliamentary Debates* (Commons), 5th ser., 226 (1929): 1404.

137. See chapter 3 for a discussion of the Anglo-German case.

138. On general Anglo-American relations of the interwar period see Allen, *Great Britain and the United States,* 724–80. On the subject of naval rivalry see Roskill, *Naval Policy between the Wars,* esp. 1:204–33, 433–66; Sprout and Sprout, *Toward a New Order of Sea Power,* esp. 66–144. The Washington Conference is examined in Buckley, *The United States and the Washington Conference,* while the London Conference is treated in O'Connor, *Perilous Equilibrium.* Useful accounts of these and the failed Geneva Conference of 1927 may also be found in Williams, *The United States and Disarmament,* 140–225; Tate, *The United States and Armaments,* 121–84.

139. J. W. Hills, 2 June 1930, *Parliamentary Debates* (Commons), 5th ser., 239 (1930): 1843.

140. Edward Denison, 11 February 1919, *Congressional Record,* 65th Cong., 3d sess., 57:3164.

141. 17 March 1920, *Parliamentary Debates* (Commons), 5th ser., 126 (1920): 2346.

142. 2 June 1930, *Parliamentary Debates* (Commons), 5th ser., 239 (1930): 1833.

143. In the United States, see *Nation,* 30 November 1918, 637, and speeches of various congressmen: George Huddleston, 4 February 1919; Edward Saunders, 6 February 1919; Gilbert Currie, 10 February 1919; *Congressional Record,* 65th Cong., 3d sess., 57:2717, 2824, 3085. In Britain, see speeches of G. Lambert, 15 May 1930; first lord of the Admiralty, A. V. Alexander, 15 May 1930; Noel Baker, 2 June 1930; *Parliamentary Debates* (Commons), 5th ser., 238 (1930): 2116, 2200, and *Parliamentary Debates* (Commons), 5th ser., 239 (1930): 1832. Of course, supporters of naval expansion vigorously denied these charges. See Lemuel Padgett, 6 February 1919, *Congressional Record,* 65th Cong., 3d sess., 57:2827; Winston Churchill, 15 May 1930, *Parliamentary Debates* (Commons), 5th ser., 238 (1930): 2104.

144. *New York Times,* 8 December 1918, sec. 3, 1.

145. *New York Times,* 11 December 1919, 12.

146. Roosevelt to Putnam, 5 December 1918, quoted in *New York Times,* 11 December 1918, 14.

147. Quoted in *Literary Digest,* 4 January 1919, 10–11.

148. Quoted in *Literary Digest,* 11 March 1922, 39.

149. 11 February 1919, *Congressional Record,* 65th Cong., 3d sess., 57:3159.

150. Ibid., 3165.

151. 15 May 1930, *Parliamentary Debates* (Commons), 5th ser., 238 (1930): 2104.

152. *Times* (London), 18 March 1921, 11.

153. 17 March 1921, *Parliamentary Debates* (Commons), 5th ser., 139 (1921): 1788, 1794–95.

154. 17 March 1920, *Parliamentary Debates* (Commons), 5th ser., 126 (1920): 2335–36.

155. It may be instructive, in this regard, that in 1935 at a second naval conference in London both the United States and Great Britain rejected Japanese demands for an agreement that would have granted Japan naval parity with the Anglo-Saxon powers.

156. Speech of 16 March 1921; quoted in *Times* (London), 18 March 1921, 14.

157. Speech of 26 January 1929; quoted in *Times* (London), 28 January 1929, 7.

158. Hurd, "The British Fleet," 402.

159. This conclusion is also reached by Rosecrance in "International Theory Revisited," 708.

Chapter 3

1. The definitive work on Anglo-German relations in the years before 1914 is Kennedy, *Anglo-German Antagonism*. Exhaustively researched and comprehensive in scope, this volume is a masterful combination of narrative and interpretive history.

2. In both its magnitude and its purpose, this accord strongly resembled the Anglo-French agreements of 1904 upon which the Entente Cordiale was based. See chapter 4.

3. Grey, *Twenty-Five Years*, 1:5, 8. Paul Kennedy has also noted that aggregate power relationships did not determine British policy. He writes: "[This] leads to one final observation about the British perception of the European balance of power throughout this whole period: namely, that it was *not merely* an automatically self-regulating instrument. While it took into account the shifts in industrial, population and military strength, it was also fundamentally concerned with the mannerisms and sometimes with the ideology of the countries concerned" (*Anglo-German Antagonism*, 431; emphasis in original).

4. The best history of the Anglo-German colonial rivalry is Gifford and Louis, *Britain and Germany in Africa*. See esp. Louis, "Great Britain and German Expansion," 3–46; Stengers, "British and German Imperial Rivalry," 337–47. For Asia and the Pacific, see Kennedy and Moses, *Germany in the Pacific and Far East*.

5. 12 March 1885, *Parliamentary Debates*, 3d ser., 295 (1885): 979.

6. A good account is Kennedy, *Anglo-German Antagonism*, chap. 10.

7. Kennedy, *Anglo-German Antagonism*, 214. See also Louis, "Great Britain and German Expansion," 20–22.

8. Carroll, *Germany and the Great Powers*, 363. See also Spring Rice to Villiers, 17 January and 21 March 1896, quoted in Louis, "Great Britain and German Expansion," 25.

9. Louis, "Great Britain and German Expansion," 24.

10. See Butler, "The German Factor in Anglo-Transvaal Relations," 179–214.

11. Hale, *Publicity and Diplomacy*, 86–88.

12. Kennedy, "Anglo-German Relations," 56–72. See also Kennedy, *The Samoan Tangle*, 189–239.

13. Langhorne, "Anglo-German Negotiations," 365–67; Carroll, *Germany and the Great Powers*, 406–8.

14. See chapter 4.

15. 13 December 1911, quoted in Kennedy, *Anglo-German Antagonism*, 414.

16. Memo by Marschall, 17 April 1897, Germany, Auswärtiges Amt, *Die grosse Politik*, 13:15–16.

17. 1 October 1899, quoted in Kennedy, *Anglo-German Antagonism*, 312.

18. Hatzfeldt to Holstein, 4 June 1894, quoted in Rich, *Friedrich von Holstein*, 1:371.

19. 30 January 1896, quoted in Pauline Relyea Anderson, *Anti-English Feeling in Germany*, 242.

20. 28 August 1897, cited in Pauline Relyea Anderson, *Anti-English Feeling in Germany*, 189.

21. See Woodward, *Great Britain and the German Navy*; Padfield, *The Great Naval Race*. See also Kennedy, *British Naval Mastery*; Marder, *The Anatomy of British Sea Power*.

22. H. W. Wilson, "The Menace of the German Navy," 376; Woodward, *Great Britain and the German Navy*, 449–54.

23. H. W. Wilson, "The Menace of the German Navy," 377–78; Marder, *The Anatomy of British Sea Power*, 456.

24. Memorandum attached to the Second Navy Bill of 1900, quoted in Padfield, *The Great Naval Race*, 93.

25. Quoted in Berghahn, *Germany and the Approach of War*, 40.

26. In fact, there is evidence, and considerable logic, to suggest that Tirpitz had even grander plans and that his risk theory, which did not require a fleet as large as that of Great Britain, was nothing more than a public relations ploy aimed at concealing his true aim—naval superiority. See Kennedy, "Anglo-German Naval Race," 127–60.

27. Marder, *The Anatomy of British Sea Power*, 463.

28. Ibid., 464.

29. Memo by Selborne, "Naval Estimates 1903–1904," 17 October 1902, quoted in Monger, *The End of Isolation*, 82.

30. Kennedy, *Anglo-German Antagonism*, 255–56.

31. Marder, *The Anatomy of British Sea Power*, 465.

32. Monger, *The End of Isolation*, 175–76.

33. For an excellent description and explanation of this phenomenon see Steinberg, "The Copenhagen Complex," 23–46.

34. Kennedy, *Anglo-German Antagonism*, 422.

35. Mitchell, *European Historical Statistics*, 30, 383, 420.

36. Kennedy, *Anglo-German Antagonism*, 423.

37. Ibid., 278, 423–24. A second, and related, event was the bloody winter revolution, which exposed to an unprecedented extent the internal weakness of the tsarist regime.

38. Grey to Spring Rice, 19 February 1906, quoted in Monger, *The End of Isolation*, 281.

39. Seymour, *The Diplomatic Background of the War*, 155. The change in British strategic thinking after 1905 from an emphasis on "blue water" to concern over the continental balance has been admirably treated by Paul Kennedy in his essay, "Mahan *versus* Mackinder," 43–85. It is important to note that while the immediate focus of British strategy shifted, its larger objective—the maintenance of naval supremacy—did not. Indeed, as Kennedy makes clear, British fear of Ger-

man hegemony in Europe was grounded mainly in the belief that an unchallenged position would greatly improve Germany's ability to compete with Britain for command of the seas. Not until 1905, with the sudden and unexpected collapse of Russia, did this nightmare threaten to become a reality. Britain's response, to undertake a continental commitment, thus reflected a changed set of international conditions but was fundamentally a continuation of, rather than a departure from, her traditional policy. It was certainly consistent with her past actions, for under similar circumstances and for similar reasons she had adopted the same strategy during the Napoleonic era.

40. 1912, quoted in Kennedy, *Anglo-German Antagonism,* 428.

41. 11 July 1912, quoted in Kennedy, *Anglo-German Antagonism,* 428–29.

42. Quoted in Kennedy, *Anglo-German Antagonism,* 280.

43. Bertie to Mallet, 15 April 1907, quoted in Monger, *The End of Isolation,* 326.

44. Minute to dispatch from Goschen to Grey, 11 April 1910, Great Britain, Foreign Office, *British Documents,* 6:461. Some Germans understood Britain's dilemma in this regard. See Metternich to Bethmann-Hollweg, 5 November 1909, Germany, Auswärtiges Amt, *Die grosse Politik,* 28:266–67.

45. Monger, *The End of Isolation,* 301.

46. Ibid., 328–29.

47. A good account is Koch, "The Anglo-German Alliance Negotiations," 378–92. Koch concludes that the chances for an agreement were never very good.

48. For the texts of the draft treaties see Great Britain, Foreign Office, *British Documents,* 2:66–68. For the diplomatic record of the negotiations see Great Britain, Foreign Office, *British Documents,* 1:100–105, 2:60–88; and Germany, Auswärtiges Amt, *Die grosse Politik,* 14:193–255, 17:1–129.

49. For example, Holstein minuted on a dispatch from Hatzfeldt that an Anglo-German understanding could come about only when "1. Russia threatens Germany and 2. England acts less haughty than today" (dispatch of 26 April 1898, Germany, Auswärtiges Amt, *Die grosse Politik,* 14:227).

50. At his first meeting with Tirpitz and William, upon becoming foreign minister, Bülow admitted, "If we bind ourselves by treaty to England, this more or less means the renunciation of the implementation of our fleet plans, since they would be scarcely reconcilable with a really honest and trustworthy Anglo-German alliance" (quoted in Kennedy, "German World Policy," 610).

51. Memo by Salisbury, 29 May 1901, Great Britain, Foreign Office, *British Documents,* 2:68; emphasis in original.

52. See this chapter below.

53. Mitchell, *European Historical Statistics,* 510, 512, 514, 517, 547, 599–600.

54. Kennedy, *Anglo-German Antagonism,* 299–300.

55. Metternich to Bülow, 1 January 1909, Germany, Auswärtiges Amt, *Die grosse Politik,* 28:47.

56. Hoffman, *Great Britain and the German Trade Rivalry,* provides the most comprehensive account, though it considers the issue primarily from the British perspective.

57. Kennedy, *Anglo-German Antagonism,* 293–98.

58. Hoffman, *Great Britain and the German Trade Rivalry,* 109.

59. Ibid., 115–38.

60. *Parliamentary Papers,* 1897, 5–6.

61. Kennedy, *Anglo-German Antagonism,* 292.

62. H. W. W., "England and Germany," 650–64.

63. Ernest E. Williams, "Made in Germany," 14–28, 113–27, 253–68, 376–91, 492–506, 636–50.

64. "England and Germany," *Saturday Review,* 11 September 1897, 278.

65. This phrase, quoted by Hoffman, Hale, and Langer, among others, does not actually appear in the article itself.

66. Barker, "Emperor William II," 29–30. This comparison was, of course, implicit in the *Saturday Review* article as well.

67. "The Foreign Policy of Germany," 1017.

68. Rathgen, "Ueber den Plan eines britischen Reichszollvereins," 522.

69. Kennedy, *Anglo-German Antagonism,* 231.

70. Ballin to William, Spring 1910, quoted in Huldermann, *Albert Ballin,* 159–60.

71. 25 December 1897, quoted in Hale, *Publicity and Diplomacy,* 166.

72. Quoted in Steinberg, "The Copenhagen Complex," 27.

73. 29 March 1900, quoted in Bülow, *Memoirs of Prince von Bülow,* 1:479.

74. Minute to dispatch from Monts to Hohenlohe, 31 July 1897, Germany, Auswärtiges Amt, *Die grosse Politik,* 13:34.

75. Hoffman, *Great Britain and the German Trade Rivalry,* 284–85; Pauline Relyea Anderson, *Anti-English Feeling in Germany,* 283.

76. For this reason, nationalists in both countries were often, somewhat ironically, more concerned with the effects of commercial competition than were the economic interest groups most directly involved. See Kennedy, *Anglo-German Antagonism,* 314–16.

77. Quoted in Kennedy, *Anglo-German Antagonism,* 314.

78. Schulze-Gävernitz, "England and Germany—Peace or War?," 602.

79. Northcliffe to Wilson, 19 May 1909, quoted in Kennedy, *Anglo-German Antagonism,* 315.

80. Fitzgerald to Maxse, 18 November 1905, quoted in Kennedy, *Anglo-German Antagonism,* 314–15.

81. Speech to the Association of Chambers of Commerce of the United Kingdom, 13 March 1901, quoted in "The Defence of the Empire," 468. This article was a scathing criticism of such complacent attitudes.

82. Quoted in Kennedy, *Anglo-German Antagonism,* 316.

83. Metternich to Bülow, 1 January 1909, Germany, Auswärtiges Amt, *Die grosse Politik,* 28:47; Holstein, diary entry of 13 January 1909, *The Holstein Papers,* 1:159–60. Bülow quoted by Collins in the House of Commons, 20 March 1911, *Parliamentary Debates* (Commons), 5th ser., 23 (1911): 137.

84. Kennedy, *Anglo-German Antagonism,* 318–20.

85. As the failure of the tariff reform movement indicated, the Germans were not completely accurate in their assessment of the situation; the British ultimately decided that protection would do them more harm than good. But it was a very close call, and the Germans had every reason to be concerned.

86. Quoted by J. King, 13 March 1911, *Parliamentary Debates* (Commons), 5th ser., 22 (1911): 1901–2.

87. Quoted in Balfour, *The Kaiser and His Times,* 234. William's attitude toward England, which has been analyzed by many writers, was far from consistent and might best be described as one of "love-hate." Although he claimed to have strong feelings of friendship for England because of his blood relationship to her royal family, he was utterly unwilling to temper his ambitions for the sake of Anglo-

German amity and was, in fact, grievously offended by British requests that he do so.

88. Quoted in Kennedy, *Anglo-German Antagonism*, 386.

89. W. W. Barton, 14 December 1911, *Parliamentary Debates* (Commons), 5th ser., 32 (1911): 2628–29.

90. Stephen Collins, 20 March 1911, *Parliamentary Debates* (Commons), 5th ser., 23 (1911): 137.

91. W. P. Byles, 13 March 1911, *Parliamentary Debates* (Commons), 5th ser., 22 (1911): 1950.

92. *Times* (London), 1 December 1899, 9.

93. Lichnowsky, "Deutsch-englische Missverständnisse," 15–16.

94. Sarolea, *The Anglo-German Problem*, 11. Sarolea was, in fact, a native of Belgium, but the sentiments he expressed were held by many Britons as well.

95. "A Better Understanding with Germany," *Spectator*, 9 December 1905, 967.

96. See chapter 2.

97. Kennedy, *Anglo-German Antagonism*, chap. 4.

98. Ibid., 164.

99. Ibid., 397.

100. Arno J. Mayer argues that the landed classes in Britain continued to dominate British politics and society until World War I. See *The Persistence of the Old Regime*, 88–95. This, if true, was not recognized by most Germans.

101. Kehr, *Battleship Building*, 189–90; Kennedy, *Anglo-German Antagonism*, 349.

102. Pauline Relyea Anderson, *Anti-English Feeling in Germany*, 361.

103. Meinecke, *Geschichte des deutsch-englischen Bündnisproblems*, 234.

104. Kennedy, *Anglo-German Antagonism*, 153, 465.

Chapter 4

1. There exists no comprehensive history of Anglo-French relations. Important dates and events may be found in Langer, *An Encyclopedia of World History*.

2. A good history of the period after 1815 may be found in Rolo, *Entente Cordiale*, esp. 16–109.

3. On the Anglo-French colonial rivalry in Africa see Gifford and Louis, *France and Britain in Africa*, esp. the following chapters: Ramm, "Great Britain and France in Egypt," 73–119; Sanderson, "Anglo-French Confrontation at Fashoda," 285–331; Guillen, "The Entente of 1904," 333–68.

4. For an account see Rolo, *Entente Cordiale*, 28–91.

5. See Monson to Salisbury, 13 January 1899, Great Britain, Foreign Office, *British Documents*, 1:199.

6. Rolo, *Entente Cordiale*, 102–6. The London press was at the same time engaged in an equally bitter anti-French campaign in response to the unpopular verdict in the celebrated Dreyfus Case.

7. For a comprehensive treatment of the proposed intervention see Andrew, *Théophile Delcassé*, 158–79. British apprehensions were not unfounded; Delcassé was clearly interested in the project, but was unable to secure the cooperation of other European states, particularly Germany.

8. Cambon to d'Estournelles de Constant, 28 October 1899, Cambon, *Correspondance*, 2:30.

9. Cambon to Delcassé, 11 November 1899, France, Ministère des affaires étrangères, *Documents diplomatiques françaises, 1871-1914*, 1st ser., 15:514-17.

10. Guillen, "Les accords coloniaux," 316-17.

11. Cambon to Jules Cambon, 22 March 1900, Cambon, *Correspondance*, 2:41.

12. Lanessan, *Histoire de l'entente cordiale*, 209-11.

13. Ibid., 220-21.

14. *Times* (London), 27 November 1896, 9.

15. Quoted in Lanessan, *Histoire de l'entente cordiale*, 218-19.

16. Quoted by Earl Wemyss, 27 January 1902, *Parliamentary Debates*, 4th ser., 101 (1902): 912.

17. Cambon to Delcassé, 25 March 1903, Cambon, *Correspondance*, 2:91.

18. For an official British account of this visit see Monson to Lansdowne, 5 and 8 May 1903, Great Britain, Foreign Office, *British Documents*, 6:762-68.

19. Ponsonby, *Recollections of Three Reigns*, 170.

20. Rolo, *Entente Cordiale*, 166.

21. Quoted in *Times* (London), 22 December 1920, 12.

22. Rolo, *Entente Cordiale*, 177.

23. Cambon to Delcassé, 31 July 1903, France, Ministère des affaires étrangères, *Documents diplomatiques françaises*, 2d ser., 3:502-3.

24. 11 July 1903, quoted in Goudswaard, *Britain's "Splendid Isolation," 1898-1904*, 108.

25. See Lanessan, *Histoire de l'entente cordiale*, 248-53, for an account of this visit. Lanessan was a member of the visiting deputation.

26. For Barclay's own somewhat self-serving account see his *Thirty Years, Anglo-French Reminiscences*.

27. The text of the Arbitration Treaty, in French and English, is in *Archives diplomatiques* 89 (March 1904): 276-77.

28. *Parliamentary Debates*, 4th ser., 129 (1904): 14.

29. For a day-by-day account of the negotiations see Rolo, *Entente Cordiale*, 171-270.

30. The texts of the agreements, in both French and English, are in *Archives diplomatiques* 90 (April 1904): 413-36.

31. H. W. Wilson, "The Menace of the German Navy," 388.

32. Louis-Jaray, "L'accord entre la France et l'Angleterre," 607.

33. 6 December 1904, France, Assemblée nationale, *1871-1942*, Sénat, *Journal officiel de la République française*, 66:201.

34. Cited in *Times* (London), 11 April 1904, 3.

35. Doumer, "The Anglo-French Agreement," 560.

36. *Times* (London), 9 April 1904, 9.

37. Dillon, "Our Friends," 609-11.

38. 1 June 1904, *Parliamentary Debates*, 4th ser., 135 (1904): 562-63.

39. The collaborationist Vichy government of Philippe Pétain was, of course, hostile to Great Britain, and vice versa.

40. Marder, *The Anatomy of British Sea Power*, 469-72.

41. Hurd, "French Friendship and Naval Economy," 660.

42. Marder, *The Anatomy of British Sea Power*, 472. See also Hurd, "Naval Concentration—and a Moral," 694. In 1908, *Jane's Fighting Ships* wrote, "the decline of the French Navy is remarkable. A few years ago it occupied second place; it has now sunk to the fifth place" (429).

43. Delcassé to his wife, 22 October 1898, quoted in Andrew, *Théophile Delcassé*, 102. See also Renouvin, *La politique extérieure de Th. Delcassé*, 6–8.

44. As foreign minister, Hanotaux was actually pro-British—he opposed the Nile expedition because it would destroy any hope for an entente with England—but, weakened by domestic political events, especially the Dreyfus Affair, he felt unable to resist pressures for a forward colonial policy. See Brown, *Fashoda Reconsidered*, 27–32.

45. Andrew, *Théophile Delcassé*, 158–79. Delcassé's interest in this scheme is curious because most evidence suggests that by 1898, when he became foreign minister, he saw Germany as France's principal adversary and strongly favored an understanding with Great Britain. See Brown, *Fashoda Reconsidered*, 120–26.

46. Montebello to Delcassé, 15 March 1900, quoted in Andrew, *Théophile Delcassé*, 173.

47. Andrew, *Théophile Delcassé*, 173.

48. Eugene N. Anderson, *The First Moroccan Crisis*, 2–3.

49. Andrew, *Théophile Delcassé*, 186–87, 197.

50. Chailley-Bert to Delcassé, July 1903, quoted in Andrew, *Théophile Delcassé*, 211.

51. Andrew, *Théophile Delcassé*, 106–7, 180–200.

52. Renouvin, *La politique extérieure de Th. Delcassé*, 6–8. See also Andrew and Kanya-Forstner, "Gabriel Hanotaux," quoted below.

53. Rolo, *Entente Cordiale*, 23.

54. Andrew, *Théophile Delcassé*, 249–50.

55. Delcassé to Montebello, 28 May 1901, France, Ministère des affaires étrangères, *Documents diplomatiques françaises*, 2d ser., 1:298.

56. Paléologue, *The Turning Point*, 29.

57. Hurd, "French Friendship and Naval Economy," 659.

58. 3 April 1900, quoted in Stuart, *French Foreign Policy*, 43.

59. Lansdowne to Monson, 2 July 1903, Great Britain, Foreign Office, *British Documents*, 2:293.

60. Paléologue, *The Turning Point*, 25. See also Andrew, *Théophile Delcassé*, 228.

61. Lansdowne to Monson, 11 December 1903, Great Britain, Foreign Office, *British Documents*, 2:224.

62. See A. J. P. Taylor, *The Struggle for Mastery in Europe*, 412; Seaman, *From Vienna to Versailles*, 147; Eugene N. Anderson, *The First Moroccan Crisis*, 101.

63. Quoted in Brown, *Fashoda Reconsidered*, 123–24; emphasis in original.

64. Lansdowne to Cromer, 8 June 1903, quoted in Monger, *The End of Isolation*, 128; Cromer to Lansdowne, 29 May 1903, quoted in Monger, *The End of Isolation*, 128.

65. Cromer to Lansdowne, 14 March 1904, Great Britain, Foreign Office, *British Documents*, 2:355.

66. Lansdowne to Cromer, 17 November 1903, quoted in Monger, *The End of Isolation*, 145.

67. Monger, *The End of Isolation*, 159.

68. Kennedy, *Anglo-German Antagonism*, 251.

69. Cambon to Delcassé, 13 March 1903, France, Ministère des affaires étrangères, *Documents diplomatiques françaises*, 2d ser., 3:184.

70. "France and England," *Spectator*, 8 February 1902, 200.

71. Garvin, "The Revival of France," 795–96. This argument, somewhat ironically, suggests that Tirpitz's risk theory was valid; the British, however, seeing the Germans as the principal danger, were motivated to make concessions to France instead of to Germany.

72. Lee, *Europe's Crucial Years*, 79. For an example, see Garvin, "The Bankruptcy of Bismarckian Policy," 765–77.

73. Lee, *Europe's Crucial Years*, 64. See also Cambon to Delcassé, 22 January 1903, France, Ministère des affaires étrangères, *Documents diplomatiques françaises*, 2d ser., 3:47–48.

74. Hardinge to Bertie, 11 March 1904, quoted in Monger, *The End of Isolation*, 100.

75. Mallet to Bertie, 2 June 1904, quoted in Monger, *The End of Isolation*, 100.

76. Bertie to Mallet, 11 June 1904, quoted in Monger, *The End of Isolation*, 100–101.

77. Lee, *Europe's Crucial Years*, 64; Monger, *The End of Isolation*, 134–35.

78. Memo by Balfour, 30 November 1903, quoted in Monger, *The End of Isolation*, 95.

79. Memo by Balfour, 30 April 1903, quoted in Monger, *The End of Isolation*, 97.

80. Hamilton to Curzon, December 1899, quoted in Ronaldshay, *The Life of Lord Curzon*, 2:100.

81. Hamilton to Curzon, 8 April 1903, quoted in Monger, *The End of Isolation*, 109.

82. Monger, *The End of Isolation*, 7.

83. Ibid., 97.

84. Ibid., 110–11; memo by Chamberlain, 7 December 1903, quoted in Monger, *The End of Isolation*, 147.

85. Selborne to Curzon, 4 January 1903, quoted in Monger, *The End of Isolation*, 110.

86. Cromer to Balfour, 15 October 1903, quoted in Monger, *The End of Isolation*, 137.

87. Memo by Lansdowne, 10 September 1903, quoted in Monger, *The End of Isolation*, 133.

88. Balfour and Ritchie, the home secretary, did in fact see this outcome as likely and expressed their reservations to Lansdowne. However, in the end, they, like many of their colleagues, were unwilling to oppose the foreign secretary, and the treaty was made despite the fact that much of the cabinet had grave doubts about its wisdom. See Monger, *The End of Isolation*, 58–65.

89. Blanche E. C. Dugdale, *Arthur James Balfour*, 1:378.

90. Eugene N. Anderson, *The First Moroccan Crisis*, 83–84.

91. It might be argued that her difficulties in the Far East should have led Britain to seek an understanding with Germany rather than with France since this, too, could have restrained Russia or deterred France from entering a conflict. Indeed, Joseph Chamberlain's abortive alliance negotiations with Berlin from 1898 to 1901 reflected at least the former motivation. But this course of action was never a very realistic one. In the first place, Germany had no desire to pull Britain's chestnuts from the fire. She would have been more than happy to see her major adversaries, Britain, Russia, and France, embroiled with one another in the Far East. The kinds of concessions that Berlin would have required for her cooperation in such an effort would have been virtually impossible for London to make. In addition,

by 1902 or so, the growth of the German navy, German economic competition, distaste for the German political system, and a profound distrust of German diplomacy had rendered British opinion strongly opposed to even the hint of collaboration with Berlin. An arrangement with Germany, the primary enemy, was widely held to be neither possible nor desirable, and not merely among the general population but within the government as well. See chapter 3.

92. Similarly, one cannot say how far the French would have been willing to go had the British been less compliant.

93. Mitchell, *European Historical Statistics,* 510, 512, 514, 517, 543–45, 599–600.

94. For a listing of the major commodities traded between England and France see *Economist,* 28 January 1899, 117.

95. Mathews, "Anglo-French Entente of 1904," 47–48.

96. For a fairly complete list of the organizations declaring themselves in favor of the Arbitration Treaty see Barclay, *Thirty Years, Anglo-French Reminiscences,* 346–53.

97. Renouvin, *La politique extérieure de Th. Delcassé,* 34–35.

98. Quoted in *Times* (London), 10 March 1903, 5.

99. Leroy-Beaulieu, "Les relations économiques," 815.

100. Garvin, "The Revival of France," 800.

101. "France, Germany, and England," *Spectator,* 23 August 1902, 244. The contrast between France and Germany in this regard was, of course, obvious, whether it was explicitly stated or not.

102. Cambon to Delcassé, 13 March 1903, France, Ministère des affaires étrangères, *Documents diplomatiques françaises,* 2d ser., 3:185.

103. 7 December 1904, France, Assemblée nationale, 1871–1942, Sénat, *Journal officiel de la République française,* 66:209.

104. See, for example, the speeches of d'Aunay, 6 December 1904, France, Assemblée nationale, 1871–1942, Sénat, *Journal officiel de la République française,* 66:201; and Vigoroux, 7 November 1904, France, Assemblée nationale, 1871–1942, Chambre des députés, *Journal officiel de la République française,* 74:309.

105. Monson to Lansdowne, 20 January 1902, Great Britain, Foreign Office, *British Documents,* 2:261.

106. 2 February 1904, *Parliamentary Debates,* 4th ser., 129 (1904): 7.

107. 1 June 1904, *Parliamentary Debates,* 4th ser., 135 (1904): 563.

108. Paléologue, *The Turning Point,* 20. See also Viner, "International Finance," 410–17; Harry D. White, *The French International Accounts,* 106, 269; Feis, *Europe, The World's Banker,* 47, 51.

109. Bülow to Alvensleben, 13 May 1903, Germany, Auswärtiges Amt, *Die grosse Politik,* 17:570. Although Lansdowne favored pressuring Japan into a negotiated settlement, he was opposed by others in the cabinet, and the British refused to restrain Japan as she proceeded to overrun Russia in the war that followed. See Monger, *The End of Isolation,* 184–85.

110. Eckardstein to Bülow, 10 May 1903, Germany, Auswärtiges Amt, *Die grosse Politik,* 17:568–70. See also Hallgarten, *Imperialismus vor 1914,* 1:470–71. Hallgarten asserts that French high finance planted in Delcassé's mind the idea of a rapprochement, but there is little or no evidence for this.

111. Lee, *Europe's Crucial Years,* 62; Viner, "International Finance," 416–17.

112. Leroy-Beaulieu, "Les relations économiques," 814–15. See also "La fortune

française a l'étranger," 450–83. This was probably the study to which Leroy-Beau-lieu refers.

113. See, for example, Leroy-Beaulieu, "Les relations économiques," 815.

114. *Economist*, 21 May 1904, 858.

115. Bloomfield, *Short-Term Capital Movements*, 67. In contrast, British hold-ings of French securities, both long-term and short-term, were insignificant. See Feis, *Europe, The World's Banker*, 23.

116. Cambon to Henri Cambon, 5 February 1904, Cambon, *Correspondance*, 2:119; Cambon to Henri Cambon, 19 February 1904, Cambon, *Correspondance*, 2:124.

117. Harry D. White, *The French International Accounts*, 195.

118. One might say, therefore, that the economic connections between England and France served as a motivating factor for the business classes and as a facilitat-ing factor for the governments of the two countries.

119. Matthew, *The Liberal Imperialists*, 210–11.

120. Quoted in Matthew, *The Liberal Imperialists*, 211.

121. "An Understanding with France," *Spectator*, 5 December 1903, 962.

122. "The Duration of the 'Entente Cordiale,'" *Spectator*, 12 August 1905, 213.

123. Quoted in *Times* (London), 10 July 1903, 3.

124. Quoted in Stuart, *French Foreign Policy*, 116.

125. 6 December 1904, France, Assemblée nationale, 1871–1942, Sénat, *Journal officiel de la République française*, 66:201.

126. Andrew and Kanya-Forstner, "Gabriel Hanotaux," 93; emphasis added.

127. Lebow, *Between Peace and War*, 72.

128. On the competition between the Colonial Ministry and the Foreign Minis-try for control of French foreign policy see Brown, *Fashoda Reconsidered*.

129. Lebow, *Between Peace and War*, 328.

130. It is ironic that Delcassé, who sought and concluded the Entente Cordiale, had been colonial minister from 1894–95 and an ardent colonialist. However, by 1898, when he took the helm at the Foreign Ministry, he had adopted a much more continentalist perspective. The reason for this change in attitude has never been satisfactorily explained. See Brown, *Fashoda Reconsidered*, 120–26.

131. See chapter 2.

132. Others have credited the Fashoda Crisis with facilitating the Anglo-French rapprochement. In addition to Lebow, see Lockhart, "Conflict Actions and Out-comes," 572–75.

Chapter 5

1. See Herwig, *Politics of Frustration*, 40–109; Turk, "Defending the New Empire," 188–89. See also Vagts, "Hopes and Fears," 54:514–35 and 55:53–76.

2. The classic work on German-American relations during the years preceding the First World War is Vagts, *Deutschland und die Vereinigten Staaten*. Also especially useful are Keim, *German-American Political Relations*; Small, "The American Image of Germany."

3. For a good treatment of the Samoan problem, see Kennedy, *The Samoan Tangle*. See also Keim, *German-American Political Relations*, 112–215; Vagts, *Deutschland und die Vereinigten Staaten*, 1:636–938.

4. See Jonas, *The United States and Germany,* 46.

5. Herwig, *Politics of Frustration,* 15. See also Keim, *German-American Political Relations,* 189–91; Vagts, *Deutschland und die Vereinigten Staaten,* 1:649.

6. 30 January 1889, *Congressional Record,* 50th Cong., 2d sess., 20:1337.

7. Herwig, *Politics of Frustration,* 17.

8. *New York World,* 31 March 1889, 4.

9. Herwig, *Politics of Frustration,* 25.

10. Quoted in Herwig, *Politics of Frustration,* 25.

11. Bülow to Hatzfeldt, 8 June 1898, Germany, Auswärtiges Amt, *Die grosse Politik,* 14:259–61.

12. Quoted in Herwig, *Politics of Frustration,* 26.

13. Herwig, *Politics of Frustration,* 27, 29–30.

14. Quoted in Vagts, *Deutschland und die Vereinigten Staaten,* 2:1423; emphasis in original.

15. Memo by Richthofen, 10 July 1898, Germany, Auswärtiges Amt, *Die grosse Politik,* 15:54–59. See also Herwig, *Politics of Frustration,* 32.

16. Kennedy, *The Samoan Tangle,* 140.

17. Herwig, *Politics of Frustration,* 26.

18. Ibid., 29.

19. Kennedy, *The Samoan Tangle,* 139.

20. Quoted in Herwig, *Politics of Frustration,* 31. See also Keim, *German-American Political Relations,* 216–43.

21. Keim, *German-American Political Relations,* 230–31; Shippee, "Germany and the Spanish-American War," 774, 774–75n. Herwig notes that, in fact, the crisis occurred while Bülow, Tirpitz, and William were all on vacation (Herwig, *Politics of Frustration,* 29).

22. 18 September 1898, quoted in Herwig, *Politics of Frustration,* 33.

23. 25 November 1898, quoted in Herwig, *Politics of Frustration,* 34.

24. 5 October 1898, quoted in Herwig, *Politics of Frustration,* 33–34.

25. Kennedy, *The Samoan Tangle,* 189–239; Kennedy, "Anglo-German Relations."

26. Quoted in Kennedy, *The Samoan Tangle,* 144.

27. Quoted in Schierbrand, *Germany,* 352.

28. 24 October 1897, quoted in Vagts, *Deutschland und die Vereinigten Staaten,* 2:1706.

29. Quoted in Baum, "German Political Designs," 588.

30. Note on dispatch from German envoy in Mexico, 19 January 1900, quoted in Vagts, *Deutschland und die Vereinigten Staaten,* 2:1476n; emphasis in original.

31. Holleben to German Foreign Office, 31 August 1898, Germany, Auswärtiges Amt, *Die grosse Politik,* 15:109–10.

32. 18 November 1901, quoted in Vagts, *Deutschland und die Vereinigten Staaten,* 2:1537.

33. Sternberg, "The Phantom Peril," 641–50. In 1903, upon his arrival in the United States to take up his duties as ambassador, Sternberg had informed his hosts, "The Emperor understands the Monroe Doctrine thoroughly. . . . He would no more think of violating that doctrine than he would of colonizing the moon" (*New York Herald,* 31 January 1903, quoted in Jonas, *The United States and Germany,* 73).

34. Memo by de Kay, 1 February 1896, quoted in Vagts, *Deutschland und die Vereinigten Staaten,* 1:619.

35. Roosevelt to Moore, 5 February 1898, Roosevelt, *The Letters of Theodore Roosevelt*, 1:769.

36. Sprout and Sprout, *American Naval Power*, 253.

37. Stuart Anderson, *Race and Rapprochement*, 67.

38. *Harper's Weekly*, 3 January 1903, 16, and 11 July 1903, 1141.

39. U.S. Navy, General Board, report to the secretary of the navy, 1906, quoted in Charles Carlisle Taylor, *The Life of Admiral Mahan*, 150–51.

40. Herbert to Lansdowne, 29 December 1902, Great Britain, Foreign Office, *British Documents*, 2:164.

41. Roosevelt to Spring Rice, 1 November 1905, Spring Rice, *The Letters and Friendships*, 2:10.

42. Quoted in Small, "The American Image of Germany," 141.

43. Jackson to Knox, 20 March 1911, quoted in Small, "The American Image of Germany," 142.

44. 2 February 1889, *Congressional Record*, 50th Cong., 2d sess., 20:1441.

45. Roosevelt to Spring Rice, 13 August 1897, Roosevelt, *The Letters of Theodore Roosevelt*, 1:645.

46. Herwig, *Politics of Frustration*, 33.

47. July 1898, quoted in Vagts, *Deutschland und die Vereinigten Staaten*, 2:1374n.

48. Cartwright to Grey, 20 August 1906, Great Britain, Foreign Office, *British Documents*, 3:371–72.

49. Vagts, *Deutschland und die Vereinigten Staaten*, 2:1914–2019.

50. Bureau of the Census, *Historical Statistics*, 550–53; Mitchell, *European Historical Statistics*, 510, 514, 547.

51. Frank H. Mason, U.S. consul-general in Frankfurt, report of 8 February 1893, Department of State, *Consular Reports*, 42 (1893): 103–4; Oscar Gottschalk, consular agent in Markneukirchen, report of 20 March 1895, Department of State, *Consular Reports*, 48 (1895): 513–14; Julius Goldschmidt, U.S. consul-general in Berlin, report of 24 December 1897, Department of State, *Commercial Relations of the United States*, 1897, 325; *Parliamentary Papers*, 1909, 178. Both *Consular Reports* and *Commercial Relations of the United States* were published by the Department of Commerce and Labor beginning in 1903.

52. *Parliamentary Papers*, 1909, 206.

53. Pauline Relyea Anderson, *Anti-English Feeling in Germany*, 153–54.

54. See Simon W. Hanauer, U.S. vice-consul-general in Frankfurt, report of 14 July 1899, Department of State, *Consular Reports*, 61 (1899): 202.

55. James H. Smith, U.S. commercial agent in Mainz, report of 23 June 1891, Department of State, *Consular Reports*, 36 (1891): 637.

56. A good account is Keim, *German-American Political Relations*, 64–111. See also Vagts, *Deutschland und die Vereinigten Staaten*, 1:1–425.

57. It should be noted that each of these restrictions was eventually eased or lifted entirely, but not before causing considerable ill feeling.

58. Keim, *German-American Political Relations*, 64–111; Vagts, *Deutschland und die Vereinigten Staaten*, 1:1–344.

59. The American tariff laws (see above) did place heavy duties on manufactured goods, which angered German producers attempting to gain a share of the American market.

60. J. C. Monaghan, U.S. consul in Chemnitz, report of 1 November 1898, Department of State, *Consular Reports*, 59 (1899): 257.

61. Frank H. Mason, U.S. consul-general in Berlin, report of 2 October 1901, Department of State, *Consular Reports*, 68 (1902): 64.

62. Vagts, *Deutschland und die Vereinigten Staaten*, 1:349.

63. Department of State, *Commercial Relations of the United States*, 1904, xx–xxi.

64. Small, "The American Image of Germany," 221–35.

65. Andrew Dickson White, *The Autobiography*, 2:144.

66. William D. Warner, U.S. consul in Cologne, report of 27 December 1895, Department of State, *Consular Reports*, 51 (1896): 163.

67. Frank H. Mason, U.S. consul-general in Berlin, report of 20 September 1899, Department of State, *Commercial Relations of the United States*, 1899, 2:244–45.

68. Charles Neuer, U.S. consular agent in Gera, report of 22 December 1903, Department of State, *Consular Reports*, 75 (1904): 64–65.

69. 24 May 1902, quoted in Deicke, "Das Amerikabild," 90.

70. Karl Bünz, German consul-general in New York, report of 6 June 1904, quoted in Vagts, *Deutschland und die Vereinigten Staaten*, 1:379.

71. Vagts, *Deutschland und die Vereinigten Staaten*, 1:391.

72. Ibid., 1:357–58; Pauline Relyea Anderson, *Anti-English Feeling in Germany*, 363; Deicke, "Das Amerikabild," 86–87.

73. May, *Imperial Democracy*, 187.

74. Memo by Halle, 1 August 1901, quoted in Vagts, *Deutschland und die Vereinigten Staaten*, 1:360. Halle was a prominent professor at the University of Marburg who served as Tirpitz's economic advisor.

75. Extracts from the book contained in Simon Hanauer, U.S. vice-consul-general in Frankfurt, report of 13 October 1900, Department of State, *Consular Reports*, 65 (1901): 69.

76. Small, "The American Image of Germany," 217.

77. Holleben to German Foreign Office, 1 January 1898, quoted in Vagts, *Deutschland und die Vereinigten Staaten*, 1:149.

78. Margerie to Delcassé, 19 November 1901, France, Ministère des affaires étrangères, *Documents diplomatiques français*, 2d ser., 1:610.

79. Bingham, *The Monroe Doctrine*, 99.

80. Quoted in Schilling, "Admirals and Foreign Policy," 17. See also Herwig, *Politics of Frustration*, 98–109.

81. Holleben to German Foreign Office, 1 January 1898, quoted in Vagts, *Deutschland und die Vereinigten Staaten*, 1:149.

82. Vagts, *Deutschland und die Vereinigten Staaten*, 1:149.

83. Holleben to Hohenlohe, 6 December 1899, quoted in Herwig, *Politics of Frustration*, 39.

84. Herwig, *Politics of Frustration*, 19.

85. For German-American financial relations see Vagts, *Deutschland und die Vereinigten Staaten*, 1:426–81.

86. Vagts, *Deutschland und die Vereinigten Staaten*, 1:466–67; Deicke, "Das Amerikabild," 85.

87. Bacon, "American International Indebtedness," 270–71.

88. Vagts, *Deutschland und die Vereinigten Staaten*, 1:462–63.

89. Christof, "Deutsch-Amerikanische Entfremdung," 23.

90. Charles de Kay, report of 27 January 1896, quoted in Vagts, *Deutschland und die Vereinigten Staaten,* 1:617. See also Jackson to Hay, 12 March 1902, quoted in Vagts, *Deutschland und die Vereinigten Staaten,* 2:1939.

91. Fraenkel, *Amerika im Spiegel des deutschen politischen Denkens,* 36–37n.

92. Fraenkel, *Amerika im Spiegel des deutschen politischen Denkens,* 33–34; Deicke, "Das Amerikabild," 73–74.

93. Fraenkel, *Amerika im Spiegel des deutschen politischen Denkens,* 34.

94. Münsterberg, *Die Amerikaner,* 1:8; Christof, "Deutsch-Amerikanische Entfremdung," 22.

95. Keim, *German-American Political Relations,* 29–35.

96. 7 February 1871, quoted in Keim, *German-American Political Relations,* 32–33n.

97. Schieber, *The Transformation of American Sentiment,* cites a number of examples; see esp. 213–37.

98. Davidson, "The Imperialization of Germany," 247.

99. Petersen, "The New Era in Germany," 110.

100. *New York World,* 4 August 1914, 8.

101. *New York Times,* 5 August 1914, 12.

102. *New York World,* 5 August 1914, 8.

103. House to Wilson, 3 February 1916, quoted in Levin, *Woodrow Wilson and World Politics,* 39.

104. See memo by Lansing, September 1916, quoted in Sondermann, "The Wilson Administration's Image of Germany," 319.

105. Memo by Lansing, 11 July 1915, quoted in Smith, *Robert Lansing and American Neutrality,* 60.

106. Gatzke, "The United States and Germany," 283.

107. Faust, *The German Element,* 2:27.

108. Small, "The American Image of Germany," 123.

109. Quoted in Gatzke, *Germany and the United States,* 38.

110. Flynt, "The German and the German-American," 655. See also Vagts, *Deutschland und die Vereinigten Staaten,* 1:600.

111. Charles de Kay, 7 May 1896, quoted in Vagts, *Deutschland und die Vereinigten Staaten,* 1:579.

112. See Stolberg-Wernigerode, *Germany and the United States,* 179–80.

113. Glazer, "America's Ethnic Pattern," 403; emphasis in original. A contemporary observer noted in 1898 that to Americans of German as well as of English origin, Great Britain was the "Old Country" (Waldstein, "The English-Speaking Brotherhood," 230).

114. 23 February 1884, quoted in Stolberg-Wernigerode, *Germany and the United States,* 163.

115. 21 February 1884, quoted in Stolberg-Wernigerode, *Germany and the United States,* 163.

Chapter 6

1. In the jargon of the social sciences, which I have tried generally to avoid, I employ three independent variables: exercise of power, economic activities, and

societal attributes, plus one intervening variable, catalytic crisis. These account for variation along the dependent variable, states' relationships with one another.

2. Table 5 is a summary of tables 1–4, found in the preceding four chapters and based on the evidence presented in each. The pairs of countries involved in the "positive" cases were characterized by higher levels of heterogeneity in the exercise of power and in their economic activities and by greater homogeneity of societal attributes than were the pairs involved in the "negative" cases. It should be noted, however, that this would not have to be true. In the framework presented in this study, relations between states are determined not by a single factor, but by three combined elements. Because of this, two states achieving a reconciliation could conceivably score lower on one, or even two, dimensions than two states not achieving a reconciliation, provided that their score on the other(s) was sufficiently higher. This would not mean, as the logic of elimination might seem to suggest, that these dimensions were irrelevant to the outcome, or that their causality was reversed (e.g., heterogeneity of societal attributes is conducive to peace). Nevertheless, the possibility of such an interpretation illustrates one of the shortcomings of the comparative method discussed in the first chapter. When analyzing a small number of cases, it is difficult, if not impossible, to deal adequately with varying degrees of (multiple) explanatory factors, as well as with their cumulative and interactive effects, using the logic of elimination alone.

3. A good account of Soviet-American relations through the 1960s can be found in Louis J. Halle, *The Cold War as History* (New York: Harper & Row, 1967). Another excellent volume is Thomas B. Larson, *Soviet-American Rivalry* (New York: W. W. Norton & Co., 1978), which analyzes separately the military, economic, and ideological aspects of the competition between the two countries.

4. The effect of the use of proxy states, a relatively recent development in international politics, is difficult to gauge. On the one hand, it may lessen the impact of particular conflicts, since the superpowers are only indirectly involved. On the other hand, it probably increases the range of geopolitical competition, since the United States and USSR can exert influence in areas where they might be unwilling to play a direct role.

5. In 1971, for example, Soviet Defense Minister Grechko stated that "imperialism has always sought and will continue to seek to crush socialism by force of arms, to change the balance of forces in its favor and to recover its lost positions" ("The Homeland's Invincible Shield," *Pravda*, 23 February 1971, quoted in *Current Digest of the Soviet Press*, 23 March 1971, 4).

6. As Robert Daniels argues, "An American hearing the Marxian *prediction* [of the triumph of socialism] can only understand it as a statement of *intent*, of intent, furthermore, that is going to be acted upon" ("What the Russians Mean," *Commentary* 34 [October 1962]: 322; emphasis in original).

7. See Caldwell, "The Future of Soviet-American Relations," 22–23, for a brief description of the nonideological aspects of Soviet-American societal/cultural alienation.

8. United Nations, Department of International Economic and Social Affairs, *1982 Yearbook of International Trade Statistics*, 1:1023, 1049.

9. Examples are the Jackson-Vanik Amendment to the Trade Reform Act of 1974, which required the Soviet Union to ease restrictions on emigration in order to

obtain most-favored-nation status, and the grain embargo imposed by the Carter administration following the Soviet invasion of Afghanistan in December 1979.

10. See Caldwell, "The Future of Soviet-American Relations," esp. 52–61, 111–18. See also Christopher E. Stowell, *Soviet Industrial Import Priorities, with Marketing Considerations for Exporting to the USSR*, Praeger Special Studies in International Economics and Development (New York: Praeger, 1975); Marshall I. Goldman, *Détente and Dollars: Doing Business with the Soviets* (New York: Basic Books, 1975). These last two volumes were published during the era of détente, a period when prospects for Soviet-American economic cooperation seemed particularly bright.

11. The crisis did, of course, lead to some modest improvement in Soviet-American relations during the mid-1960s. See Lebow, *Between Peace and War*, 326–33.

12. This occurrence might not be desirable, of course. If the improvement in relations between the Soviet Union and the United States were more than offset by the deterioration in Sino-Soviet and Sino-American relations, the net level of conflict in the international system might actually increase and the world be more dangerous than it is now.

13. See Marshall I. Goldman, "The Shifting Balance of World Power," *Technology Review* 90 (April 1987): 20–21.

14. Goldman writes, "It is the Soviet Union that faces the biggest threat to its economic and political standing. Unless Gorbachev prompts an economic and social revolution, the Soviet Union will find itself contending for power and influence not only with the United States but also with Japan and conceivably China as well. Despite its wealth of raw materials and vast population, I prophesy that the Soviet Union will become a second-rate military power by the next century" ("The Shifting Balance of World Power," *Technology Review* 90 [April 1987]: 20–21).

15. There exists, of course, the unpleasant possibility that economic or other domestic problems in the United States and USSR would make the two countries more aggressive internationally, in order to forestall a feared deterioration in their global positions.

16. See Harvey Wheeler, "The Role of Myth Systems in American-Soviet Relations," *Journal of Conflict Resolution* 4 (June 1960): 179–84, for a discussion of this problem.

17. Whether this represents a lasting change in Chinese politics, or is only a temporary and reversible phenomenon, is still open to debate.

18. On this issue, see Mandelbaum, *The Nuclear Revolution*.

19. On this subject, see Lebow, *Nuclear Crisis Management*.

20. There are other examples of this phenomenon: the Chinese decision to enter the Korean War against the United States and the Egyptian assault on Israel in 1973. Of course, the case of a nonnuclear state challenging a nuclear state is almost certainly characterized by different dynamics than a case involving two nuclear states. In particular, a nonnuclear state may feel confident that a nuclear state will not employ its nuclear capabilities because such use would be grossly disproportionate, provoking widespread outrage both domestically and internationally. Moreover, the specter of a globally catastrophic nuclear conflagration would not haunt decision makers in such instances.

21. It should be noted that ideological/cultural relations reflecting societal attributes are also open to some influence. For example, Bismarck's anti-British

campaign contributed greatly to the ideological animosity felt toward Britain by many of the German people. See chapter 3.

22. It is even more difficult to see how British or American leaders could have made concessions to Germany on these matters since national security was so clearly at stake and public opinion was so unified.

23. See the discussion of "environmental possibilism," "probabilism," and "determinism" in Sprout and Sprout, *The Ecological Perspective.*

24. One place where this may be most true is at a point of crisis, when the quality of statesmanship may determine whether the crisis will lead to a further deterioration of relations or will serve as a positive catalyst, enhancing the prospects for peace.

Bibliography

International Relations Theory and the Comparative Method

Angell, Robert C. *Peace on the March: Transnational Participation*. New Perspectives in Political Science, 19. New York: Van Nostrand Reinhold Co., 1969.

Aron, Raymond. *Peace and War: A Theory of International Relations*. Translated by Richard Howard and Annette Baker Fox. Garden City, N.Y.: Doubleday & Co., 1966.

Baldwin, David A. "Power Analysis and World Politics: New Trends versus Old Tendencies." *World Politics* 31 (January 1979): 161-94.

——. "Interdependence and Power: A Conceptual Analysis." *International Organization* 34 (Autumn 1980): 471-506.

Boulding, Kenneth E. *Conflict and Defense: A General Theory*. A publication of the Center for Research in Conflict Resolution at the University of Michigan. New York: Harper & Bros., 1962.

——. *Stable Peace*. Austin: University of Texas Press, 1978.

Brinton, Clarence Crane. *From Many One: The Process of Political Integration, The Problem of World Government*. Cambridge: Harvard University Press, 1948.

Bull, Hedley. *The Anarchical Society: A Study of Order in World Politics*. New York: Columbia University Press, 1977.

Burke, Edmund. "First Letter on a Regicide Peace." In *The Works of the Right Honorable Edmund Burke*, 5:233-341. Rev. ed. 12 vols. Boston: Little, Brown & Co., 1866-67.

Butterfield, Herbert, and Wight, Martin, eds. *Diplomatic Investigations: Essays in the Theory of International Politics*. Cambridge: Harvard University Press, 1966.

Carr, E. H. *The Twenty Years' Crisis, 1919-1939: An Introduction to the Study of International Relations*. London: Macmillan & Co., 1941.

Caves, Richard E., and Jones, Ronald W. *World Trade and Payments: An Introduction*. 3d ed. Boston: Little, Brown & Co., 1981.

Claude, Inis L., Jr. *Power and International Relations*. New York: Random House, 1962.

Cobb, Roger W., and Elder, Charles. *International Community: A Regional and Global Study*. New York: Holt, Rinehart & Winston, 1970.

Cohen, Benjamin J. *The Question of Imperialism: The Political Economy of Dominance and Dependence*. New York: Basic Books, 1973.

Craig, Gordon A., and George, Alexander L. *Force and Statecraft: Diplomatic Problems of Our Time*. New York: Oxford University Press, 1983.

Deutsch, Karl W. *Political Community at the International Level: Prob-

lems of Definition and Measurement. Garden City, N.Y.: Doubleday & Co., 1954.

———. *Tides among Nations.* New York: Free Press, 1979.

Deutsch, Karl W.; Burrell, Sidney A.; Kann, Robert A.; Lee, Maurice, Jr.; Lichterman, Martin; Lindgren, Raymond E.; Loewenheim, Francis L.; and Van Wagenen, Richard W. *Political Community and the North Atlantic Area: International Organization in the Light of Historical Experience.* A publication of the Center for Research on World Political Institutions at Princeton University. Princeton: Princeton University Press, 1957.

Doyle, Michael W. "Kant, Liberal Legacies, and Foreign Affairs." *Philosophy and Public Affairs* 12 (Summer, Fall 1983): 205-35, 323-53.

George, Alexander L. "Case Studies and Theory Development: The Method of Structured, Focused Comparison." In *Diplomacy: New Approaches in History, Theory, and Policy,* edited by Paul Gordon Lauren, 43-68. New York: Free Press, 1979.

———. "Case Studies and Theory Development." Paper presented at the Second Annual Symposium on Information Processing in Organizations, Carnegie-Mellon University, Pittsburgh, 15-16 October 1982.

Gilpin, Robert. *War and Change in World Politics.* Cambridge: Cambridge University Press, 1981.

Gulick, Edward Vose. *Europe's Classical Balance of Power: A Case History of the Theory and Practice of One of the Great Concepts of European Statecraft.* Ithaca: Cornell University Press for the American Historical Association, 1955.

Haas, Ernst B. "The Balance of Power: Prescription, Concept, or Propaganda?" *World Politics* 5 (July 1953): 442-77.

———. "The Challenge of Regionalism." *International Organization* 12 (Autumn 1958): 440-58.

Hardy, Thomas. *The Dynasts: A Drama of the Napoleonic Wars, in Three Parts, Nineteen Acts, and One Hundred and Thirty Scenes.* New York: Macmillan Co., 1936.

Hartmann, Frederick H. *The Conservation of Enemies: A Study in Enmity.* Westport, Conn.: Greenwood Press, 1982.

Hinsley, F. H. *Power and the Pursuit of Peace: Theory and Practice in the History of Relations between States.* Cambridge: Cambridge University Press, 1963.

Hobbes, Thomas. *Leviathan.* Edited by Herbert W. Schneider. Indianapolis: Bobbs-Merrill Publishing Co., 1958.

Hobson, J. A. *Imperialism: A Study.* New York: James Pott & Co., 1902.

Janis, Irving L., and Mann, Leon. *Decision-Making: A Psychological Analysis of Conflict, Choice, and Commitment.* New York: Free Press, 1977.

Jervis, Robert. *Perception and Misperception in International Politics.* Princeton: Princeton University Press, 1976.

Johnson, L. Gunnar. *Conflicting Concepts of Peace in Contemporary*

Peace Studies. Sage Professional Paper in International Studies, vol. 4, no. 02–001. Beverly Hills: Sage Publications, 1976.

Kaplan, Morton A. *System and Process in International Politics.* New York: John Wiley & Sons, 1957.

Kelman, Herbert C. "International Interchanges: Some Contributions from Theories of Attitude Change." In *Analyzing International Relations: A Multimethod Introduction,* edited by William D. Coplin and Charles W. Kegley, Jr., 205–18. New York: Praeger, 1975.

Keohane, Robert O., and Nye, Joseph S., Jr. "International Interdependence and Integration." In *Handbook of Political Science.* Vol. 8, *International Politics,* edited by Fred I. Greenstein and Nelson W. Polsby, 363–414. Reading, Mass.: Addison-Wesley Publishing Co., 1975.

———. *Power and Interdependence: World Politics in Transition.* Boston: Little, Brown & Co., 1977.

———, eds. *Transnational Relations and World Politics.* Cambridge: Harvard University Press, 1972.

Krasner, Stephen D., ed. *International Regimes.* Ithaca: Cornell University Press, 1983.

Lebow, Richard Ned. *Between Peace and War: The Nature of International Crisis.* Baltimore: Johns Hopkins University Press, 1981.

———. *Nuclear Crisis Management: A Dangerous Illusion.* Ithaca: Cornell University Press, 1987.

Lenin, V. I. *Imperialism, the Highest Stage of Capitalism: A Popular Outline.* Little Lenin Library, vol. 15. New York: International Publishers Co., 1933.

Levy, Jack S. "Theories of General War." *World Politics* 37 (April 1985): 344–74.

Lijphart, Arend. "Comparative Politics and the Comparative Method." *American Political Science Review* 65 (September 1971): 682–93.

———. "The Comparable-Cases Strategy in Comparative Research." *Comparative Political Studies* 8 (July 1975): 158–77.

Lindberg, Leon N., and Scheingold, Stuart A., eds. *Regional Integration: Theory and Research.* Cambridge: Harvard University Press, 1971.

Locke, John. *The Second Treatise of Government.* Edited by Thomas P. Peardon. Indianapolis: Bobbs-Merrill Publishing Co., 1952.

Lockhart, Charles. "Conflict Actions and Outcomes: Long-Term Impacts." *Journal of Conflict Resolution* 22 (December 1978): 565–98.

Mandelbaum, Michael. *The Nuclear Revolution: International Politics before and after Hiroshima.* Cambridge: Cambridge University Press, 1981.

Mill, John Stuart. *A System of Logic: Ratiocinative and Inductive.* 8th ed. 2 vols. London: Longmans, Green, Reader, & Dyer, 1872.

Modelski, George. "The Long Cycle of Global Politics and the Nation-State." *Comparative Studies in Society and History* 20 (April 1978): 214–35.

————. *Long Cycles in World Politics.* Seattle: University of Washington Press, 1986.

Morgenthau, Hans J. *Politics among Nations: The Struggle for Power and Peace.* 5th ed. New York: Alfred A. Knopf, 1973.

Nelson, Keith L., and Olin, Spencer C., Jr. *Why War?: Ideology, Theory, and History.* Berkeley: University of California Press, 1979.

Nye, Joseph S. "Comparative Regional Integration: Concept and Measurement." *International Organization* 22 (Autumn 1968): 855–80.

————. *Peace in Parts: Integration and Conflict in Regional Organization.* Boston: Little, Brown & Co., 1971.

Organski, A. F. K. *World Politics.* 2d ed. New York: Alfred A. Knopf, 1968.

Organski, A. F. K., and Kugler, Jacek. *The War Ledger.* Chicago: University of Chicago Press, 1980.

Przeworski, Adam, and Teune, Henry. *The Logic of Comparative Social Inquiry.* New York: Wiley Interscience, 1970.

Rosecrance, Richard. "International Theory Revisited." *International Organization* 35 (Autumn 1981): 691–713.

————. "Long Cycle Theory and International Relations." *International Organization* 41 (Spring 1987): 283–301.

Russett, Bruce, and Starr, Harvey. *World Politics: The Menu for Choice.* 2d ed. New York: W. H. Freeman & Co., 1985.

Sabrosky, Alan Ned. "From Bosnia to Sarajevo: A Comparative Discussion of Interstate Crises." *Journal of Conflict Resolution* 19 (March 1975): 3–24.

Skocpol, Theda, and Somers, Margaret. "The Uses of Comparative History in Macrosocial Inquiry." *Comparative Studies in Society and History* 22 (April 1980): 174–97.

Sprout, Harold, and Sprout, Margaret. *The Ecological Perspective on Human Affairs, with Special Reference to International Politics.* Princeton: Princeton University Press for the Princeton Center of International Studies, 1965.

Spykman, Nicholas John. *America's Strategy in World Politics: The United States and the Balance of Power.* New York: Harcourt, Brace & Co., 1942.

Van Wagenen, Richard W. *Research in the International Organization Field: Some Notes on a Possible Focus.* Princeton: Center for Research on World Political Institutions, Woodrow Wilson School of Public and International Affairs, Princeton University, 1952.

Walt, Stephen M. "Alliance Formation and the Balance of World Power." *International Security* 9 (Spring 1985): 3–43.

————. *The Origins of Alliances.* Ithaca: Cornell University Press, 1987.

Waltz, Kenneth N. *Man, the State, and War: A Theoretical Analysis.* New York: Columbia University Press, 1959.

————. *Theory of International Politics.* Reading, Mass.: Addison-Wesley Publishing Co., 1979.

Warwick, Donald P. "Transnational Participation and International Peace." In *Transnational Relations and World Politics*, edited by Robert O. Keohane and Joseph S. Nye, Jr., 305–24. Cambridge: Harvard University Press, 1972.

Wight, Martin. *Power Politics*. Rev. and exp. ed. Edited by Hedley Bull and Carsten Holbraad. New York: Holmes & Meier, 1978.

Case Studies

Primary Sources

Government Documents and Publications

Dugdale, E. T. S., comp. and trans. *German Diplomatic Documents, 1871–1914*. 4 vols. London: Methuen & Co., 1928–31.

France. Assemblée nationale, 1871–1942. Chambre des députés. *Journal officiel de la République française. Annales. Débats parlementaires*, 1900–1905.

——. Sénat. *Journal officiel de la République française. Annales. Débats parlementaires*, 1900–1905.

——. Ministère des affaires étrangères. Commission de publication des documents relatifs aux origines de la guerre de 1914. *Documents diplomatiques françaises, 1871–1914*, 1st series, 1871–1900, 16 vols.; 2d series, 1901–10, 14 vols.; 3d series, 1911–14, 11 vols. Paris: Imprimerie nationale, 1929–59, 1930–55, 1929–36.

Germany. Auswärtiges Amt. *Die grosse Politik der europäischen Kabinette, 1871–1914: Sammlung der diplomatischen Akten des Auswärtigen Amtes*. Compiled by Johannes Lepsius, Albrecht Mendelssohn Bartholdy, and Friedrich Thimme. 40 vols. Berlin: Deutsche Verlagsgesellschaft für Politik und Geschichte, 1922–27.

——. Reichstag. *Stenographische Berichte über die Verhandlungen*, 1890–1908.

Great Britain. Foreign Office. *British Documents on the Origins of the War, 1898–1914*. Edited by G. P. Gooch and Harold Temperley, with the assistance of Lillian M. Penson. 11 vols. London: His Majesty's Stationery Office, 1926–38.

——. Parliament. *Parliamentary Debates*. 3d series, 1830–91; 4th series, 1892–1908; Commons, 5th series, 1909–; House of Lords, 5th series, 1909–.

——. *Parliamentary Papers*, 1897, vol. 60 (Accounts and Papers, vol. 9). Cd. 8449. "Trade of the British Empire and Foreign Competition."

——. *Parliamentary Papers*, 1903, vol. 68 (Accounts and Papers, vol. 33). "Food Supplies (Imported)."

——. *Parliamentary Papers*, 1909, vol. 102 (Accounts and Papers, vol. 53). Cd. 4954. "British and Foreign Trade and Industry (1854–1908)."

United Nations. Department of International Economic and Social Affairs. Statistical Office. *1982 Yearbook of International Trade Statistics*. 2 vols. (1984).

U.S. Bureau of Foreign and Domestic Commerce. *Statistical Abstract of the United States, 1906.* Washington, D.C.: Government Printing Office, 1907.

―――. Bureau of the Census. *Historical Statistics of the United States, Colonial Times to 1957.* Washington, D.C.: Government Printing Office, 1960.

―――. Congress. *Congressional Record*, 1889–1930. Washington, D.C.: Government Printing Office.

―――. Department of State. *Commercial Relations of the United States with Foreign Countries.* Published beginning in 1903 by the Department of Commerce and Labor, Bureau of Manufactures. Washington, D.C.: Government Printing Office, 1890–1909.

―――. *Consular Reports.* Published beginning in 1903 by the Department of Commerce and Labor. Title varies. Washington, D.C.: Government Printing Office, 1890–1910.

―――. *Papers Relating to the Foreign Relations of the United States.* Washington, D.C.: Government Printing Office, 1890–1930.

―――. National Monetary Commission. *Statistics for Great Britain, Germany, and France, 1867–1909.* Washington, D.C.: Government Printing Office, 1910.

―――. *Statistics for the United States, 1867–1909.* Compiled by A. Piatt Andrew. Washington, D.C.: Government Printing Office, 1910.

―――. *The Trade Balance of the United States.* By George Paish. Washington, D.C.: Government Printing Office, 1910.

Letters, Diaries, and Memoirs

Barclay, Thomas. *Thirty Years, Anglo-French Reminiscences (1876–1906).* London: Constable & Co., 1914.

Bülow, Bernhard von. *Imperial Germany.* Translated by Marie A. Lewenz. New York: Dodd, Mead & Co., 1914.

―――. *Memoirs of Prince von Bülow.* 4 vols. Translated by Geoffrey Dunlop and F. A. Voigt. Boston: Little, Brown & Co., 1931–32.

Cambon, Paul. *Correspondance (1870–1924).* Commentary and notes by Henri Cambon. 3 vols. Paris: Editions Bernard Grasset, 1940–46.

Fisher, John. *Fear God and Dread Nought: The Correspondence of Admiral of the Fleet Lord Fisher of Kilverstone.* Selected and edited by Arthur J. Marder. Cambridge: Harvard University Press, 1952.

Grey, Edward, Viscount of Fallodon, K.G. *Twenty-Five Years, 1892–1916.* 2 vols. New York: Frederick A. Stokes, 1925.

Hay, John. *Addresses of John Hay.* New York: Century Co., 1906.

―――. Papers. Library of Congress, Washington, D.C.

Holstein, Friedrich von. *The Holstein Papers: The Memoirs, Diaries, and Correspondence of Friedrich von Holstein, 1837–1909.* Edited by Norman Rich and M. H. Fisher. 4 vols. Cambridge: Cambridge University Press, 1955–63.

House, Edward Mandell. *The Intimate Papers of Colonel House.* Arranged as a narrative by Charles Seymour. 4 vols. Boston: Houghton Mifflin Co., 1926–28.

Mahan, Alfred Thayer. *Letters and Papers of Alfred Thayer Mahan.* Edited by Robert Seager II and Doris D. Maguire. 3 vols. Annapolis: Naval Institute Press, 1975.

Richardson, James D., ed. *A Compilation of the Messages and Papers of the Presidents.* 20 vols. New York: Bureau of National Literature, 1897–1914.

Roosevelt, Theodore. *The Letters of Theodore Roosevelt.* Selected and edited by Elting E. Morison. 8 vols. Cambridge: Harvard University Press, 1951–54.

Roosevelt, Theodore, and Lodge, Henry Cabot. *Selections from the Correspondence of Theodore Roosevelt and Henry Cabot Lodge, 1884–1918.* Edited by Henry Cabot Lodge. 2 vols. New York: Charles Scribner's Sons, 1925.

Spring Rice, Cecil. *The Letters and Friendships of Sir Cecil Spring Rice: A Record.* Edited by Stephen Gwynn. 2 vols. Boston: Houghton Mifflin Co., 1929.

Tirpitz, Alfred von. *My Memoirs.* 2 vols. New York: Dodd, Mead & Co., 1919.

White, Andrew Dickson. *The Autobiography of Andrew Dickson White.* 2 vols. New York: Century Co., 1905.

Wilson, Woodrow. *The Papers of Woodrow Wilson.* Edited by Arthur S. Link. 46 vols. Princeton: Princeton University Press, 1966–84.

Witte, Emil. *Revelations of a German Attaché: Ten Years of German-American Diplomacy.* Translated by Florence Clarkson Taylor. New York: George H. Doran Co., 1916.

Articles and Books

Abbott, Lyman. "The Basis of an Anglo-American Understanding." *North American Review* 166 (May 1898): 513–21.

Abrami, Léon. "Le traité d'arbitrage du 14 Octobre 1903 et les relations anglo-françaises." *Revue politique et parlementaire* 38 (10 December 1903): 535–55.

Adams, Brooks. "The Spanish War and the Equilibrium of the World." *Forum* 25 (August 1898): 641–51.

Annual Review 7 (1808).

Atkinson, Edward. "The Cost of an Anglo-American War." *Forum* 21 (March 1896): 74–88.

Bacon, Nathaniel T. "American International Indebtedness." *Yale Review* 9 (November 1900): 265–85.

Barclay, Thomas. "A General Treaty of Arbitration between England and France." *Fortnightly Review,* o.s. 75 (June 1901): 1022–29.

Barker, J. Ellis. "The Foreign Policy of the Emperor William II." *Nineteenth Century* 63 (January 1908): 26–37.

Barrett, John. "The United States and Latin America." *North American Review* 183 (September 1906): 474–83.

Beresford, Charles. "The Anglo-American Entente." *Pall Mall Magazine* 18 (July 1899): 379–83.

Bigelow, Poultney. "The German Press and the United States." *North American Review* 164 (January 1897): 12–23.

Bingham, Hiram. *The Monroe Doctrine: An Obsolete Shibboleth.* New Haven: Yale University Press, 1913.

Brooks, Sydney. "England and Germany." *Atlantic Monthly* 105 (April 1910): 617–27.

Bruce, Philip Alexander. "American Feeling Toward England." *Westminster Review* 154 (October 1900): 451–63.

Bryce, James. "British Feeling on the Venezuelan Question." *North American Review* 162 (February 1896): 145–53.

―――. "America Revisited: The Changes of a Quarter-Century." *Outlook* 79 (April 1905): 846–55.

Carnegie, Andrew. "The Venezuelan Question." *North American Review* 162 (February 1896): 129–44.

―――. "An Anglo-French-American Understanding." *North American Review* 181 (October 1905): 510–17.

Clarke, G. S. "England and America." *Nineteenth Century* 44 (August 1898): 186–95.

Clowes, William Laird. "American Expansion and the Inheritance of the Race." *Fortnightly Review*, o.s. 70 (December 1898): 884–92.

Conrad, Joseph. "Autocracy and War." *North American Review* 181 (July 1905): 33–55.

Cox, Harold. "American Progress and British Commerce." *North American Review* 173 (July 1901): 91–101.

Davidson, Thomas. "The Imperialization of Germany." *Forum* 23 (April 1897): 246–56.

"The Defence of the Empire: An Open Letter to Lord Salisbury." *Contemporary Review* 79 (April 1901): 457–71.

Dicey, A. V. "A Common Citizenship for the English Race." *Contemporary Review* 71 (April 1897): 457–76.

Dicey, Edward. "The New American Imperialism." *Nineteenth Century* 44 (September 1898): 487–501.

Dillon, E. J. "Our Friends, Our Ally, and Our Rivals." *Contemporary Review* 85 (May 1904): 609–26.

Diplomaticus [pseud.]. "Is There an Anglo-American Understanding?" *Fortnightly Review*, o.s. 70 (July 1898): 163–74.

―――. "Is It Peace? The Progress of Anglo-French Negotiations." *Fortnightly Review*, o.s. 71 (March 1899): 500–510.

Dooley, W. H. "German and American Methods of Production." *Atlantic Monthly* 107 (April 1911): 649–60.

Doumer, Paul. "The Anglo-French Agreement." *National Review* 43 (June 1904): 556–65.

Dunnell, Mark B. "The Hay-Pauncefote Treaty." *North American Review* 171 (December 1900): 829–46.

Edinburgh Review 5 (October 1804).

Einstein, Lewis [A Diplomatist]. *American Foreign Policy.* Boston: Houghton Mifflin Co., 1909.

Einstein, Lewis [Washington]. "The United States and Anglo-German Rivalry." *National Review* 60 (January 1913): 736–50.

Eltzbacher, O. "The German Emperor as a Political Factor." *Fortnightly Review*, o.s. 78 (November 1902): 806–19.

———. "German Colonial Ambitions and Anglo-Saxon Interests." *Fortnightly Review*, o.s. 79 (March 1903): 469–88.

———. "The Social Democratic Party in Germany." *Nineteenth Century* 53 (May 1903): 755–72.

Fiske, Bradley A. "Naval Power." *Proceedings of the United States Naval Institute* 37 (September 1911): 683–736.

Flynt, Josiah. "The German and the German-American." *Atlantic Monthly* 78 (November 1896): 655–64.

"The Foreign Policy of Germany." *Fortnightly Review*, o.s. 84 (December 1905): 1005–21.

"La fortune française a l'étranger." *Bulletin de statistique et de législation comparée* 52 (July 1902): 450–83.

Garvin, J. L. [Calchas]. "The Revival of France." *Fortnightly Review*, o.s. 77 (May 1902): 785–800.

———. "The Bankruptcy of Bismarckian Policy." *Fortnightly Review*, o.s. 81 (May 1904): 765–77.

Gleig, Charles. "British Food Supply in War." *Naval Annual* (1898): 152–66.

Goltz, C. von der. "Seemacht und Landkrieg." *Deutsche Rundschau* 102 (March 1900): 335–52.

Greenwood, Frederick. "The Anglo-American Future." *Nineteenth Century* 44 (July 1898): 1–11.

Harvey, George. "The United States and Great Britain: Their Past, Present, and Future Relations." *Nineteenth Century* 55 (April 1904): 529–37.

Hazeltine, Mayo W. "The United States and Great Britain: A Reply to Mr. David A. Wells." *North American Review* 162 (May 1896): 594–606.

———. "The United States and the Late Lord Salisbury." *North American Review* 177 (November 1903): 720–24.

Henderson, John B., Jr. *The Monroe Doctrine and the Venezuelan Boundary Question.* N.p., n.d.

Hershey, Amos S. "Germany—The Main Obstacle to the World's Peace." *Independent*, 20 May 1909, 1071–76.

Hobson, J. A. "The Approaching Abandonment of Free Trade." *Fortnightly Review*, o.s. 77 (March 1902): 434–44.

Hobson, Richmond Pearson. "America Must Be Mistress of the Seas." *North American Review* 175 (October 1902): 544–57.

Horwill, Herbert W. "Anglo-American Arbitration." *Contemporary Review* 101 (April 1912): 475–86.

Hurd, Archibald S. "French Friendship and Naval Economy." *Fortnightly Review*, o.s. 80 (October 1903): 654–62.

———. "Naval Concentration—and a Moral." *Fortnightly Review*, o.s. 81 (April 1904): 685–98.

———. "The British Fleet 'Dips Its Ensign.'" *Fortnightly Review*, o.s. 117 (March 1922): 396–409.

H. W. W. "England and Germany." *Westminster Review* 136 (December 1891): 650–64.

Jane's Fighting Ships, 1908.

[Kerr, Philip.] "Foreign Affairs: Anglo-German Rivalry." *Round Table* 1 (November 1910): 7–40.

Lees, Frederic. "Some Promoters of Anglo-French Amity." *Fortnightly Review*, o.s. 80 (July 1903): 132–40.

Leroy-Beaulieu, Pierre. "Les relations économiques entre la France et l'Angleterre." *Revue des deux mondes* 18 (15 December 1903): 786–816.

Lichnowsky, Karl Max [von]. "Deutsch-englische Missverständnisse." *Nord und Süd* 142 (July 1912): 15–19.

Lodge, Henry Cabot. *One Hundred Years of Peace.* New York: Macmillan Co., 1913.

Louis-Jaray, Gabriel. "Notre accord avec l'Angleterre et la politique franco-anglaise." *Revue politique et parlementaire* 40 (10 June 1904): 462–506.

———. "L'accord entre la France et l'Angleterre—L'opinion publique et le rapprochement franco-anglais." *Questions diplomatiques et coloniales; revue de politique extérieure* 18 (16 November 1904): 593–608.

Low, A. Maurice. "The German Emperor." *Atlantic Monthly* 97 (March 1906): 300–308.

Mahan, Alfred Thayer. *The Interest of America in International Conditions.* Boston: Little, Brown & Co., 1910.

Mead, Edwin D. "England and Germany." *Atlantic Monthly* 101 (March 1908): 397–407.

Méringhoc, A. "Le traité d'arbitrage permanent au XXe siècle: accords franco-anglais et franco-italien des 14 Octobre et 25 Decembre 1903." *Revue politique et parlementaire* 40 (10 May 1904): 281–301.

Mommsen, Theodor. "German Feeling Toward England and America." *North American Review* 170 (February 1900): 240–43.

Münsterberg, Hugo. *Die Amerikaner.* 2 vols. Berlin: Ernst Siegfried Mittler und Sohn, 1904.

Olney, Richard. "International Isolation of the United States." *Atlantic Monthly* 81 (May 1898): 577–88.

Petersen, George D. "The New Era in Germany." *Independent*, 27 January 1898, 110.

Pressensé, Francis de. "The Relations of France and England." *Nineteenth Century* 39 (February 1896): 189–203.

Rathgen, Karl. "Ueber den Plan eines britischen Reichszollvereins." *Preussische Jahrbücher* 86 (December 1896): 481–523.

Saint-Charles, Fleury de. "L'accord franco-anglais et l'Europe." *Revue d'histoire diplomatique* 18 (July 1904): 454–75.

Sarolea, Charles. *The Anglo-German Problem*. New York: Thomas Nelson & Sons, 1912.

Schapiro, J. Salwyn. "Significant Tendencies in German Politics." *Forum* 47 (June 1912): 685–98.

[Schlieffen, Alfred von]. "Der Krieg in der Gegenwart." *Deutsche Revue* 34 (January 1909): 13–24.

Schulze-Gävernitz, Gerhardt von. "England and Germany—Peace or War?" *American Review of Reviews* 40 (November 1909): 602–5.

Seton-Karr, H. "England's Food Supply in Time of War." *North American Review* 164 (June 1897): 651–63.

Sherwood, Sidney. "An Alliance with England the Basis of a Rational Foreign Policy." *Forum* 21 (March 1896): 89–99.

Simon, Jules. "France and England." *Contemporary Review* 67 (June 1895): 783–87.

Spender, J. A. "Great Britain and Germany." *Fortnightly Review*, o.s. 84 (November 1905): 811–28.

Sternberg, Speck von. "The Phantom Peril of German Emigration and South-American Settlements." *North American Review* 182 (May 1906): 641–50.

Tardieu, André. *France and the Alliances: The Struggle for the Balance of Power*. New York: Macmillan Co., 1908.

Waldstein, Charles. "The English-Speaking Brotherhood." *North American Review* 167 (August 1898): 223–38.

Wells, David A. "Great Britain and the United States: Their True Relations." *North American Review* 162 (April 1896): 385–405.

Whelpley, J. D. "American Control of England's Food Supply." *North American Review* 174 (June 1902): 796–806.

White, Arthur Silva. "An Anglo-American Alliance." *North American Review* 158 (April 1894): 484–93.

Williams, Ernest E. "Made in Germany." *New Review* 14 (January 1896): 14–28, (February 1896): 113–27, (March 1896): 253–68, (April 1896): 376–91, (May 1896): 492–506, (June 1896): 636–50.

———. "Made in Germany—Five Years After." *National Review* 38 (September 1901): 130–44.

Wilson, H. W. "The Menace of the German Navy." *National Review* 43 (May 1904): 375–92.

Secondary Sources

Adams, William Scovell. *Edwardian Heritage: A Study in British History, 1901–1906*. London: Frederick Muller, 1949.

Albertini, Luigi. *The Origins of the War of 1914*. Translated and edited by Isabella M. Massey. 3 vols. London: Oxford University Press, 1952–57.

Albrecht-Carrié, René. *A Diplomatic History of Europe since the Congress of Vienna.* New York: Harper & Bros., 1958.

Allen, H. C. *Great Britain and the United States: A History of Anglo-American Relations (1783–1952).* London: Odhams Press, 1954.

Anderson, Eugene N. *The First Moroccan Crisis, 1904–1906.* Chicago: University of Chicago Press, 1930.

Anderson, Pauline Relyea. *The Background of Anti-English Feeling in Germany, 1890–1902.* Washington, D.C.: American University Press, 1939; reprint ed., New York: Octagon Books, 1969.

Anderson, Stuart. *Race and Rapprochement: Anglo-Saxonism and Anglo-American Relations, 1895–1904.* East Brunswick, N.J.: Associated University Presses, 1981.

Andrew, Christopher M. "German World Policy and the Reshaping of the Dual Alliance." *Journal of Contemporary History* 1 (July 1966): 137–51.

———. "France and the Making of the Entente Cordiale." *Historical Journal* 10 (1967): 89–105.

———. *Théophile Delcassé and the Making of the Entente Cordiale: A Reappraisal of French Foreign Policy, 1898–1905.* London: Macmillan & Co.; New York: St. Martin's Press, 1968.

———. "The Entente Cordiale from Its Origins to 1914." In *Troubled Neighbours: Franco-British Relations in the Twentieth Century,* edited by Neville Waites, 11–39. London: Weidenfeld & Nicolson, 1971.

———. "The French Colonialist Movement during the Third Republic: The Unofficial Mind of Imperialism." *Transactions of the Royal Historical Society,* 5th series, 26 (1976): 143–66.

Andrew, Christopher M.; Grupp, P.; and Kanya-Forstner, A. S. "Le mouvement colonial français et ses principales personalités (1890–1914)." *Revue d'histoire d'outre-mer* 62 (1975): 640–73.

Andrew, Christopher M., and Kanya-Forstner, A. S. "The French 'Colonial Party': Its Composition, Aims and Influence, 1885–1914." *Historical Journal* 14 (March 1971): 99–128.

———. "Gabriel Hanotaux, the Colonial Party and the Fashoda Strategy." In *European Imperialism and the Partition of Africa,* edited by E. F. Penrose, 55–104. New Orientations Series, no. 2. London: Frank Cass & Co., 1975.

———. *France Overseas: The Great War and the Climax of French Imperial Expansion.* London: Thames & Hudson, 1981.

Aydelotte, William Osgood. *Bismarck and British Colonial Policy: The Problem of South West Africa, 1883–1885.* Philadelphia: University of Pennsylvania Press, 1937; reprint ed., Westport, Conn.: Negro University sities Press, 1970.

Balfour, Michael. *The Kaiser and His Times.* London: Cresset Press, 1964.

Barnett, Correlli. *The Collapse of British Power.* New York: William Morrow & Co., 1972.

Baum, Loretta. "German Political Designs with Reference to Brazil." *Hispanic American Historical Review* 2 (November 1919): 586–99.

Beale, Howard K. *Theodore Roosevelt and the Rise of America to World*

Power. Albert Shaw Lectures on Diplomatic History, 1953. Baltimore: Johns Hopkins University Press, 1956.

Beisner, Robert L. *Twelve against Empire: The Anti-Imperialists, 1898-1900.* New York: McGraw-Hill Book Co., 1968.

──────. *From the Old Diplomacy to the New, 1865-1900.* New York: Thomas Y. Crowell Co., 1975.

Beloff, Max. "Is There an Anglo-American Political Tradition?" *History* 36 (February–June 1951): 73–91.

──────. *Imperial Sunset.* Vol. 1, *Britain's Liberal Empire, 1897-1921.* New York: Alfred A. Knopf, 1970.

Berghahn, V. R. *Germany and the Approach of War in 1914.* London: Macmillan & Co., 1973.

Blake, Nelson M. "The Olney-Pauncefote Treaty of 1897." *American Historical Review* 50 (January 1945): 228–43.

Bloomfield, Arthur I. *Short-term Capital Movements under the Pre-1914 Gold Standard.* Princeton Studies in International Finance, no. 11. Princeton: International Finance Section, Department of Economics, Princeton University, 1963.

Bonnet, Georges. *Miracle de la France (1870-1919).* Les Grandes Etudes Contemporaines. Paris: Librairie Arthème Fayard, 1965.

Bourne, Kenneth. *Britain and the Balance of Power in North America, 1815-1908.* Berkeley: University of California Press, 1967.

──────. *The Foreign Policy of Victorian England, 1830-1902.* Oxford: Clarendon Press, 1970.

Boyle, T. "The Venezuela Crisis and the Liberal Opposition, 1895-96." *Journal of Modern History* 50 (September 1979, on-demand supplement): D1185-1212.

Brebner, John Bartlet. *North Atlantic Triangle: The Interplay of Canada, the United States and Great Britain.* New Haven: Yale University Press for the Carnegie Endowment for International Peace, Division of Economics and History, 1945.

Brown, Roger Glenn. *Fashoda Reconsidered: The Impact of Domestic Politics on French Policy in Africa, 1893-1898.* Baltimore: Johns Hopkins University Press, 1970.

Brunschwig, Henri. *French Colonialism, 1871-1914: Myths and Realities.* Translated by William Granville Brown. London: Pall Mall Press, 1966.

Buckley, Thomas. *The United States and the Washington Conference, 1921-1922.* Knoxville: University of Tennessee Press, 1970.

Butler, Jeffrey. "The German Factor in Anglo-Transvaal Relations." In *Britain and Germany in Africa: Imperial Rivalry and Colonial Rule,* edited by Prosser Gifford and William Roger Louis, with the assistance of Alison Smith, 179-214. New Haven: Yale University Press, 1967.

Cairncross, Alexander Kirkland. *Home and Foreign Investment, 1870-1913: Studies in Capital Accumulation.* Cambridge: Cambridge University Press, 1953.

Caldwell, Lawrence T. "The Future of Soviet-American Relations." In

Soviet-American Relations in the 1980's: Superpower Politics and East-West Trade, by Lawrence T. Caldwell and William Diebold, Jr., 21-230. New York: McGraw-Hill Book Co., 1981.

Calvert, P. A. R. "Great Britain and the New World, 1905-1914." In *British Foreign Policy under Sir Edward Grey*, edited by F. H. Hinsley, 382-94. Cambridge: Cambridge University Press, 1977.

Campbell, A. E. *Great Britain and the United States, 1895-1903.* London: Longmans, Green & Co., 1960.

Campbell, Charles S., Jr. *Anglo-American Understanding, 1898-1903.* Baltimore: Johns Hopkins University Press, 1957.

———. *From Revolution to Rapprochement: The United States and Great Britain, 1783-1900.* New York: John Wiley & Sons, 1974.

———. *The Transformation of American Foreign Relations, 1865-1900.* New York: Harper & Row, 1976.

Carroll, E. Malcolm. *Germany and the Great Powers, 1866-1914: A Study in Public Opinion and Foreign Policy.* New York: Prentice-Hall, 1938.

———. *French Public Opinion and Foreign Affairs, 1870-1914.* New York: Century Co., 1931; reprint ed., Hamden, Conn.: Archon Books, 1964.

Christof, Horst. "Deutsch-amerikanische Entfremdung: Studien zu den deutsch-amerikanischen Beziehungen von 1913 bis zum Mai 1916." Ph.D. diss., Julius-Maximilians-Universität zu Würzburg, 1975.

Clement, Wilhelm. "Die Monroedoktrine und die deutsch-amerikanischen Beziehungen im Zeitalter des Imperialismus." *Jahrbuch für Amerikastudien* 1 (1956): 153-67.

Coolidge, Archibald Cary. *The United States as a World Power.* New York: Macmillan Co., 1908.

Cortissoz, Royal. *The Life of Whitelaw Reid.* 2 vols. New York: Charles Scribner's Sons, 1921.

Cross, Colin. *The Liberals in Power, 1905-1914.* London: Barrie & Rockliff with Pall Mall Press, 1963.

Davis, George Theron. *A Navy Second to None: The Development of Modern American Naval Policy.* New York: Harcourt, Brace, Jovanovich, 1940; reprint ed., Westport, Conn.: Greenwood Press, 1971.

Dawson, Raymond, and Rosecrance, Richard. "Theory and Reality in the Anglo-American Alliance." *World Politics* 19 (October 1966): 21-51.

Deckart, Gerald. *Deutsch-englische Verständigung: eine Darstellung der nichtoffiziellen Bemühungen um einer Wiederannäherung der beiden Länder zwischen 1905 und 1914.* Bamberg: Offsetdruckerei K. Urlaub, 1970.

Deicke, Gertrud. "Das Amerikabild der deutschen öffentlichen Meinung von 1898-1914." Thesis, University of Hamburg, 1956.

Dennett, Tyler. *John Hay: From Poetry to Politics.* New York: Dodd, Mead & Co., 1933.

Dennis, Alfred L. P. *Adventures in American Diplomacy, 1896-1906 (From Unpublished Documents).* New York: E. P. Dutton & Co., 1928.

Dugdale, Blanche E. C. *Arthur James Balfour, First Earl of Balfour, K.G., O.M., F.R.S., Etc.* 2 vols. New York: G. P. Putnam's Sons, 1937.

Eckardstein, Hermann von. *Ten Years at the Court of St. James, 1895–1905.* Translated and edited by George Young. London: Thornton Butterworth, 1921.

Edwards, E. W. "The Japanese Alliance and the Anglo-French Agreement of 1904." *History* 42 (February 1957): 19–27.

Eggert, Gerald G. *Richard Olney: Evolution of a Statesman.* University Park: Pennsylvania State University Press, 1974.

Eubank, Keith. "The Fashoda Crisis Re-examined." *Historian* 22 (February 1960): 145–62.

————. *Paul Cambon: Master Diplomatist.* Norman: University of Oklahoma Press, 1960.

Faust, Albert Bernhardt. *The German Element in the United States, with Special Reference to Its Political, Moral, Social, and Educational Influence.* 2 vols. New York: Steuben Society of America, 1927.

Feis, Herbert. *Europe, the World's Banker, 1870–1914: An Account of European Foreign Investment and the Connection of World Finance with Diplomacy before the War.* New Haven: Yale University Press for the Council on Foreign Relations, 1930.

Foot, M. R. D. *British Foreign Policy since 1898.* London: Hutchinson's University Library, 1956.

Fraenkel, Ernst, comp. *Amerika im Spiegel des deutschen politischen Denkens: Ausserungen deutscher Staatsmänner und Staatsdenker über Staat und Gesellschaft in den Vereinigten Staaten von Amerika.* Cologne: Westdeutscher Verlag, 1959.

Gall, Wilhelm. *Sir Charles Hardinge und die englische Vorkriegspolitik, 1903–1910.* Historische Studien, Heft 352. Berlin: Dr. Emil Ebering, 1939.

Ganiage, Jean. *L'expansion coloniale de la France sous la Troisième République, 1871–1914.* Paris: Payot, 1968.

Gardner, Lloyd C. "Ideology and American Foreign Policy." In *Ideology and Foreign Policy: A Global Perspective,* edited by George Schwab, 133–42. New York: Cyrco Press, 1978.

Garvin, J. L. *The Life of Joseph Chamberlain.* 4 vols. London: Macmillan & Co., 1932–51. Vol. 4 by Julian Amery.

Gatzke, Hans W. "The United States and Germany on the Eve of World War I." In *Deutschland in der Weltpolitik des 19. und 20. Jahrhunderts,* edited by Imanuel Geiss and Bernd Jürgen Wendt, 271–86. Düsseldorf: Bertelsmann Universitätsverlag, 1973.

————. *Germany and the United States: A Special Relationship?* Cambridge: Harvard University Press, 1980.

Gelber, Lionel M. *The Rise of Anglo-American Friendship: A Study in World Politics, 1898–1906.* London: Oxford University Press, 1938.

Gerschenkron, Alexander. *Bread and Democracy in Germany.* New York: Howard Fertig, 1966.

Gifford, Prosser, and Louis, William Roger, eds. With the assistance of Alison Smith. *Britain and Germany in Africa: Imperial Rivalry and Colonial Rule.* New Haven: Yale University Press, 1967.

Gifford, Prosser, and Louis, William Roger, eds. *France and Britain in Africa: Imperial Rivalry and Colonial Rule.* New Haven: Yale University Press, 1971.

Glazer, Nathan. "America's Ethnic Pattern." *Commentary* 15 (April 1953): 401–8.

Gooch, G. P. *Franco-German Relations, 1871–1914.* The Creighton Lecture for 1923. London: Longmans, Green, & Co., 1923.

Gooch, G. P., and Masterman, J. H. B. *A Century of British Foreign Policy.* London: George Allen & Unwin, 1917.

Goudswaard, Johan Marius. *Some Aspects of the End of Britain's "Splendid Isolation," 1898–1904.* Rotterdam: W. L. & J. Brusse, 1952.

Grenville, J. A. S. "Lansdowne's Abortive Project of 12 March 1901 for a Secret Agreement with Germany." *Bulletin of the Institute of Historical Research* 27 (November 1954): 201–13.

———. *Lord Salisbury and Foreign Policy: The Close of the Nineteenth Century.* London: University of London, Athlone Press, 1964.

Grenville, J. A. S., and Young, George Berkeley. *Politics, Strategy, and American Diplomacy: Studies in Foreign Policy, 1873–1917.* New Haven: Yale University Press, 1966.

Guillen, Pierre. "Les accords coloniaux franco-anglais de 1904 et la naissance de l'entente cordiale." *Revue d'histoire diplomatique* 82 (October–December 1968): 315–57.

———. "The Entente of 1904 as a Colonial Settlement." In *France and Britain in Africa: Imperial Rivalry and Colonial Rule,* edited by Prosser Gifford and William Roger Louis, 333–68. New Haven: Yale University Press, 1971.

Hale, Oron James. *Germany and the Diplomatic Revolution: A Study in Diplomacy and the Press, 1904–1906.* Philadelphia: University of Pennsylvania Press, 1931.

———. *Publicity and Diplomacy, with Special Reference to England and Germany, 1890–1914.* New York: D. Appleton-Century Co. for the Institute for Research in the Social Sciences, University of Virginia, 1940.

Hallgarten, George W. F. *Imperialismus vor 1914: Theoretisches-Soziologische Skizzen der aussenpolitischen Entwicklung in England und Frankreich, soziologische Darstellung der deutschen Aussenpolitik bis zum ersten Weltkrieg.* 2 vols. Munich: C. H. Beck'sche Verlagsbuchhandlung, 1951.

Hargreaves, J. D. "The Origin of the Anglo-French Military Conversations in 1905." *History* 36 (October 1951): 244–48.

Hauser, Oswald. *Deutschland und der englisch-russische Gegensatz, 1900–1914.* Göttinger Bausteine zur Geschichtswissenschaft, Band 30. Göttingen: Musterschmidt-Verlag, 1958.

Healy, David. *US Expansionism: The Imperialist Urge in the 1890s.* Madison: University of Wisconsin Press, 1970.

Heggoy, Alf Andrew. *The African Policies of Gabriel Hanotaux, 1874–1898.* Athens: University of Georgia Press, 1972.

Heindel, Richard Heathcote. *The American Impact on Great Britain.* Philadelphia: University of Pennsylvania Press, 1940.

Herwig, Holger H. *Politics of Frustration: The United States in German Naval Planning, 1889–1941.* Boston: Little, Brown & Co., 1976.

Hoffman, Ross J. S. *Great Britain and the German Trade Rivalry, 1875–1914.* Philadelphia: University of Pennsylvania Press, 1933.

Holt, W. Stull. *Treaties Defeated by the Senate: A Study of the Struggle between President and Senate over the Conduct of Foreign Relations.* Baltimore: Johns Hopkins University Press, 1933.

Huldermann, Bernhard. *Albert Ballin.* Translated by W. J. Eggers. London: Cassell & Co., 1922.

James, Henry. *Richard Olney and His Public Service.* Boston: Houghton Mifflin Co., 1923.

Jenkins, Roy. *Asquith.* London: Collins Press, 1964.

Jonas, Manfred. *The United States and Germany: A Diplomatic History.* Ithaca: Cornell University Press, 1984.

Judd, Denis. *Balfour and the British Empire: A Study in Imperial Evolution, 1874–1932.* London: Macmillan & Co., 1968.

Kehr, Eckart. "Deutsch-englisches Bundnisproblem der Jahrhundertwende." In *Der Primat der Innenpolitik: Gesammelte Aufsätze zur preussisch-deutschen Sozialgeschichte in 19. und 20. Jahrhundert,* edited by Hans-Ulrich Wehler, 176–83. Veröffentlichungen der Historischen Kommission zu Berlin beim Friedrich-Meinecke-Institut der Freien Universität Berlin, Band 19. Berlin: Walter de Gruyter & Co., 1965.

―――. "Englandhass und Weltpolitik." In *Der Primat der Innenpolitik: Gesammelte Aufsätze zur preussisch-deutschen Sozialgeschichte in 19. und 20. Jahrhundert,* edited by Hans-Ulrich Wehler, 149–75. Veröffentlichungen der Historischen Kommission zu Berlin beim Friedrich-Meinecke-Institut der Freien Universität Berlin, Band 19. Berlin: Walter de Gruyter & Co., 1965.

―――. *Battleship Building and Party Politics in Germany, 1894–1901: A Cross-Section of the Political, Social, and Ideological Preconditions of German Imperialism.* Translated and edited by Pauline R. Anderson and Eugene N. Anderson. Chicago: University of Chicago Press, 1973.

Keiger, John F. V. *France and the Origins of the First World War.* New York: St. Martin's Press, 1983.

Keim, Jeanette. *Forty Years of German-American Political Relations.* Philadelphia: William J. Dornan, 1919.

Kendrick, John W. *Productivity Trends in the United States.* National Bureau of Economic Research, general series, no. 71. Princeton: Princeton University Press, 1961.

Kennedy, Paul M. "Tirpitz, England and the Second Navy Law of 1900: A Strategical Critique." *Militärgeschichtliche Mitteilungen* (1970): 33–57.
———. "Anglo-German Relations in the Pacific and the Partition of Samoa, 1885–1889." *Australian Journal of Politics and History* 17 (April 1971): 56–72.
———. "German World Policy and the Alliance Negotiations with England, 1897–1900." *Journal of Modern History* 45 (December 1973): 605–25.
———. *The Samoan Tangle: A Study in Anglo-German-American Relations, 1878–1900.* St. Lucia: University of Queensland Press, 1974.
———. *The Rise and Fall of British Naval Mastery.* London: Allen Lane, 1976.
———. *The Rise of the Anglo-German Antagonism, 1860–1914.* London: George Allen & Unwin, 1980.
———. *The Realities behind Diplomacy: Background Influences on British External Policy, 1865–1980.* London: George Allen & Unwin in association with Fontana Books, 1981.
———. "Mahan *versus* Mackinder: Two Interpretations of British Sea Power." In *Strategy and Diplomacy, 1870–1945: Eight Studies,* by Paul M. Kennedy, 43–85. London: George Allen & Unwin in association with Fontana Paperbacks, 1983.
———. "Strategic Aspects of the Anglo-German Naval Race." In *Strategy and Diplomacy, 1870–1945: Eight Studies,* by Paul M. Kennedy, 127–60. London: George Allen & Unwin in association with Fontana Paperbacks, 1983.
Kennedy, Paul M., and Moses, John A., eds. *Germany in the Pacific and Far East, 1870–1914.* St. Lucia: University of Queensland Press, 1977.
Kessler, Alexander. *Das deutsch-englische Verhältnis von Amtsantritt Bethmann Hollwegs bis zur Haldane-Mission.* Erlanger Abhandlungen zur mittleren und neueren Geschichte. Neue Folge, zweiter Band. Erlangen: Verlag von Palm und Enke, 1938.
Koch, H. W. "The Anglo-German Alliance Negotiations: Missed Opportunity or Myth?" *History* 54 (October 1969): 378–92.
Kunz-Lack, Ilse. *Die deutsch-amerikanischen Beziehungen, 1890–1914.* Beiträge zur Geschichte der nachbismarckischen Zeit und des Weltkriegs, Heft 30 (Neue Folge, Heft 10). Stuttgart: W. Kohlhammer, 1935.
LaFeber, Walter. "The American Business Community and Cleveland's Venezuelan Message." *Business History Review* 34 (Winter 1960): 393–402.
———. *The New Empire: An Interpretation of American Expansion, 1860–1898.* Ithaca: Cornell University Press for the American Historical Association, 1963.
Lamer, Reinhard J. *Der englische Parlamentarismus in der deutschen politischen Theorie im Zeitalter Bismarcks (1857–1890): ein Beitrag*

zur Vorgeschichte des deutschen Parlamentarismus. Historische Studien, Heft 387. Lübeck: Matthiesen Verlag, 1963.

Lanessan, J.-L. de. Histoire de l'entente cordiale franco-anglaise: les relations de la France et de l'Angleterre depuis le XVI siècle jusqu' à nos jours. Paris: Librairie Félix Alcan, 1916.

Langer, William L. The Diplomacy of Imperialism, 1890–1902. 2 vols. New York: Alfred A. Knopf, 1935.

———, comp. and ed. An Encyclopedia of World History: Ancient, Medieval, and Modern, Chronologically Arranged. Rev. ed. Boston: Houghton Mifflin Co., 1948.

Langhorne, Richard. "The Naval Question in Anglo-German Relations, 1912–1914." Historical Journal 14 (June 1971): 359–70.

———. "Anglo-German Negotiations Concerning the Future of the Portuguese Colonies, 1911–1914." Historical Journal 16 (June 1973): 361–87.

Lee, Dwight E. Europe's Crucial Years: The Diplomatic Background of World War I, 1902–1914. Hanover, N.H.: University Press of New England for Clark University Press, 1974.

Leusser, Hermann. Ein Jahrzehnt deutsch-amerikanischer Politik (1897–1906). Beiheft 13 der Historischen Zeitschrift. Munich: R. Oldenbourg, 1928.

Levin, N. Gordon, Jr. Woodrow Wilson and World Politics: America's Response to War and Revolution. New York: Oxford University Press, 1968.

Lewis, Cleona. Assisted by Karl T. Schlotterbeck. America's Stake in International Investments. The Institute of Economics of the Brookings Institution, Publication no. 75. Washington, D.C.: Brookings Institution, 1938.

Liebig, Hans von. Die Politik von Bethmann Hollwegs. Munich: J. F. Lehmanns Verlag, 1919.

Louis, William Roger. "Great Britain and German Expansion in Africa, 1884–1919." In Britain and Germany in Africa: Imperial Rivalry and Colonial Rule, edited by Prosser Gifford and William Roger Louis, with the assistance of Alison Smith, 3–46. New Haven: Yale University Press, 1967.

McElroy, Robert. Grover Cleveland: The Man and the Statesman. 2 vols. New York: Harper & Bros., 1923.

Mackenzie, Kenneth. "Some British Reactions to German Colonial Methods, 1885–1907." Historical Journal 17 (March 1974): 165–75.

Marder, Arthur J. The Anatomy of British Sea Power: A History of British Naval Policy in the Pre-Dreadnought Era, 1880–1905. New York: Alfred A. Knopf, 1940.

Mathews, Joseph James. "Egypt and the Formation of the Anglo-French Entente of 1904." Ph.D. diss., University of Pennsylvania, 1939.

Matthew, H. C. G. The Liberal Imperialists: The Ideas and Politics of a Post-Gladstonian Elite. London: Oxford University Press, 1973.

May, Ernest R. The World War and American Isolation, 1914–1917. Cambridge: Harvard University Press, 1959.

————. *Imperial Democracy: The Emergence of America as a Great Power.* New York: Harcourt, Brace & World, 1961.

Mayer, Arno J. *The Persistence of the Old Regime: Europe to the Great War.* New York: Pantheon Books, 1981.

Meinecke, Friedrich. *Geschichte des deutsch-englischen Bündnisproblems, 1890–1901.* Munich: R. Oldenbourg, 1927.

Mencken, H. L. *The American Language: An Inquiry into the Development of English in the United States.* 4th ed., corr., rev., and enl. New York: Alfred A. Knopf, 1936.

Millis, Walter. *Road to War: America, 1914–1917.* Boston: Houghton Mifflin Co., 1935.

Mitchell, B. R. *European Historical Statistics, 1750–1975.* 2d rev. ed. New York: Facts on File, 1981.

Monger, George. *The End of Isolation: British Foreign Policy, 1900–1907.* London: Thomas Nelson & Sons, 1963.

Morris, A. J. A. *The Scaremongers: The Advocacy of War and Rearmament, 1896–1914.* London: Routledge and Kegan Paul, 1984.

Mowat, R. B. *The Diplomatic Relations of Great Britain and the United States.* New York: Longmans, Green & Co., 1925.

————. *The Life of Lord Pauncefote, First Ambassador to the United States.* Boston: Houghton Mifflin Co., 1929.

Mowrey, George E. *The Era of Theodore Roosevelt, 1900–1912.* New York: Harper & Row, 1958.

Neale, R. G. *Great Britain and United States Expansion, 1898–1900.* East Lansing: Michigan State University Press, 1966.

Neton, Albéric. *Delcassé (1852–1923).* Paris: Académie Diplomatique Internationale, 1952.

Newton, Thomas Wodehouse Legh, 2d baron. *Lord Lansdowne: A Biography.* London: Macmillan & Co., 1929.

Nicholas, H. G. *The United States and Britain.* Chicago: University of Chicago Press, 1975.

Notter, Harley. *The Origins of the Foreign Policy of Woodrow Wilson.* Baltimore: Johns Hopkins University Press, 1937.

O'Connor, Raymond G. *Perilous Equilibrium: The United States and the London Naval Conference of 1930.* Lawrence: University of Kansas Press, 1962.

Osgood, Robert Endicott. *Ideals and Self-Interest in America's Foreign Relations: The Great Transformation of the Twentieth Century.* Chicago: University of Chicago Press, 1953.

Padfield, Peter. *The Great Naval Race: The Anglo-German Naval Rivalry, 1900–1914.* New York: David McKay Co., 1974.

Paléologue, Georges Maurice. *The Turning Point: Three Critical Years, 1904–1906.* Translated by F. Appleby Holt. London: Hutchinson & Co., 1935.

Papadopoulos, G. S. "Lord Salisbury and the Projected Anglo-German Alliance of 1898." *Bulletin of the Institute of Historical Research* 26 (November 1953): 214–18.

Perkins, Bradford. *The Great Rapprochement: England and the United States, 1895–1914.* New York: Atheneum, 1968.

Perkins, Dexter. *The Monroe Doctrine, 1867–1907.* Albert Shaw Lectures on Diplomatic History, 1937, The Walter Hines Page School of International Relations. Baltimore: Johns Hopkins University Press, 1937.

———. *Hands Off: A History of the Monroe Doctrine.* Boston: Little, Brown & Co., 1941.

Persell, Stuart Michael. *The French Colonial Lobby, 1889–1938.* Stanford: Hoover Institution Press, 1983.

Playne, Caroline E. *The Pre-War Mind in Britain: An Historical Review.* London: George Allen & Unwin, 1928.

Ponsonby, Frederick, First Lord Sysonby. *Recollections of Three Reigns.* London: Eyre & Spottiswoode, 1951.

Porter, Charles W. "The Career of Théophile Delcassé." Ph.D. diss., University of Pennsylvania, 1936.

Pratt, Julius W. *Expansionists of 1898: The Acquisition of Hawaii and the Spanish Islands.* Albert Shaw Lectures on Diplomatic History, 1936, The Walter Hines Page School of International Relations. Baltimore: Johns Hopkins University Press, 1936.

Pribram, Alfred Francis. *England and the International Policy of the European Great Powers, 1871–1914.* Oxford: Clarendon Press, 1931.

Puhle, Hans-Jürgen. *Agrarische Interessenpolitik und preussischer Konservatismus in wilhelminischen Reich (1893–1914): Ein Beitrag zur Analyse des Nationalismus in Deutschland am Beispiel des Bundes der Landwirte und der Deutsch-Konservativen Partei.* Schriftenreihe des Forschunginstituts der Friedrich-Ebert-Stiftung, Band 51. Bonn: Verlag Neue Gesellschaft, 1975.

Ramm, Agatha. "Great Britain and France in Egypt, 1876–1882." In *France and Britain in Africa: Imperial Rivalry and Colonial Rule,* edited by Prosser Gifford and William Roger Louis, 73–119. New Haven: Yale University Press, 1971.

Renouvin, Pierre. *La politique extérieure de Th. Delcassé (1898–1905).* Paris: Institut d'Etudes Politiques, Université de Paris, 1962.

Rich, Norman. *Friedrich von Holstein: Politics and Diplomacy in the Era of Bismarck and Wilhelm II.* 2 vols. Cambridge: Cambridge University Press, 1965.

Ritter, Gerhard. *The Sword and the Scepter: The Problem of Militarism in Germany.* Translated by Heinz Norden. 4 vols. Coral Gables, Fla.: University of Miami Press, 1969–1973.

Rolo, P. J. V. *Entente Cordiale: The Origins and Negotiation of the Anglo-French Agreements of 8 April 1904.* London: Macmillan & Co.; New York: St. Martin's Press, 1969.

Ronaldshay, Lawrence John Lumley Dundas, earl of. *The Life of Lord Curzon: Being the Authorized Biography of George Nathaniel, Marquess Curzon of Kedleston, K.G.* 3 vols. New York: Boni & Liveright, n.d.

Rosen, Philip T. "The Treaty Navy, 1919–1937." In *In Peace and War:*

Interpretations of American Naval History, 1775–1978, edited by Kenneth J. Hagan, 221–36. Contributions in Military History, no. 16. Westport, Conn.: Greenwood Press, 1978.

Roskill, Stephen. *Naval Policy between the Wars.* 2 vols. London: Collins Press, 1968.

Rowland, Peter. *The Last Liberal Governments: The Promised Land, 1905–1910.* London: Barrie & Rockliff, Cresset Press, 1968.

Russett, Bruce M. *Community and Contention: Britain and America in the Twentieth Century.* Cambridge: MIT Press, 1963.

Ryden, George Herbert. *The Foreign Policy of the United States in Relation to Samoa.* Yale Historical Publications, no. 24. New Haven: Yale University Press, 1933.

Sanderson, G. N. "The Origins and Significance of the Anglo-French Confrontation at Fashoda, 1898." In *France and Britain in Africa: Imperial Rivalry and Colonial Rule,* edited by Prosser Gifford and William Roger Louis, 285–331. New Haven: Yale University Press, 1971.

Schieber, Clara Eve. *The Transformation of American Sentiment toward Germany, 1870–1914.* Boston: Cornhill Publishing Co., 1923.

Schierbrand, Wolf von. *Germany: The Welding of a World Power.* New York: Doubleday, Page & Co., 1902.

Schilling, Warner Roller. "Admirals and Foreign Policy, 1913–1919." Ph.D. diss., Yale University, 1954.

———. "Civil-Naval Politics in World War I." *World Politics* 7 (July 1955): 572–91.

Schmitt, Bernadotte Everly. *England and Germany, 1740–1914.* Princeton: Princeton University Press, 1916.

Schuman, Frederick L. *War and Diplomacy in the French Republic: An Inquiry into Political Motivations and the Control of Foreign Policy.* New York: Whittlesey House, McGraw-Hill Book Co., 1931.

Schüssler, Wilhelm. *Deutschland zwischen Russland und England: Studien zur Aussenpolitik des Bismarck'schen Reiches, 1879–1914.* 2d rev. ed. Leipzig: Koehler und Amelang, 1940.

Seager, Robert II. *Alfred Thayer Mahan: The Man and His Letters.* Annapolis: Naval Institute Press, 1977.

Seaman, L. C. B. *From Vienna to Versailles.* New York: Coward-McCann, 1956.

Seed, Geoffrey. "British Reactions to American Imperialism Reflected in Journals of Opinion, 1898–1900." *Political Science Quarterly* 73 (June 1958): 254–72.

Seton-Watson, R. W. *Britain in Europe, 1789–1914: A Survey of Foreign Policy.* New York: Howard Fertig, 1968.

Seymour, Charles. *The Diplomatic Background of the War, 1870–1914.* New Haven: Yale University Press, 1916.

Shippee, Lester Burrell. "Germany and the Spanish-American War." *American Historical Review* 30 (July 1925): 754–77.

———. "German-American Relations, 1890–1914." *Journal of Modern History* 8 (December 1936): 479–88.

Sloan, Jennie A. "Anglo-American Relations and the Venezuelan Bound-
ary Dispute." *Hispanic American Historical Review* 8 (November
1938): 486–506.
Small, Melvin. "The American Image of Germany, 1906–1914." Ph.D.
diss., University of Michigan, 1965.
Smith, Daniel M. *Robert Lansing and American Neutrality, 1914–1917.*
University of California Publications in History, vol. 59. Berkeley:
University of California Press, 1958.
Sondermann, Fred Albert. "The Wilson Administration's Image of Ger-
many." Ph.D. diss., Yale University, 1953.
Sontag, Raymond James. "German Foreign Policy, 1904–1906." *American
Historical Review* 33 (January 1928): 278–301.
———. *Germany and England: Background of Conflict, 1848–1898.*
New York: D. Appleton-Century Co., 1938.
Spender, J. A. *The Life of the Right Hon. Sir Henry Campbell-Banner-
man, G.C.B.* 2 vols. London: Hodder & Stoughton, 1923.
Sprout, Harold, and Sprout, Margaret. *Toward a New Order of Sea
Power: American Naval Policy and the World Scene, 1918–1922.* 2d
ed. Princeton: Princeton University Press, 1943.
———. *The Rise of American Naval Power, 1776–1918.* Rev. ed. Prince-
ton: Princeton University Press, 1944.
Steinberg, Jonathan. "The Copenhagen Complex." *Journal of Contempo-
rary History* 1 (July 1966): 23–46.
———. "The German Background to Anglo-German Relations,
1905–1914." In *British Foreign Policy under Sir Edward Grey,* edited by
F. H. Hinsley, 193–215. Cambridge: Cambridge University Press, 1977.
Steiner, Zara S. *The Foreign Office and Foreign Policy, 1898–1914.* Cam-
bridge: Cambridge University Press, 1969.
———. *Britain and the Origins of the First World War.* New York: St.
Martin's Press, 1977.
Stengers, Jean. "British and German Imperial Rivalry: A Conclusion." In
Britain and Germany in Africa: Imperial Rivalry and Colonial Rule,
edited by Prosser Gifford and William Roger Louis, with the assistance
of Alison Smith, 337–47. New Haven: Yale University Press, 1967.
Stolberg-Wernigerode, Otto zu. *Germany and the United States of
America during the Era of Bismarck.* Translated by Otto E. Lessing.
Reading, Pa.: Henry Janssen Foundation under the auspices of the Carl
Schurz Memorial Foundation, 1937.
Strong, Theron G. *Joseph H. Choate: New Englander, New Yorker, Law-
yer, Ambassador.* New York: Dodd, Mead & Co., 1917.
Stuart, Graham H. *French Foreign Policy from Fashoda to Sarajevo
(1898–1914).* New York: Century Co., 1921.
Sweet, D. W. "Great Britain and Germany, 1905–1911." In *British Foreign
Policy under Sir Edward Grey,* edited by F. H. Hinsley, 216–35. Cam-
bridge: Cambridge University Press, 1977.

Tansill, Charles Callan. *The Purchase of the Danish West Indies.* New York: Greenwood Press, 1968.

Tate, Merze. *The United States and Armaments.* Cambridge: Harvard University Press, 1948.

Taylor, A. J. P. *The Struggle for Mastery in Europe, 1848-1918.* Oxford: Clarendon Press, 1954.

Taylor, Charles Carlisle. *The Life of Admiral Mahan; Naval Philosopher; Rear-Admiral United States Navy; D.C.L. Oxford; LL.D. Cambridge; LL.D. Harvard, Yale, Columbia, Magill, and Dartmouth; President of the United States Naval War College; President of the American Historical Association; Etc.; Etc.* London: John Murray, 1920.

Thayer, William Roscoe. *The Life and Letters of John Hay.* 2 vols. Boston: Houghton Mifflin Co., 1915.

Thierry, Adrien. *L'Angleterre au Temps de Paul Cambon.* Paris: La Palatine, 1961.

Tinneman, Ethel Mary, Sister. "Count Johann von Bernstorff and German-American Relations, 1908-1917." Ph.D. diss., University of California, Berkeley, 1960.

Turk, Richard W. "Defending the New Empire, 1900-1914." In *In Peace and War: Interpretations of American Naval History, 1775-1978*, edited by Kenneth J. Hagan, 186-204. Contributions in Military History, no. 16. Westport, Conn.: Greenwood Press, 1978.

Turner, Arthur Campbell. *The Unique Partnership: Britain and the United States.* New York: Bobbs-Merrill Publishing Co., 1971.

Tyler, J. E. *The British Army and the Continent, 1904-1914.* London: Edward Arnold & Co., 1938.

Vagts, Alfred. *Deutschland und die Vereinigten Staaten in der Weltpolitik.* 2 vols. New York: Macmillan Co., 1935.

―――. "Hopes and Fears of an American-German War, 1870-1915." *Political Science Quarterly* 54 (December 1939): 514-35; 55 (March 1940): 53-76.

Valentin, Veit. *Deutschlands Aussenpolitik von Bismarcks Abgang bis zum Ende des Weltkrieges.* Berlin: Deutsche Verlagsgesellschaft für Politik und Geschichte, 1921.

Viner, Jacob. "International Finance and Balance of Power Diplomacy, 1880-1914." *Southwestern Political and Social Science Quarterly* 9 (March 1929): 407-51.

Ward, Sir A. W., and Gooch, G. P., eds. *The Cambridge History of British Foreign Policy, 1783-1919.* 3 vols. Cambridge: Cambridge University Press, 1922-23.

Wehler, Hans-Ulrich. *Der Aufsteig des amerikanischen Imperialismus: Studien zur Entwicklung des Imperium Americanum, 1865-1900.* Kritische Studien zur Geschichtswissenschaft, Band 10. Göttingen: Vandenhoeck & Ruprecht, 1974.

Weiner, Joel H., ed. *Great Britain: Foreign Policy and Span of Empire,*

1689–1971. A Documentary History. 3 vols. New York: Chelsea House Publishers in association with McGraw-Hill Book Co., 1972.

Wells, Samuel F., Jr. "British Strategic Withdrawal from the Western Hemisphere, 1904–1906." *Canadian Historical Review* 49 (December 1968): 335–56.

Werner, Lothar. *Der Alldeutsche Verband, 1890–1918: Ein Beitrag zur Geschichte der öffentlichen Meinung in Deutschland in den Jahren vor und während des Weltkrieges.* Historische Studien, Heft 278. Berlin: Dr. Emil Ebering, 1935.

Wertheimer, Mildred S. "The Pan-German League, 1890–1914." Ph.D. diss., Columbia University, 1924.

White, Harry D. *The French International Accounts, 1880–1913.* Harvard Economic Studies, vol. 40. Cambridge: Harvard University Press, 1933.

Widenor, William C. *Henry Cabot Lodge and the Search for an American Foreign Policy.* Berkeley: University of California Press, 1980.

Williams, Benjamin H. *The United States and Disarmament.* New York: Whittlesey House, McGraw-Hill Book Co., 1931.

Wilson, Keith M. *The Policy of the Entente: Essays on the Determinants of British Foreign Policy, 1904–1914.* Cambridge: Cambridge University Press, 1985.

Winzen, Peter. "Die Englandpolitik Friedrich von Holsteins, 1895–1901." Ph.D. diss., University of Cologne, 1975.

———. *Bülows Weltmachtkonzept: Untersuching zur Frühphase seiner Aussenpolitik, 1897–1901.* Boppard: Boldt, 1977.

Woodward, E. L. *Great Britain and the German Navy.* Oxford: Clarendon Press, 1935; reprint ed., London: Frank Cass & Co., 1964.

Zetland, Lawrence John Lumley Dundas, 2d marquis of. *Lord Cromer: Being the Authorized Life of Evelyn Baring, First Earl of Cromer, G.C.B., O.M., G.C.M.B., K.C.S.I.* London: Hodder & Stoughton, 1932.

Index